Fully Revised and Updated Edition

A Parent's Guide to CHILD CARE

Dr. Suresh Keshan
M.D. (Paediatrics)

PUSTAK MAHAL®

Publishers
Pustak Mahal®

J-3/16 , Daryaganj, New Delhi-110002
☎ 23276539, 23272783, 23272784 • *Fax:* 011-23260518
E-mail: info@pustakmahal.com • *Website:* www.pustakmahal.com

Sales Centre

- 10-B, Netaji Subhash Marg, Daryaganj, New Delhi-110002
  ☎ 23268292, 23268293, 23279900 • *Fax:* 011-23280567
  E-mail: rapidexdelhi@indiatimes.com
- 6686, Khari Baoli, Delhi-110006
  ☎ 23944314, 23911979

Branches

Bengaluru: ☎ 080-22234025 • *Telefax:* 080-22240209
E-mail: pustak@airtelmail.in • pustak@sancharnet.in
Mumbai: ☎ 022-22010941, 022-22053387
E-mail: rapidex@bom5.vsnl.net.in
Patna: ☎ 0612-3294193 • *Telefax:* 0612-2302719
E-mail: rapidexptn@rediffmail.com
Hyderabad: *Telefax:* 040-24737290
E-mail: pustakmahalhyd@yahoo.co.in

ISBN 978-81-223-0001-7

Edition: 2012

Printed at : Param Offsetters, Okhla, Delhi

Dedication

I have a genuine and fond affection for children, primarily because they reciprocate my love for them by loving me back more, without any strings attached. So it is most appropriate that I dedicate this book to all the children because they are innocent, adorable and make the life of their parents so meaningful. I dedicate this book to all the children whose love and innocence provide the foundation for the optimal development of family bond as a unit.

ACKNOWLEDGEMENTS

For the compilation of this book, I had to go through a lot of literature, particularly from medical textbooks and literature provided by medical journals, medical companies etc. I have included a few figures, text, tables etc. from them in this book. I wish to share whatever useful information I found suitable in them with all the readers of this book. I am grateful to all these medical textbooks etc. for having taught me how to care better for the small children and help me in writing this book so that the parents are also able to care better for their small children.

I am thankful to the institution in which I am currently working as "Head of Department" Paediatrics i.e. Nazareth Hospital, Shillong, Meghalaya. It is a fully computerised hospital with state-of-the-art technology providing yeomen medical services, particularly to the poor and the needy. I thank the director (Sister Mary Paul) of the institution for allowing me free access to the computers and other facilities of the hospital in my endeavour to write this book.

I also extend my thanks to the Principal (Father Steven Mavley) of St. Anthony's College, Shillong, Meghalaya, who helped me off and on and also let me allow to use the college facilities in compiling this book.

I also extend my thanks to **Mrs. Patricia Mukhim, Padma Shree, a leading journalist and author,** for going through the manuscript and giving valuable suggestions to make it better and interesting to the readers.

I am grateful to the publishers of this book (PUSTAK MAHAL) and their editorial staff who have done a fantastic work to make the book see the light of the day in such a wonderful format.

Lastly but not the least, I am eternally grateful to my wife and my one and only daughter for bearing with me and letting me spend so much time in writing this book. They never let me feel that I am neglecting my duties as a father/husband. My wife also encouraged me and gave valuable suggestions regarding the writing of this book.

CONTENTS

PREFACE

Compiling a book on child-care is always a challenge, the prime concern being to make the book as comprehensive as possible, while still keeping it simple and reader-friendly.

In this endeavour, I have referred to numerous medical writings (*Nelson's Textbook of Paediatrics* and *Rudolf's Paediatrics* to name just two) and taken the liberty of including some of what I read in this book. I'm sure these inclusions will be a great source of inspiration to readers.

Most parents, especially first-time ones, have many anxieties regarding child-care, not all of which are grounded in reality – which is why the book deals with 40 myths about child-care. The book also covers a slew of other problems, such as common problems amongst newborns, common parental anxieties, the advantages of breast-feeding, advice on toilet training and other relevant issues.

The attempt has also been to ensure that parents know enough to handle an emergency situation until expert help is at hand. Besides common childhood diseases and immunisation guidelines, you will also learn something about antibiotics used, particularly in respiratory infections and diarrhoea.

Furthermore, you will learn how to let your child develop his full potential, without unduly pressurising him to perform like a perfectionist. By the time you have gone through the pages of *A Parent's Guide to Child-care*, your child's upbringing will have transformed from a painful challenge into a pleasurable one.

—Dr Suresh Keshan

FOREWORD TO THE THIRD EDITION

***A professor after reading a thesis commented, "This thesis is original and good, but I am sorry to reject it as the good part is not original and the original part is not good." ***

There are a lot of books available regarding child care in the market. All of them help the parents in some way or the other in knowing facts and thus be able to care for their child in a better way. However, the truth is that parents do not require a Ph.D. to learn the complexities of child care. What comes naturally and instinctively to them is usually correct and should be followed rather than trying to bring up the child in a copy book fashion. Endeavour to learn all that you can, but don't get caught up in trying to understand all the myriad advices, some going to lengthy and unnecessary details like how to tie the diapers of a baby, how to massage him, how to dress him up etc., which are more theoretical than of practical use. For example it does not matter to the baby how you massage him; also your way of massage does not have any impact on his health.

Many books pay particular attention to the nutrition of the child and give detailed dietary charts and figures; what foods should be given to the child, in what amounts, when etc. It appears to me that we are so enamoured by what modern science thinks we ought to eat, that we tend to forget that our bodies have known this for millions of years **(that is what to eat, when to eat and how much to eat)**. Because of this enamouration, the mother wants her child to get a balanced diet. BUT how can the mother be sure that the child is receiving a balanced diet? After all, the child eats a variety of things. To calculate the quantity and the nutritional composition of each food item that the child takes and then compare them with standard nutritional tables and dietary charts is practically impossible on a day to day basis. *Fortunately calculations are not needed as what we eat daily tends to be balanced by itself over a period of time*. **Else every human being would have become malnourished!**

That is why I reiterate parents do not require a Ph.D. in child care. Rather they should do what comes naturally to them and be relaxed. Remember experience is the best teacher and as you learn from your mistakes; your confidence as parents goes up. At the same time parents should not feel handicapped by lack of simple, practical and common sense knowledge regarding the child care. **This is what this book is all about**.

In my continuous and sincere efforts, I have tried to address the full spectrum of diseases and problems related to the health and welfare of children that are faced by the parents.

I gain immense satisfaction and pride in the role of a teacher and am ever ready to teach the medical personnel and the medical students, doctors etc. whatever I know and at the same time am a willing student, i.e. learning from them. This passion for teaching led me to write this book so that the parents can also be made aware of the medical facts, particularly regarding child care.

The second edition was brought out 2 years back. The third edition has been edited so as to incorporate the latest scientific information and facts so that the parents are also kept up-to-date with the recent advances and developments in the field of medical science. Every chapter of the book has been carefully scrutinized for possible improvement and updated. I hope that the changes made in the third edition are useful to the parents.

With my blessings for your child that he/she blossoms and attains his/her full potential.

***Both adultery and adulteration come from the word "adults." This is because babies don't do these things. ***

***Incidentally, adulation also comes from the word "adults", which both adults and children do and reciprocate. ***

CHAPTER 1

INTRODUCTION

***A patient came to the doctor's chamber with bruises on his face. On being asked the reason for those bruises, he replied that his friend had just come back from honeymoon. The doctor couldn't understand the relation between the two events whence he elaborated "you see; it was me who had suggested marriage to my friend." ***

There is an ideal about motherhood, which presumes that a woman is overjoyed when she finds that she is pregnant and going to have a baby in the near future. She spends her time dreaming about her baby. When the baby is born she slips into the maternal role with consummate ease and delight. *This, alas, is true only to a limited extent.* Actually there are a lot of worries connected with pregnancy, particularly with the first one. There is often a let-down for the mother when the first baby actually is born.

In USA, they have devised dolls whose behaviour is similar to a newborn. It cries, sleeps, feeds and evacuates i.e. does everything that a newborn does. *The only hitch with it is that there is no "Off" button.* So once it starts crying, it will go on crying till fed or it may go on crying for a prolonged time without any reason and refuse to be soothed. Plus it has odd hours of crying. Thus it may cry at 2 A.M. when the parents are in deep sleep, disturbing their peace of mind. Why such a doll was devised? This is to make the prospective parents realise what childcare is like, how difficult and tough it is, how much sacrifices they have to make of their personal life. Interestingly, 60% of the prospective mothers after their experience with the doll dropped the idea of having a child, at least in the near future.

***When a couple is fresh and newly wed, they are young and carefree. After having two children, they reach middle age. Middle age should be defined as the age in which the middle portion of the body bulges out (i.e. they acquire a paunch). ***

When the child is born, it spells the end of the exuberance of youth and also the freedom of the parents, a thing that the father and the mother both so much cherish and may not want to give up. The maidenly figure and the sprightly grace of the woman goes into eclipse and is replaced with a sober, portly mother. The woman realizes with a feeling of dismay that there are limitations set upon everything e.g. social life, late night parties, pursuing hobbies and so many other enjoyments of life. No more going shopping at the spur of the moment or coming home at odd hours. Instead these type of incidents become far and few, and have to be planned instead of the freedom of decision at the spur of the moment. The spouse's attention, which used to be exclusively meant for the other,

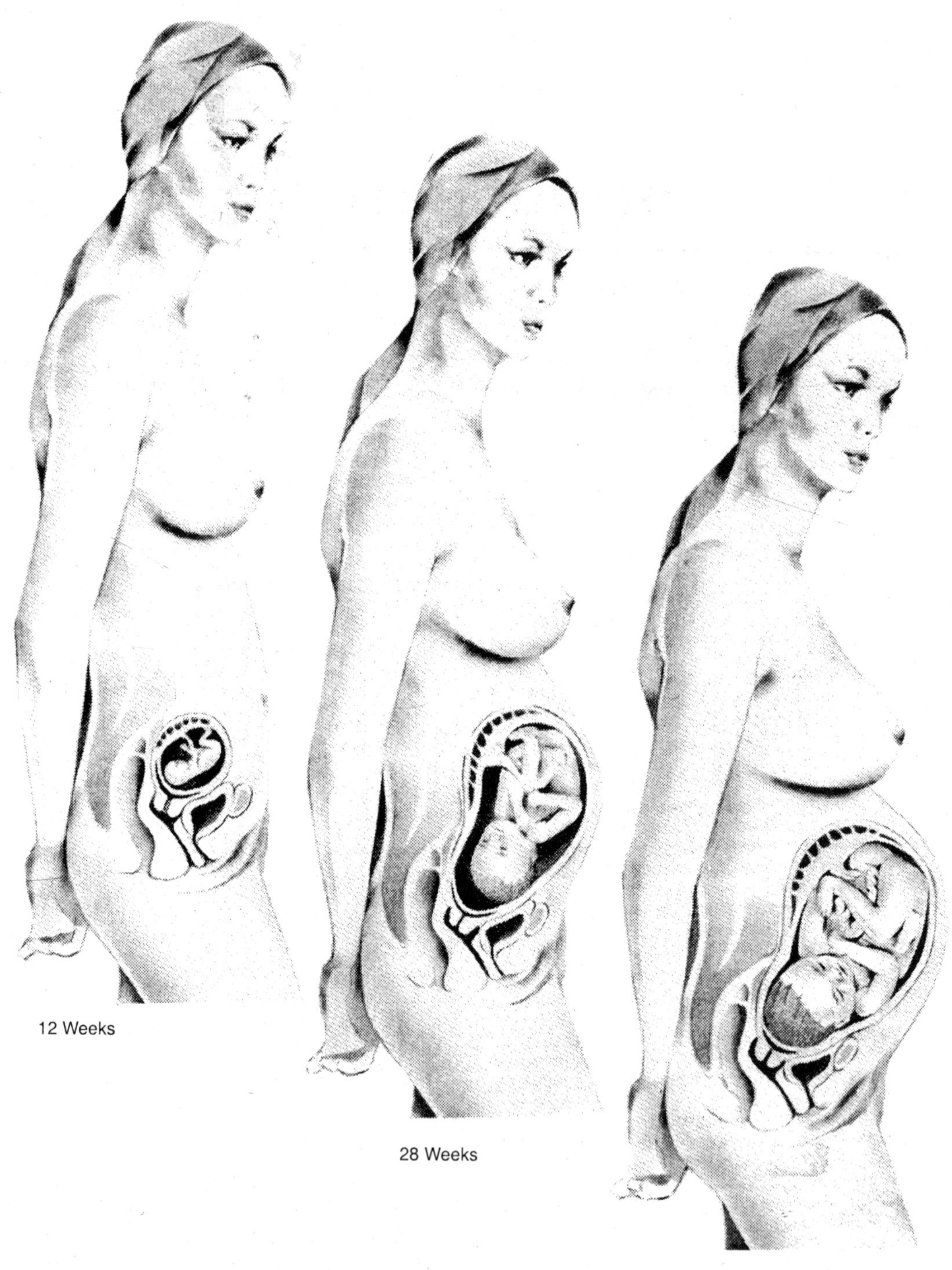

A New Life: Development of the prenatal baby in the womb of its mother.

is now divided, as the baby gets its share too. Often the husband feels that he is at the receiving end, as the mother is now more concerned and preoccupied with the baby.

Love for the newborn comes gradually. The mother may expect to recognise the baby as her own blood and flesh at the first instance and to feel an overwhelming surge of maternal feelings of love and affection towards it immediately. *But this doesn't happen the first day and takes time.* Thus maternal expectations may be belied leading to a feeling of disappointment in the mother, who should understand that it is a gradual process rather than an instantaneous "love at first sight" affair. As the mother and child interact with each other daily, they gradually but steadily develop strong emotional bonds based on mutual love and affection.

After delivery there is a common phase, which many mothers undergo, known as "post partum blues." The mother is depressed, and may burst out into tears spontaneously on petty things. This feeling occurs with a lot of mothers and is transient. Coping with it is easier if the mother is aware of it, knows that a lot of others also face the same situation and is reassured that it is a temporary phase. The mother can pursue some hobby or talk it out with his husband or friends. She can have cheerful company of friends around to lessen the feeling of loneliness and depression. The mother may feel "blue" because she may perceive the husband to be indifferent. The husband may feel left out because of the attention being showered on the baby. Thus it may become a vicious cycle. So the mother should remember to pay some of her attention to the husband plus encourage him in the care of the baby. The husband should also be aware of this phenomenon and try to lift the spirits of the wife rather than thinking that post-delivery her attitude has changed and she has become "attention seeking."

For the second or third child also, the parents, particularly the mother may have periods of doubts and negative feelings. She may have doubts as to whether she will have the time and energy to devote for the care of the next child. These types of reactions occur in the best of parents and usually are temporary, as they have already gone through the challenges and ordeals of the first childbirth and so are experienced. Further the child's arrival proves less of a challenge than the parents anticipated and sooner rather than later everything falls into groove and life, with some more adjustments, again becomes smooth and mundane.

***In a sermon, a priest said, "God created us all." A youngster stood up and shouted, "You are wrong. My father is a scientist and he says that we came from monkeys." The priest said, "He is right, because we are not talking about your family, but the rest of us."* **

For the parents, the birth of a baby, after 9 long months in the womb of the mother, is a very important event. The baby signals its arrival by crying, as if protesting against leaving the warmth and security of the mother's womb to arrive in a new, unknown world. What is compelling about the baby is its innocence and tenderness. For the mother, it is a blissful moment of contentment. She was carrying it up so far, dreaming about it and now it is just like a dream come true.

A few days with the baby and the parents come rapidly to the ground realities. They start realising that the small bundle of joy, which cannot do anything by itself, is in fact a very tremendous responsibility. Blissfully unaware of the commotion it has created and "life will never be the same again" sobering feeling of the parents, it cries and sleeps, cries and sleeps; a cycle punctuated only by its feeding.

How to rear this soft and delicate, helpless but very sweet and tiny replica of the parents?

This book is not an exhaustive treatise on child-care. It is meant to be simple, easily understandable and to make for enjoyable reading. If this book makes parents more confident and less anxious in baby care, I will consider I have succeeded, for the purpose of this book is to make child-care better and enjoyable.

CHAPTER 2

PARENTAL CONCERNS AND ANXIETIES

KEY POINTS

- **Parental care:** Don't be obsessed with perfect baby care. The natural love and care that you give to your child is priceless and more important than knowing how to handle babies expertly. Some parents are over-conscientious and feel self-guilt about small things, because they take baby care too seriously and righteously. This impedes the natural parental care.
- **Childcare is hard:** Unless you are mentally prepared to go through the "grind" of child rearing, don't go for a child immediately. The fact that you won't trade places with a childless couple for the entire world doesn't alter the basic fact that childcare is at best a lot of hard work and deprivation. As child rearing leaves parents exhausted and drained, they should "recharge their batteries"; i.e. take some quality time off from baby care and enjoy.
- **Enjoy your baby:** Parents are scared at the prospect of taking sole charge of a helpless baby for the first time. The overwhelmed parents push themselves too hard and feel only the burden of responsibility towards the baby rather than enjoying and playing with the child. Remember that the baby is born to be a reasonable and friendly human being. The best way to cope up with your child and enjoy him is to be open with your spouse about your feelings and laugh aloud at the child's "silliness" together. Remember the child doesn't do all this "silliness" to irritate you.
- **Sex of the baby:** Mothers in India are under a lot of pressure to deliver "preferentially" a male baby. The irony is that the mother has nothing to do with the sex of the baby. The sex of the child depends upon the chromosome which the baby gets from the father, and not from the mother.
- A newborn though it looks so frail, is in fact a very strong and robust creature. Its defence mechanisms (immunity) are well developed to ward off the common infections.
- **Parental expectations:** Parents have high expectations from their children, wanting them to be "perfect." All this puts a lot of pressure on the child who strives to live up to the expectations of his parents. Simply stating the high expectations of the parents are creating neurotic children.
- **Working parents:** Self-guilt particularly affects the mother. To overcome the feeling of guilt, the parents tend to be extra sensitive towards their child. Working or not working, the parents should shower that much love and attention as comes naturally to them. They should act like self-confident, firm parents without letting guilt complex bow them down. The child may plead for the mother to stay at home. This is a sensitive issue and should be tackled delicately. Don't waver. Rather explain to the child, truthfully, why both of you must go to work. The caretaker (in your absence) should be affectionate and self-confident. Another very important aspect is the permanence of the caretaker.

***A nurse and a doctor fell in love, got married and had a child. The nurse said, "I am not the mother of this child." The doctor said, "I am not the father of this child." What was the real situation? ** (answer at the end of this chapter)*

***The doctor completed an examination of the patient, shaking his head, "I can't find a cause for your complaints. Frankly I think it is due to drinking."*

"In that case", said the sympathetic patient. "I'll come back when you are sober."

"It is established that human beings are more valuable than all other living creatures - at least so human beings believe. Baba has interpreted this to believe that he is the centre of all activities and that everything has to be done to serve him and serve him alone.

Baba has been able to qualify this. For example while a kilo of chicken costs Rs. 100/- , for a newborn to put a kg of weight costs thousands of rupees. Decades later, they spend thousands more to get rid of that extra kilo of weight. There are regular visits to the child specialist only to be told that your child is doing fine.

Baba has laid down the rules of the game. He has a single objective. He must get what he wants when he wants it. He must be fed on demand. He also has only a single medium for effective communication, crying with varying intensities, cry, cry louder, and still louder.

After his arrival, my routine has been permanently altered. I am awakened at 2 am in the early morning and can go back to bed only several hours later, after Baba has been fed. A baby falls asleep immediately, while an adult takes varied time to go back to sleep, a thing which the baby is blissfully unaware of. When you then see him as a cherubic angel, no one will ever believe the trauma that he has caused only a short time ago - the acting and deception is perfect.

When everything is going on alright, Baba believes that it is time for a change that some variety should come in the otherwise mundane and routine life. Something must go wrong-otherwise people will get casual and complacent. He will thus get choked when the mother is not around and make you run to the grand mothers in the vicinity and in the neighbourhood, who you discover are useless, out of touch and depth to handle a 21st century child. And he is most unreliable when it comes to passing stool or urine, his bowel moves like the unpredictable stock exchange index.

But like the stars on the silver screen, you love him because of the suspense, excitement and entertainment he brings from day to day. Infact he is more like a TV serial with each day bringing a new episode."

You are going to be a proud parent or already are one. Naturally you must be having some doubts and anxieties regarding your baby. The doctors and nurses must have given you instructions, sometimes complicated. On top of that is the advice, often conflicting, given by friends, relatives, neighbours etc (e.g. one may say give water to your baby, another may say, don't). **My advice is to trust your common sense**. The natural love and care that parents give to their child is a hundred times more valuable than their knowing how to handle their babies in an expert way. Every time you pick your baby up, smile and cuddle, caress and hug her; and do small things for her (e.g. changing diapers, feeding etc.), even if you do it awkwardly and sometimes make a mess of it; gives a feeling to your baby that she belongs to you and that you belong to her. Nobody else in the world, however, expert he or she is in the art of baby care, can give that to her. **So my recommendation is, don't be obsessed with the idea of the perfect baby care.** Instead trust your natural instincts because what good mothers and fathers instinctively feel like doing for their babies is usually the best. It is better to be natural, than to do everything perfectly in a copybook manner. Aiming for ideal care will lead to a feeling of worry and anxiety about your performance as the ideal parents; and so take away the pleasure of enjoying your child.

Three important principles regarding parenthood are:

1. Be Mentally Prepared for Parenthood

Parents are a little scared at the prospect of taking sole charge of a helpless baby for the first time. For those who are fortunate enough to have the support of the grandparents of the baby, this is easier. But for those parents who are alone (particularly if they are young and therefore mentally less prepared for this responsibility and/or both are working parents), child-care may be a big mental stress. With the coming of the baby, their life style completely changes. Not only is their freedom gone, but they feel overwhelmed by all that has to be done for the baby. They may not get a proper sleep in the night because of the baby's odd hours of crying, which disturbs their blissful sleep. If the baby doesn't go off to sleep again quickly and goes on crying, the parents really start feeling the pressures of parenthood. On top of that the parents may start feeling that their spouse is not doing enough in the care of the baby, i.e. sharing the "workload of baby care 50-50." This may lead to a feeling of irritation that why should they only be responsible for child-care. So they may start shifting the responsibility on one another. Because of all these factors, the parents should realise that child rearing is a very serious business in which they have to sacrifice a lot AND can leave the parents mentally, physically and emotionally exhausted. Therefore I strongly advise that unless you are mature enough, mentally ready and emotionally prepared to go through the "grind" of child rearing, don't go for a child immediately. There is no rigid rule that you should have a child within a year or two of marriage. You can wait, enjoy life with your spouse, and settle your career etc. before considering having a child. Otherwise the baby becomes a "task"; the overwhelmed parents push themselves too hard and feel only the burden of responsibility towards the baby.

2. Parents are Humans

All good parents naturally feel that it is their duty and moral responsibility to rear their child in the best way possible. But many times (particularly in the case of over conscientious, young parents), this may be carried to excessive limits. They feel that their whole attention and time must be for the baby, so they give up their freedom and personal hobbies etc., not as a matter of practicality but as a matter of principle! So even if they sneak off to enjoy some free time when they get a chance, they feel too guilty to enjoy fully. In the long run they chafe at this "imprisonment."

Another concept the parents have is that for them to be the right sort of parents, they should have unlimited patience and tolerance towards their baby. But this is not humanly possible. When a child disobeys a reasonable rule, is not listening to you repetitively and goes on doing something that he should not do, you can't remain cool like a robot with no emotions. You are bound to feel indignant. So you blow your top once in a while and give a good scolding to the child or sometimes even beat him. There is nothing to feel guilty or bad about it afterwards. The child was asking for it and deserved it. Certainly parents should not take out their own mental stress, frustrations and tensions on the child i.e. they are irritated at something else but take it out on the child.

Having children does mean giving up so much, that parents naturally do and should expect something from their child in return; if not much, at least that he would be reasonable, considerate and willing to accept the parents' standards and ideals of right and wrong. If parents are hesitant in asking for reasonable behaviour and overlook his mischief and unreasonable behaviour, the child, feeling no check is sure to get spoiled. **Therefore parents should be firm, because such firmness is one aspect of parental love.** Firmness keeps the child on the right track and that is for his own good.

The child also understands your outburst, if your reaction is fair. He knows that he has done something that he was not supposed to do. Naturally he accepts your being angry with him and doesn't resent it for long, as is evident by the fact that after sometime (as you cool down and accept him again); he will kiss and hug you. This means that your getting angry doesn't diminish the bond of love and affection between you and your child as long as you are consistent and reasonable i.e. you get angry on his committing some mischief, which oversteps the limits set by you upon the child.

Sometimes your resentment suddenly boils over and you are shocked by your vehemence towards the child. But if you analyse it, you may find that the child had been doing a series of irritating acts, all of which you have been trying to ignore for quite some time in a supreme bid to be patient. Finally he does a small thing (which doesn't warrant that much anger), and you suddenly lose your composure and give him a severe scolding. This again is justifiable if the child was pestering you for a long time. It is also a good idea to be open about your feelings of anger and irritation towards the child with your spouse or friends. This way you can comfortably accept these natural and humanly reactions without feeling remorse about such feelings.

There is an enormous amount of hard work in child-care - changing diapers, preparing food, struggling to make the child eat what you have so lovingly prepared, cleaning up all the mess that the child makes, stopping fights and drying up tears, listening to stories that are hard to understand, joining in games that aren't exciting to an adult, reading stories that aren't interesting, trudging around zoos and parks, helping with school homework and studies, being disturbed and hampered in your daily chores or hobby by the eager, enthusiastic, "wanting to help and participate" type of child, and so much more.

***A man whose English was so-so did not have a child (was childless) for a long time. He went to the doctor and complained. "Doctor, the problem is with my wife. She is inconceivable. No, no I mean she is impregnable. No, no, I am sorry, she is unbearable." ***

Children keep parents away from parties, theatres, outings, meeting friends etc. They will interrupt when the parents are discussing something interesting amongst themselves, the child won't let the conversation be smooth and uninterrupted. Rather he has to poke his nose in the middle and meddle, as a reminder that he is also very much there and thus not to be ignored. The fact that you won't trade places with a childless couple for the entire world doesn't alter the basic fact that child-care is at best a lot of hard work and deprivation.

So it is justifiable that the genuine needs of the parents, their frustrations associated with child rearing, how tired they get (physically and mentally), how much emotionally drained they become sometimes, how much they also want some rest and change from the routine of child-care are understood and appreciated. **Because the fact is that child rearing is a long, hard job and parents are humans just as children, and not superhuman.**

***Going to a party with your wife is just like going fishing with the game warden. ***

As child rearing is a hard, monotonous work which can leave the parents mentally, physically and emotionally exhausted, I advocate that the parents should "recharge their batteries"; i.e. take some rest and "quality" time off from baby care and enjoy themselves (e.g. go to movies, parties etc. once in a while). If there is some caretaker, then both the parents can take some time off for themselves. If there is no caretaker, one parent can look after the child for few hours, while the other parent can "loosen" himself or herself. Like this the parents will feel rejuvenated, less irritable and better able to cope with the stress of child caring.

3. Enjoy Your Baby

** (A young couple enjoying before a baby): *A young soldier was proudly showing his newly wed wife their rifle range where the trainees were practising target shooting. As a rifle went off, the girl, frightened by the sudden noise, flung herself in the arms of her cavalier husband. The visitors and the soldiers standing nearby merely smiled. The wife blushed and stepping back said, "I am sorry. I didn't mean to. But it was so sudden and frightening."*

*"Its O.K.", said the husband with a grin. "Now let's go & watch the heavy artillery." ***

You may think from the amount of attention and time the baby requires that the babies come in this world to put the parents under their thumbs. This isn't true. The baby is born to be a reasonable and friendly human being. Every baby needs to be smiled at, talked to, fondled, hugged and showered with love and affection, **which is difficult if you don't learn to enjoy your baby.**

***For family planning, Lippes loop is quite famous. The scientist, Mr. Lippe who invented* *it used the following slogan for its advertisement: "loop before you leap." ***

The parents should let the child do whatever he enjoys, including creating some mess, as long as it is harmless and within limits. Finally as long as parents are loving and conscientious, who care for their child, they should not pressurise themselves too much by self-guilt and doubts regarding the rearing of the child. Instead they should take child-care in a carefree attitude, enjoying themselves and the antics play, social interaction etc. of the baby.

A woman went to a gynaecologist and complained, 'Doctor when I wasn't married, I had three abortions and now I that I am married, I can't get pregnant."

"Evidently you don't breed in captivity", replied the gynaecologist.

That's why also, you will find grandmothers remarking wistfully, "Why couldn't I have enjoyed my own children the way I enjoy my grandchild? I suppose I was trying too hard and feeling only the responsibility."

That's why you also enjoy playing with other's child (particularly if he is smaller than your child is) more than playing with your own child, because the other's child is not your responsibility. You are completely at ease with that child, because at a moment's notice (as soon as you get bored or want to do some other work or the child starts crying and gets on your nerves), you can "pass" the child over to its mother and get "rid" of it. While with your own child, you cannot do it. You and only you have to bear his demands & tantrums stoically.

Does this mean that it is difficult to enjoy one's child? Yes, it is. After all, the child is yours and only yours responsibility and you only have to cope with it. This coping is easier, if you are emotionally mature and mentally prepared for baby care. Once you realize that what he is doing is what every child does, **that you also did the same when you were a child;** you won't feel irritated or chafed at him that much. Therefore to enjoy your child you have to accept your child as he is; knowing that it is a part and parcel of growing up and everyone passes through the same phase.

***Once a person confronted a psychiatrist and asked, "Has anyone escaped from your mental home recently?" On seeing the puzzled look on the doctor's face he explained, "Someone has ran away with my wife." ***

Another way to enjoy your child is to laugh it out with your spouse. For e.g. your child has made a mess of the food in the plate by mixing different foodstuff together and also spilling some of it. You might get irritated at the child and consider him to be always doing such "senseless" and "stupid" doings. On the other hand, if you have come to terms with your child and have a sense of humour, you will realise that what the child has done is harmless and that he enjoys doing so. So you may laugh it out with your spouse and enjoy with your child his "mischief."

There are so many other examples, where you can look at things in two entirely different and opposite ways, one with a feeling of irritation towards your child and one with laughter and merriment at your child's "silly" pranks and doings, as long as they are harmless.

The child doesn't do all this "silliness" to make you angry or to irritate you; rather he does it because he enjoys it. He wants to explore this world by experimenting in different ways. His curiosity is boundless and he is fascinated by all novel things. He is a most willing and ardent learner (e.g. if he sees you washing clothes, he will want to try it out himself. He may make a mess of it, but this is how he enjoys a new experiment.) He is a great imitator, particularly of the parents. That's why a baby girl will stand in front of the mirror and apply lipstick, comb her hair, and apply powder and other cosmetics of the mother; just like the mother. The mother may get irritated because not only the girl is spoiling her cosmetics but also making a mess of her hands and face, which now she has to clean up. But just pause for a second and see how much the baby enjoys it, how much bliss this act is for her and how much it means to her (it is a part of her learning and growing up). **So my humble request is don't spoil the mood of the baby and in the process yours**. Get the child her own cosmetics (maybe artificial) and let her play with it, i.e. device ways where the baby can enjoy without spoiling much. Then sit back and enjoy your child's antics! The child's enjoyment and the thrill she feels (in doing such acts) will be doubled if she finds that you, too, are enjoying her "play." Reciprocally your heart will also be filled with joy seeing your child enjoy.

The child's mental level is much below yours (there is a whole generation gap between you and him). The things she does, which you consider as "stupid" are not stupid (if you view it from the child's eye and mental perspective). The child cannot come up to your mental level (so she can't for instance, enjoy your hobbies and pastimes like playing cards, reading magazines, watching T.V. etc.). But, you can go down to the child's mental level! Enjoy participating in whatever "games" she plays (she also wants her parents to join in), however, foolish they might seem to you and don't feel conscious about it. I know that after sometime you will start finding it boring and will want to "quit." By all means do so! The child wants your company for sometime only. For instance, if the child requests you to "play" with her in some "game" of her own making; you can tell her that you will play for 10-15 minutes (i.e. for sometime), as you have some work of yours to do after that. The child understands this and is more than happy if you join in the fun even temporarily. But by outright refusing her (because you are busy, tired or consider the "games" of her boring and making no sense to you), you will make the child unhappy and let down. Maybe you will also end up feeling guilty (as to why didn't you concede to a simple request of your child?).

The parents have to come down to the child's mental level to enjoy her. I know it may be difficult at times (your mind may be preoccupied with caring for her and keeping everything in order or you may not be in the mood); but you can certainly try and make sincere efforts towards this. Initially you may not enjoy it that much (because you may feel awkward), but with time your awkwardness will go, you will come to terms with it and enjoy it.

** *(Life cannot be put into reverse gear, enjoy your child): A person was seen driving his car round and round, but in reverse gear. On being asked the reason, he said that he*

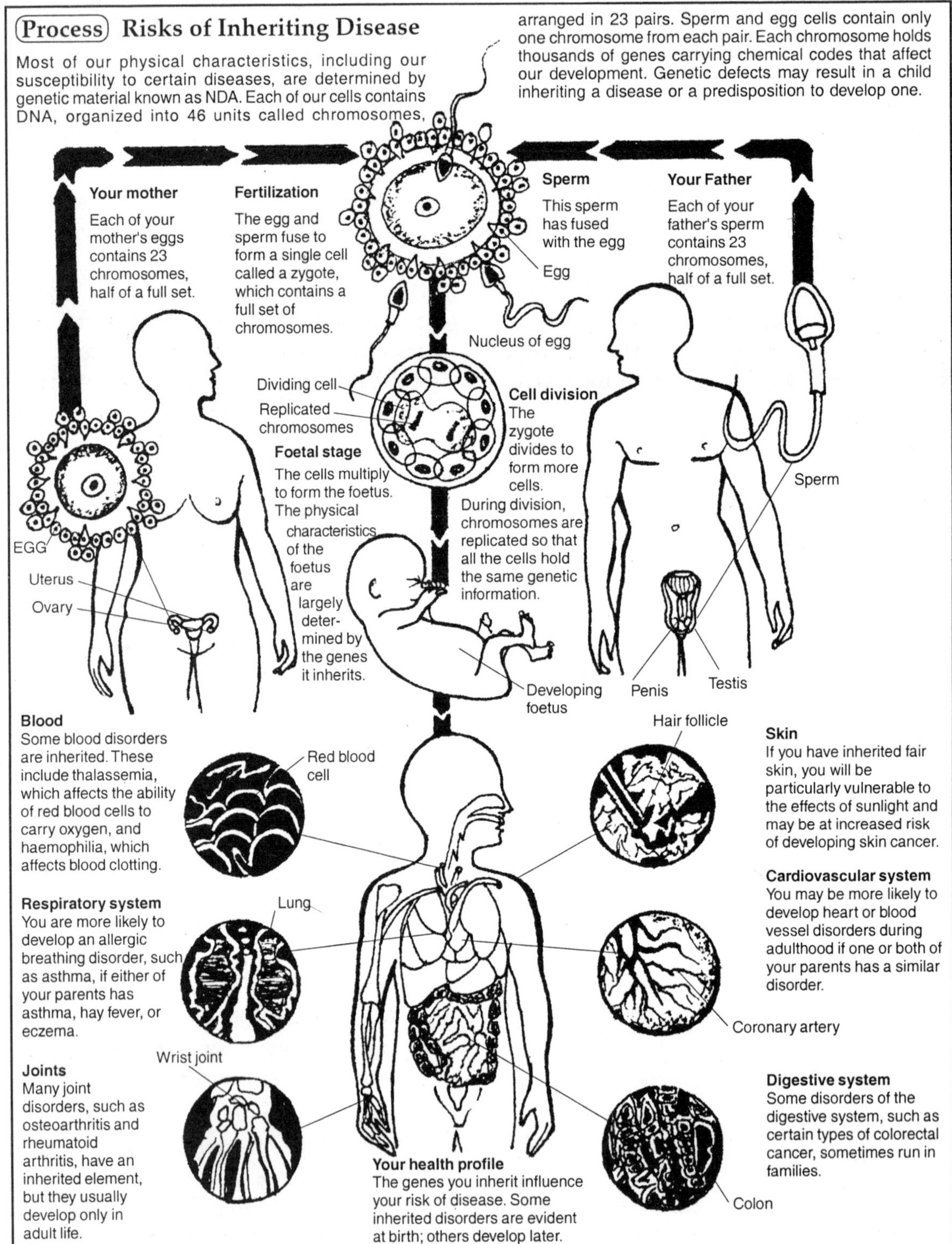

Process
Risks of Inheriting Disease
Most of our physical characteristics, including our susceptibility to certain diseases, are determined by genetic material known as NDA. Each of our cells contains DNA, organized into 46 units called chromosomes, arranged in 23 pairs. Sperm and egg cells contain only one chromosome from each pair. Each chromosome holds thousands of genes carrying chemical codes that affect our development. Genetic defects may result in a child inheriting a disease or a predisposition to develop one.
Your mother
Each of your mother's eggs contains 23 chromosomes, half of a full set.
Fertilization
The egg and sperm fuse to form a single cell called a zygote, which contains a full set of chromosomes.
Sperm
This sperm has fused with the egg
Egg
Your Father
Each of your father's sperm contains 23 chromosomes, half of a full set.
Nucleus of egg
Dividing cell
Replicated chromosomes
Cell division
The zygote divides to form more cells. During division, chromosomes are replicated so that all the cells hold the same genetic information.
Foetal stage
The cells multiply to form the foetus. The physical characteristics of the foetus are largely determined by the genes it inherits.
EGG
Uterus
Ovary
Sperm
Developing foetus
Penis
Testis
Blood
Some blood disorders are inherited. These include thalassemia, which affects the ability of red blood cells to carry oxygen, and haemophilia, which affects blood clotting.
Red blood cell
Hair follicle
Skin
If you have inherited fair skin, you will be particularly vulnerable to the effects of sunlight and may be at increased risk of developing skin cancer.
Cardiovascular system
You may be more likely to develop heart or blood vessel disorders during adulthood if one or both of your parents has a similar disorder.
Respiratory system
You are more likely to develop an allergic breathing disorder, such as asthma, if either of your parents has asthma, hay fever, or eczema.
Lung
Coronary artery
Wrist joint
Joints
Many joint disorders, such as osteoarthritis and rheumatoid arthritis, have an inherited element, but they usually develop only in adult life.
Digestive system
Some disorders of the digestive system, such as certain types of colorectal cancer, sometimes run in families.
Colon
Your health profile
The genes you inherit influence your risk of disease. Some inherited disorders are evident at birth; others develop later.

*wanted to sell his car. Therefore he wanted to reduce its mileage in order to fetch a better price.***

Why I stress so much on enjoying your child has got a forceful reason. As your child grows up, off and on, you will remember her past, bygone days, and her babyhood. At those times, you may also feel wistfully (like the grandmother mentioned earlier), "I wish I had enjoyed my baby more, rather than having felt too bogged down by the parental duties and responsibilities." But the past doesn't come back!

In brief, the best way to cope up with your child and enjoy him is to have a sense of humour, to be free and open with your spouse about your feelings, and laugh at the child's "silliness" together. Parents, apart from being parents, should also be the friends of their child.

***A smile requires only 4 muscles while a frown uses 16 muscles. Why waste more energy in worrying? Always smile. ***

COMMON PARENTAL ANXIETIES AND WORRIES

1. Normalcy of the Unborn Child

The parental anxieties may start from the time of pregnancy. The joy and pride of parenthood is mixed with a fear, "will my child be perfectly normal, i.e. without any birth defects?" The answer is a question, "why not?" The chances of a baby being born abnormal are minimal. It is just like worrying whether the roof will fall on one's head one day, which is no cause for worry simply because the chances are minimal. Various other fears, which may haunt the mother, may be like she may not abort the baby, give birth to a preterm baby, give birth to a baby with some physical handicap or mental retardation, giving birth to a dead baby etc. The chances of all these happening are very less, so less that they should not be taken seriously and sleepless nights spent over them. It is most appropriate to bundle all these worries and throw them out of the window once and for all.

Friends, neighbours, relatives etc. may narrate anecdotes about pregnancy and childbirth, which may unwittingly give rise to anxiety in the prospective mother. They may site examples about abnormal babies etc. Just don't pay any attention to their "experiences". Such "hearsay" is best discouraged. Just relax and enjoy your pregnancy. Active work and exercises in moderation during pregnancy is in no way detrimental. However, chronic mental stress can be harmful to the baby.

Caution: If there is a family history of genetic disorders e.g. Thalessemia, or you had abortions previously or a baby was born abnormal previously; go in for genetic counselling before planning your next baby.

Dear doctor, both my wife and I are sterile. Is there any chance we may pass this on to our children?

2. Sex of the Child

Another common worry is regarding the sex of the child; i.e. will it be a boy or a girl? In today's rapidly progressive world, where both the sexes are having equal opportunities and are doing equally well in the all important and meaningful spheres of education, career, independence and 'bread earning', this question has lost much of its relevance. But still due to social pressures and cultural values like propagation of the family's name, this question is not redundant. The parents should realize that a girl is in all aspects equal to a boy. Infact she is superior biologically and can absorb the shocks and tensions of life better than a man, which is much more important than physical prowess. Also the girl is of a gentler nature and sweeter. One complaint told to me by a mother of 2 boys was that she was constantly worried about their falling in bad company and more than that about their career and future settlement. "Had they been girls, this agony would not have been there", she remarked wistfully. And she was dead serious.

Mothers, particularly in India, are under a lot of pressure to deliver "preferentially" a male baby. If she doesn't do so, even after 2 pregnancies (as if she had been given 2 chances to deliver a male baby and she failed to capitalise on both of them), the patience, particularly, of the in-laws, may start wearing thin. The mother is directly or indirectly, blamed and held guilty for not being able to deliver a male child, which puts her under tremendous mental stress. **The irony is that the mother has nothing to do with the sex of the baby.** Simply stating, a baby with "XX" chromosomes becomes a female, while a baby with "XY" chromosomes becomes a male. The mother always contributes only the X chromosome (i.e. the X in "XX" and the X in "XY"). The other chromosome (i.e. the X in "XX" and the Y in "XY") comes from the father. Therefore, the sex determination of the child depends upon the chromosome which the baby gets from the father, and not from the mother. So, why the mother should be blamed for not giving birth to a male child? In fact, no one is to be blamed (either the mother or the father). It is just chance as to which of the father's chromosome (X or Y) will fuse with the X chromosome of the mother to form the first living cell of the baby and hence determine its sex. And the chances are 50% for either a male or a female baby to be born in each pregnancy.

3. Illnesses in a child

After the birth of the baby, a significant concern may be about any harm befalling the baby in the form of various illnesses. The parents worry about the baby's crying thinking that something is seriously wrong with the baby. They worry about almost everything, from a benign sneeze to some harmless spots or rash over the skin of the baby. Some "sensitive" parents may tiptoe into the baby's room to see whether the baby is breathing normally and all is well. All this is nature's way to ensure that the parents take their responsibility seriously. However, the fact is that the newborn, though it looks so frail, is in fact a very strong and robust creature. Its defence mechanisms (immunity) are well developed to ward off the common infections. Even if the newborn falls sick, by and large the infections are contained by immunity so as to not become serious. Therefore most of the common infections in a baby are by and large benign and self-limiting (as in adults). **In fact I have found in my clinical practice that babies respond very well to treatment and recover faster, even better than adults do**. This may be due to the fact that the baby's tissues are still actively dividing and therefore has a much greater regenerative power as compared to the adults. In adults, the organs, with age, start losing their "vitality". Another important reason why the babies respond better than the adult to a disease is that they don't have any psychological component (like anxiety, depression, feeling of helplessness and uncertainty etc.) attached to a disease. These psychological factors (called psychosomatic component of a disease) aggravate the disease, making healing delayed and difficult.

4. Feeding and Growth of the Child

Another common parental concern is about the feeding and the growth of the child. Mothers invariably feel that their child does not eat well, is thin and thus not healthy. This is due to a comparison between their child with other children of the same age group and finding differences between them.

As far as "poor eating" is concerned, remember that even a 1-day-old has an inborn mechanism to signal hunger by crying when it is hungry. So no child can starve of its own accord. Mother, due to her anxiety that the child is not eating well tries to force or coax extra morsels down the baby's throat. The child may resist this because something is being forced upon him against his wishes. Put yourself in the baby's shoes and imagine someone stuffing you forcibly. Won't you revolt? Not only that; with time you will lose all the pleasure of eating and consider it as a dreary task forcibly thrust upon you. Also you will feel antagonism towards the "force feeder". Same theory applies to a child also. So next time when you have the urge to somehow make the child accept that "extra morsel", **stop**.... and "put yourself in the child's shoes!" Respect the child's natural instincts and be secure in the belief that nature has so ordained that the child will signal and will accept food whenever it is hungry; **and thus cannot starve and become weak as a consequence.**

Regarding the child's weight, it is important to bear in mind that there is no "ideal weight" that you should become obsessed with and strive to achieve. To give an example, two perfectly healthy adults may weigh differently (say one is 60 kilos, another is 70 kilos). Yet both of them are normal and healthy. So we should realise that there is a range of normalcy, rather than a fixed set point. For example, a child of 1 year has a normal weight if it lies between 8-12 kilos, though if 2 children weighing 8 kilos and 12 kilos are compared side by side, one may appear robust and the other may appear thin. And finally remember that too much plumpness in the baby is also not desirable, as there is evidence that this may be the harbinger of

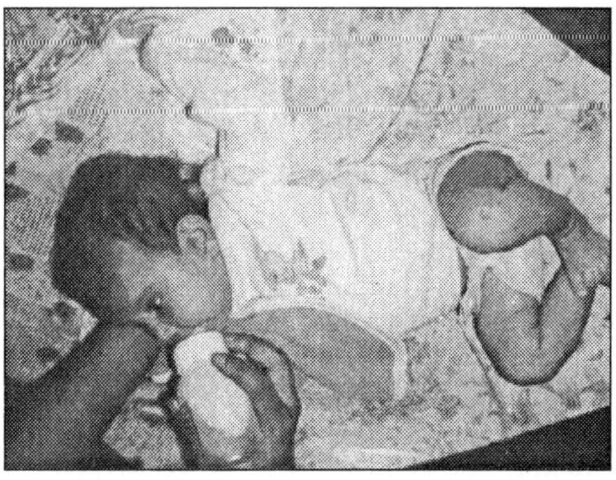

3-months old infant bottle feeding: Observe the intent facial expression of satisfaction, gratitude and intimacy towards the caretaker.

obesity in later life. I remember a doctor friend of mine whose baby tilted the scales at a hefty 8 kilos at 6 months of age. She looked so chubby that people around used to cite her as an example of a perfectly healthy baby. But the doctor father knowing that excessive fat at this age leads to obesity later; put her on diluted milk and rice water i.e. "dieting" to decrease her weight, much to the chagrin of the mother, who however, was wise enough to realise the logic of such a step.

5. Psychological and Mental Development of the Child

Psychiatrist to patient: "Maybe you don't have an inferiority complex - maybe you are inferior."

Nowadays, in this competitive world, parents pay a lot of attention to the mental and psychological development of the child. Parents have high expectations from their children, wanting them to be "perfect." They want their child to excel in academics in the school and be amongst the toppers. Not only that they also expect their child to excel in the extracurricular activities and come out with flying colours in various fields like dancing, singing, sports etc. All this puts a lot of pressure on the child because he has to constantly strive to live up to the high expectations of his parents. When in spite of his best efforts, the child performs below the high set standards; it leads to a feeling of worthlessness and inferiority in the child along with loss of self-esteem and confidence. It also leads to a feeling of disappointment in the parents. **Therefore simply stating, the high expectations of the parents create neurotic children.**

The parents should only support and guide their child to tap his full potential and not burden the child with their expectations. For example, the parents may want their child to be amongst the top ten in the class, but the child may not achieve it. Under these circumstances the parents should not let their disappointments be known to the child. Rather they should try to improve the child's performance by modifying the method of preparations for the exams. The parents should never criticise him for doing badly or compare him with others. Rather they should praise the child for his efforts. After all, the child has tried his best.

Parents, particularly educated ones, also are concerned a lot about the psychological development of their child. Some may consider their child to be timid, docile, socially withdrawn and shy. Others may consider their child to be hyperactive, aggressive and "difficult" to manage. All this may lead to the nagging feeling that there is something wrong with the child's psychological development. This in turn might lead to a feeling of guilt in the parents. They may feel that if only they had been more loving and devoted more time and attention to their child, the child's behaviour may not have been like what it is. It is important to realise that adults also are introverts and extroverts i.e. some adults may be shy and reticent while others may be boisterous, energetic and outgoing. **Yet as long as their behaviour confers to the accepted social norms, it is considered normal**. Similar is the case with the children. As long as the family as a unit is stable and the parents love their child and have a feeling of care and warmth towards him, the child will blossom normally.

Therefore parents should not pressurise themselves and harbour feelings of self-blame regarding the rearing of the child. After all parents are doing their best and no loving parent will deliberately neglect his child. Once in a while if parents blow their tops and get infuriated with the child doesn't mean that they have spoiled the psychology of the child or created an indelible negative impression on the child's mind.

Caution: There are some parents who are overly doting, who look the other way every time their child does something wrong, and instead of being firm with him; bow down to all his tantrums, whims and fancies under the umbrella of the convenient excuse that he is small. Such parents who cannot find or don't want to find any fault with their child are running the risk of making their child a spoiled "brat". Parents should set firm guidelines as to what is wrong and what is right and acceptable, and then treat the child accordingly without wavering. This is what discipline is all about (more about it in a separate chapter on "Child Psychology.")

6. Working Parents

Another common source of parental worry and self-guilt is when both parents are working. This particularly affects the mother because of the strength of the tradition that mothers are supposed to give priority to child-care and child-care is primarily their responsibility as compared to the father. Thus she is caught on the two horns of dilemma. She has to work mainly due to economic considerations, but by doing so she feels that she is not being a "good mother" and neglecting the child. This feeling is very common amongst all working mothers. This is minimised if the husband and other relatives approve and commend her for her efforts in child-care and also share some of the burden. If the mother can resolve her guilt and doubts, her child will not only accept it, but will be proud of her being a working lady. He will feel proud that his father is so and so and his mother is also so and so. **It has been studied and found out that if the mother also is working, it in no way hampers the mental and emotional development of the child**, if the family bonds are strong and based on love and affection. In fact it is the mother's extra sensitivity and doting (after the work hours to "compensate" for her being away from the child) that may have negative effects, and not her absence during the working hours. It has been shown that children whose parents are working are in the long run more autonomous, free and decisive. They become independent faster and don't depend on their parents for small things. They also interact socially more freely and are less shy and clinging.

To overcome the pangs of self-guilt, the mother and the father tend to be extra sensitive towards the child. They shower him with gifts and presents, bow to his wishes, and "literally" let him get away with "murder". When the child finds that the parents are so good appeasers, it makes him more demanding. So working or not working, the parents should shower that much love and attention as comes to them naturally. They should expect reasonable behaviour from their child. In other words they should act like self-confident, firm parents without letting the guilt complex bow them down.

What are the alternatives for such a couple where both are working?

- *The mother's and father's duty hours can be adjusted so that both are not absent for a prolonged period simultaneously.*
- *The job hours can be cut down or alternatively the mother can look for a part time or a short duration job of 3-4 hours.*
- *Engage a caretaker for the baby.*

CARETAKER AND THE CHILD

During the time that both parents are at work, there should be someone (a caretaker) who loves and is sensitive to the needs of the child. This caretaker may be the grandmother, a nanny, a servant etc. For the child it doesn't matter, as long as he is not being neglected by the caretaker. Alternatively the child can be put in a crèche, with the caveat that the crèche should be clean, the caretaker should have a genuine fondness and love for the child rather than just going through the motions. There should not be many children in the crèche as then individualised attention becomes difficult and hence the child may be neglected. The most important aspect is that the child should not feel neglected.

What qualities should parents look for in a caretaker, say an ayah or a servant?

- *Foremost is the person's disposition towards the child. She should be genuinely loving, affectionate and self-confident. She should enjoy the child. She should be able to control him without nagging, neglecting or being harsh.*
- *A common mistake parents make is to look for mainly experience in the caretaker. Experience is desirable, but more important is the right personality as enumerated above.*
- *It is better to have a person who is a bit casual and easy going rather than one who is strict, rigid and full of theories.*
- *Some parents focus on the education of the caretaker, but this is hardly of any importance. A small child does not require a tutor.*
- *A very important aspect is the permanency of the caretaker. Frequent changes in the caretaker of a child have negative consequences. A child as small as 6 months may become depressed and lose his smile, interest and appetite if the person caring for him disappears.*

These are the main points that the working mother should look for and once she finds a suitable caretaker, she can work freely without worrying or feeling guilty about the child's care.

As the child grows older, particularly at the age of 1 year+, he starts realising that both his parents are going away leaving him with someone else for a period of time. He may start pondering about it and once in a while, may request the parents not to leave him alone. He may plead and insist that one of the parents (usually the mother) stay back home to look after and play with him. This is a very critical and sensitive issue and should be tackled delicately.

The most important thing is that the parents should not waver in the face of such a request or show evidence of distress and guilt on their faces. If the mother's heart "bleeds" on such a fervent plea from the child that she starts looking guilty and tends to kiss and hug the child three times over and stays back (thinking one day off duty doesn't matter), two things happen.

Firstly, the child starts thinking that it was not all that necessary for his mother to go to work and hence by going to work daily, she was not fully concerned about him.

Secondly, the child is happy that the mother has acceded to his plea and starts using it as a "weapon" in the future. So the same story is repeated the next day. Ultimately one day the mother will have to leave the child and go to work, as she cannot take a prolonged leave without a valid reason. At that time it really hurts the child and on seeing his hurt, it cuts the mother to the quick and hurts her even more. **So, nip it in the bud and don't let the story repeat itself.** From the first day onwards, don't waver but rather explain to the child why both of you must go to work. Ideally the parents should have mentally prepared and "toughened" themselves a long time ago that such an issue will come up in the future one day. They should have decided amongst themselves (after weighing the pros and cons) that it is necessary for both of them to work and that during their absence the child will be looked after well and not neglected. So when this question comes up, as is bound to one day, the parents are mentally ready to be firm and truthful, without doubts or wavering or feeling guilt.

They should explain to the child the exact reasons why it is necessary for both of them to go to work and why they cannot forego it. They should also reassure the child that their love for him is in no way lessened by the fact that they are working. They should tell the child straightforwardly that they go to work to earn money, which is necessary for running the home and if one of them doesn't work, then the money will become less to support the family. The child understands it and after a period of time and reassurance stops his clamouring for the mother to stay at home. Never lie to the child. Supposing you are going to some party or market and find taking the child bothersome (though I advocate that you should try to take your child to all social gatherings, market for shopping etc, even though cumbersome). Don't tell the child that you are going to work while in reality, you are going out to a party. If at all you cannot take the child, explain to him that you cannot take him to the party because children are not invited there (i.e. give a valid and logical reason to the child).

***Answer to the riddle: The doctor was a female and the nurse was a male. ***

CHAPTER 3

CARE OF THE NEWBORN

KEY POINTS

- **Father's role:** There is no reason why the father can't do all that the mother does for the baby. Once they become used to this role, they feel proud and satisfied that they are good fathers and are contributing something to the upbringing of their child.
- **Bathing:** The baby is very limp and with soap on his body, becomes slippery and liable to slip out of your grasp, which may lead to injury. So be careful.
- **Diapers:** The diaper should not cover the navel as it may soil it. It should be of cotton and frequently changed, preferably after each soiling.
- **Clothing:** Often parents tend to over-clothe the baby, which may be uncomfortable to him. Head should be covered in winters because heat loss through it can be considerable.
- **Stools and urine:** There is a wide range of normalcy regarding voiding of urine and stools. The parents need not be perturbed as long as the stools are not watery or hard and infrequent. Counting the number of times the baby has voided urine or stool is not advisable.
- **Jaundice:** The skin and eyes of the baby may show a yellowish hue. In most of the babies, it is not due to a liver problem, but is due to "physiological jaundice". It requires no treatment. Mothers, who are of the "negative" blood group (e.g. O negative), may have babies with severe jaundice, if the baby's blood group is "positive."
- **Umbilicus:** A slight discharge may come from the navel after the stump has fallen off. This discharge is normal. The navel should be kept as dry as possible and exposed to air.
- **Diarrhoea:** A golden dictum is that breast-fed babies usually don't have infective diarrhoeas. Most of baby diarrhoeas are self-limiting and don't require antibiotics.

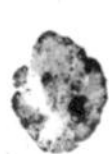

Most of the parents are unprepared and scared at the prospect of taking sole charge of such a precious commodity as their helpless baby for the first time. If there is a support system, e.g. the grandparents of the baby, the parents feel less anxious as they are reassured by the presence of someone experienced. Some of the worries and doubts of parents concern the baby's temperature, feeding, crying, sleeping, colic, burping, breathing, voiding etc. This feeling is natural and goes away with time as the parents adjust to the needs of the baby, realise that it isn't all that fragile; and thus gain confidence, both in themselves as parents and also in the "strength" of the baby.

The birth of a baby should be planned well in advance. The obstetrician should be consulted regularly during pregnancy. Diapers, clothes, baby cosmetics etc. for the baby should be bought in advance and a cot for the baby should be put in an appropriate warm and cosy place in the house.

FATHER'S ROLE

***There's nothing in this world that I wouldn't do for my wife and there is nothing she wouldn't do for me – we spend our lives doing nothing for each other. ***

***Tears: The hydraulic force by which masculine will power is defeated by feminine waterpower. ***

The role of the father is extremely important in the care of the newborn. There is no reason why the father cannot do all that the mother does for the baby, thus contributing towards the growth and development of the baby. Once they become mentally adapted to the role of child-care, they feel very satisfied that they are contributing their share towards the rearing of the baby and also feel proud in the fact that they are good fathers.

Initially what happens is that the father, just like the mother, is not ready for the responsibility and so may adopt the attitude that **he will wait** till the baby is bigger and more like a human being. Mothers, on the other hand, can't postpone it. They have to start immediately and learn quickly as the onus of baby care, culturally and socially, lies primarily with her. An understanding husband at this stage is required. He should understand that the mother has just delivered a baby and she also is not an expert in childcare. In fact she is as much a novice as he is. So if both take it as a combined duty, reassure each other and talk out their fears and anxieties, not only will they be able to better cope with the child-care, but the wife will also much appreciate the husband's maturity and understanding. However, this benefit is lost if the husband does this work as a

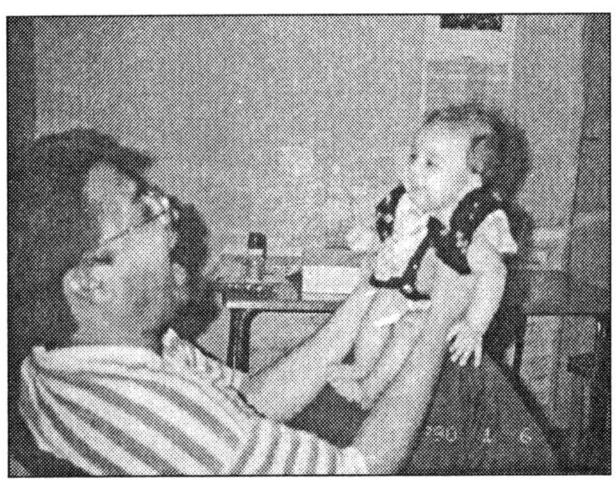

Matching the affective expression of laughter: At this age, 30% of times, infant match the expressions of the caretaker.

favour towards his wife rather than considering it as a part of his duty, since then it implies that it is not really his work, but he is doing it as a generosity towards his wife.

The husband should not feel ashamed or shy in taking care of his baby. Because the men, right from childhood, are not ingrained with the idea of baby care, they find it awkward, embarrassing and difficult to accept (particularly things like changing the soiled diapers or cleaning the stools of the child). I can understand this feeling of men, and the best way to lessen the intensity of such a feeling is by thinking:

i) Many fathers, both in Indian and western society are participating actively in the baby care and take pride in it, so why not you too? Experts in newborn care nowadays stress on an active role of the father in baby care so as to make it wholesome and complete.

ii) The most important point is that they are doing it for their own baby, and so what is wrong or embarrassing about it? Infact they should feel satisfied and proud for it.

ROUTINE BABY CARE

Parents harbour doubts whether they are doing baby care correctly e.g. is the feeding proper, the clothing suitable etc? My advice is that parents should trust their natural instincts. The very fact that you are doing something for the care of your own child (even if awkwardly) is enough for the baby to feel loved and have a sense that she belongs to you and that you belong to her. Nobody else in the world, including the most perfect baby care provider, can give this feeling to your child. You and only you can make your baby feel as a part of you by your loving care, even if this care is less than theoretically perfect. (For more details refer to the chapter on "Parental Concerns and Anxieties.")

***At 18 a woman is like a football, 22 men after her. At 28, basketball, 10 men after her. At 38 golf ball, 1 man after her. At 48, TT ball, 2 men pushing her to the other. ***

1. Bathing Your Baby

Before you bathe your baby, make sure everything you need is at hand: a baby bath tub/basin, baby soap, soft towels, some cotton wool, a set of clean clothes, a clean nappy and water that is approximately the same temperature as your body. Any standard baby soap and shampoo can be used. The mother can do the bathing sitting on the floor or standing (by keeping the bathtub at her waist level on some platform). Start by undressing your baby. One hand should always be supporting the child (the head of the baby should be supported on your forearm or wrist and the

Having a bath: An ideal way of holding your baby.

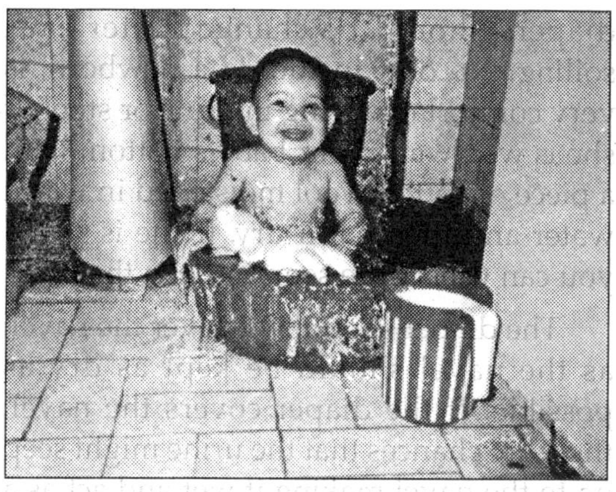

9-month old baby enjoying bathing: Note the splashing of water by the baby and her toy also having a bath with her.

fingers of that hand should hold the baby securely around her armpit) while the other can be used for applying soap, shampoo and then rinsing with water. With the other hand, wash the scalp. Gently rub some mild soap over the body and limbs. Then turn him over and soap his back. The important thing to remember is that the baby is very limp and with soap on his body, becomes slippery and liable to slip out of your grasp. That is why I stress on a bathtub, so that even if the baby slips, he remains in the bathtub only and thus not get injured. Bathing the baby on the floor or bathing the baby without a bathtub makes the baby prone to injury due to accidental slipping. So hold him firmly around the top of the arm, giving support to the shoulders. With the other hand support his bottom and lower him gently into the bath tub. Continue to support the baby's shoulders. Now rinse off all the soap by gently splashing water. Lift your baby out of the bath, wrap him in a towel and dry with another towel, paying attention to the skin creases and folds. Use a soft towel for drying. Drying should be done

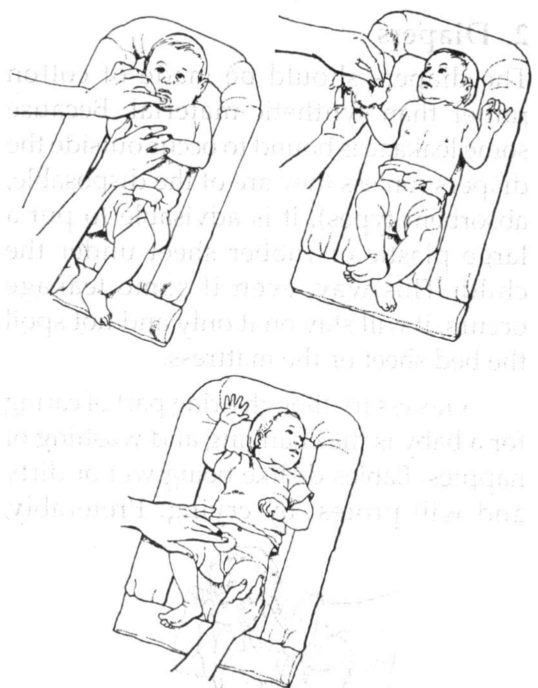

Dry cleaning: The process of sponging the face, body and genital area of the baby with warm water.

by patting rather than rubbing. Finally apply some baby cream if you use and put on a fresh nappy and clothes.

It is not essential that the baby should be bathed daily. There is no basis in the theory that babies should not be bathed till the navel is completely healed. If the navel stump is there, just dry it after giving the bath and then apply some spirit over it with clean cotton.

In cold weathers there is no need to bathe the baby daily (twice a week will do). Instead you can give a sponge bath with warm water and soft towel (if not to the whole body, then at least the diaper area should be cleaned daily with soap and water). **There is no need to clean the nose, ears, mouth, eyes and tongue of the baby.**

2. Diapers

The diapers should be made of cotton rather than synthetic material. Because some leakage is bound to occur outside the diapers (unless they are of the disposable, absorbent types), it is advisable to put a large plastic or rubber sheet under the child. This way, even if some leakage occurs, it will stay on it only and not spoil the bed sheet or the mattress.

A necessary though tiring part of caring for a baby is the changing and washing of nappies. Babies dislike being wet or dirty and will protest by crying. Preferably, diapers should be changed after each soiling. No one, including a newborn, is very comfortable lying in urine or stool. If she is wet, wash your baby's bottom with a piece of cotton wool moistened in warm water and then pat it dry. If she is soiled you can use a little soap to clean the baby.

A diaper change: Change it as soon as it is soiled

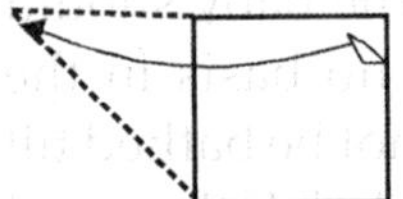

1. Take a nappy folded in four with the open edges to the top and right. Pick up the top layer by the right-hand edge.

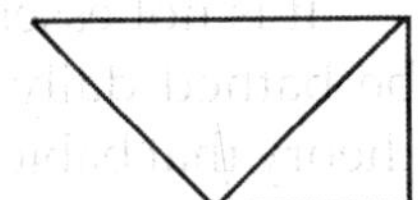

2. Pull out the top layer to form an inverted triangle up the top layer by the right-hand edge.

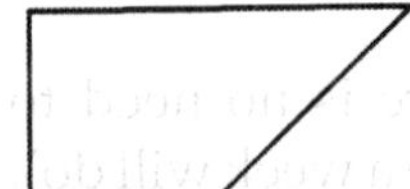

3. Carefully turn the whole nappy over so that the pointed edge is at the top right-hand side.

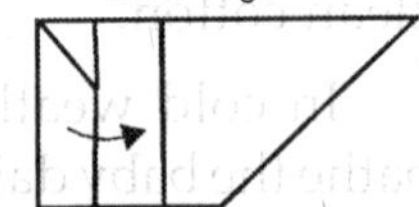

4. Fold the two middle layers into the centre by one third.

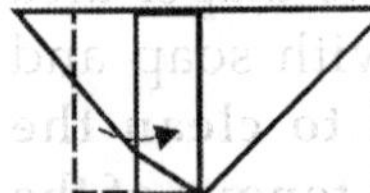

5. Fold in another third to form a thick central panel.

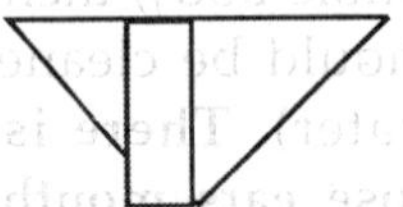

6. Put a nappy liner in the middle and have a pin ready.

The diaper should not cover the navel; as the navel should be kept as dry as possible. If the diaper covers the navel, there are chances that the urine might seep on to the navel making it wet and act as a source of infection. Plus accidental traction on the diaper by movement of the baby or during changing can apply a shearing force on the navel and lead to minor bleeding from there.

Clean soiled nappies by holding under running water. Scrape off the excess. Then wash the nappy in hot water with soap or detergent powders, and rinse thoroughly.

For going outside or undertaking journeys, excellent disposable baby diapers are available. Routine use of them is not done at home, basically because of the cost factor.

Preferably the diapers should be secured in place by tying with a knot. If you use safety pins, be careful that it doesn't accidentally open and hurt the baby. The diaper should be of generous size and the most cloth should be around the area of passage of urine and stool.

3. Care of the navel

***Once there was a search for Adam in heaven and a saint was asked to locate him quickly. He did it very rapidly, which astonished God. He asked how he could so fast, to which he replied "it is simple. He is the only one without a navel." ***

The delivering doctor cuts off the umbilical cord soon after birth. It dries and shrivels off gradually over a period of 1-2 weeks (depending on the climate) and then falls off leaving the healthy navel. During this period, the cord should be kept as dry as possible. It should be daily cleaned with spirit swab and left open to dry in the air. There is no need to apply any powder or ointment (medicated or non-medicated) over the navel.

4. Massage

Massage of the baby is good (most babies enjoy it). Any baby oil can be used for massaging. There is no harm in exposing the baby to sunshine, provided the sun is not too hot (the baby can tolerate the same amount of sun that you can). You can apply powder/lotions to the baby (at least it makes the baby smell good!). But it is best to avoid cosmetics on areas of the skin which are chapped and broken or have some rashes or allergic manifestations. One should also be aware of the fact that it is not absolutely necessary to massage or apply cosmetics on the baby.

5. Clothing

Common sense should guide the parents. In hot summers, the baby will feel comfortable in a light cotton wear. In general, a term, healthy baby is able to maintain his body temperature well and is comfortable in the same type & amount of clothing as an adult.

In winters, it is preferable to cover as much parts of the baby as possible including the head with a cap, the feet with woollen socks and the hands with woollen gloves. The covering of the head is important as it has got a large surface area and hence heat loss through it can be considerable. During sleeping, the baby may toss and turn and thus uncover himself of the blanket or the quilt. It is better to rap the baby with a blanket and if you feel that he requires more warmth, you can put a quilt on top of the baby swathed in the blanket. Often, parents tend to over-clothe (rather than under-clothe the baby), which may be pretty uncomfortable to the baby. Over-clothing the baby can lead to excessive heat retention and the baby may land up with dehydration and fever. Common sense dictates that the parents should put themselves in the baby's place and try to imagine in their minds whether they will be comfortable if covered with the same amount and type of clothes. Another precaution the parents should take is that the nose of the baby should be open to allow him to breathe easily. Any type of clothing, which can slip and cover the nose of the baby, may be dangerous.

NORMAL ASPECTS OF THE BABY

*** What similar things you prefer in your coffee and your girlfriend.*

- Should be hot
- Should be rich
- Should be creamy
- Should be able to keep you awake all night**

There are many facts and things regarding a baby that are normal. The parents should be aware of these small but significant truths, so that they don't get unnecessarily concerned.

1. Normal parameters of a newborn

A baby is term if it is 37-42 weeks' gestation. If it is less than 37 weeks, it is preterm and if it is more than 42 weeks, it is post-term. A pregnancy is typically 40 weeks. The EDD (expected date of delivery) = LMP (last menstrual period) + 9 months and 7 days. Supposing a pregnant woman had her LMP on 1.1.96. Then the EDD will be 8.10.96, which is equal to 40 weeks of pregnancy. If the baby is born between 17.9.96 (i.e. 3 weeks prior to 8.10.96 = 37 weeks) and 22.10.96 (i.e. 2 weeks after 8.10.96 = 42 weeks), then it is term.

A term baby's normal weight lies between 2.5 kilos to 3.8 kilos. A term baby loses some of its birth weight for 3-4 days and regains it by the end of 1 week. A baby weighing less than 2.5 kilos is "small for date" while a baby weighing more than 3.8 kilos is "large for date". The normal length of a term baby is approximately 48-52 cms. The normal head circumference of a term baby is 33-36 cms. When your baby is born, these parameters (i.e. the gestational age, birth weight, length and head circumference) should be preferably recorded in the discharge slip of the baby. These parameters should be monitored regularly (once every 1-2 months till the baby is 1 year old and twice a year thereafter: excepting head size which is of importance only till the age of 2 years) and plotted on a "growth card" because they are very good indicators of the growth and development of a child. A good doctor will usually record them during the time of routine immunization.

2. Feeding

Parents are requested to refer to the chapter "Feeding" for detailed advice regarding feeding. Babies may bring out some whitish, curd like semi-digested milk from the corner of their mouths after feeds. This is called "Regurgitation" and is normal. It should not be mistaken or confused with vomiting, in which the baby will throw out most of the milk in its original liquid consistency. Vomiting is not normal and a doctor should always be consulted.

3. Stool and urine

If the baby passes stools within the first 24 hours and urine within the first 48 hours, it is normal. Very often, I have seen parents worrying that their child has not passed urine even once after birth. A simple reassurance that the baby will do so within 48 hours is all that is required, as barring an occasional baby, all of them do pass it.

The stool that the baby initially passes is called "meconium." It is greenish black and sticky in consistency. After 3-4 days, the baby passes what is called "transitional stools", which is a bit soft/liquid and yellowish green in colour. By the end of 1 week, the baby passes normal stools, which in the breast-fed baby are golden yellow and soft. Formula fed babies pass stools that are pale yellow and firm to hard. Generally, the frequency of motions is more in breast-fed babies than formula fed babies. Some babies may pass stools after each feed (i.e. 10-12 times/day) while some may not pass stools even for a whole day (even if breast-fed). The next day, they may pass stools, which is soft in consistency (they may pass stools once in 1-2 days). All this is normal. Some babies groan and grunt, strain a lot and may even cry before voiding stools or urine, which again is normal.

There is such a wide range of normalcy regarding voiding of urine and stools that the parents need not be perturbed as long as the stools that are passed are not watery or hard and infrequent. Counting the number of times the baby has voided urine or stool is not advisable.

4. The skull (head)

At birth, there is a diamond shaped gap (about 1" in diameter) between the bones of the anterior part of the skull in the midline covered by a tough canvas like covering. This gap is soft and compressible. It is called "anterior fontanel", and it closes by 1-2 years of age.

The head of a baby born by operation or born breech (buttocks first) is typically round, while the head of a baby born vertex (head first) may be elongated and asymmetric, being depressed or elevated on one side. You need not worry about it as in a few days the head will assume its natural round contour. Babies who lie most of the times on one side may develop a flattening of the skull on that side. For e.g. if the baby is sleeping on his back most of the times, then the back of the head may become flat. Again this is no cause for concern as the head resumes its natural shape when the baby starts sitting up.

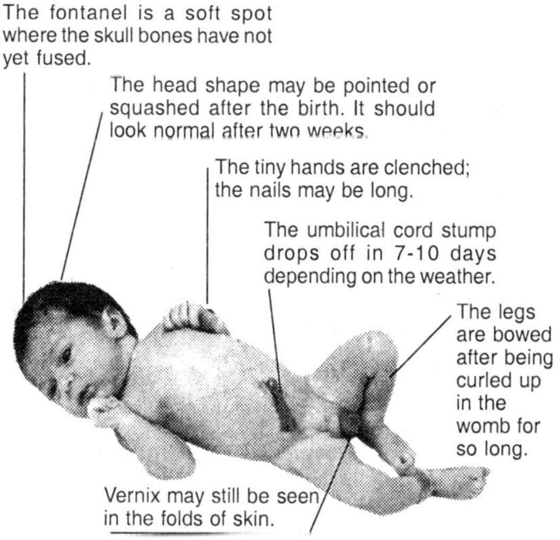

A newborn infant: Parts of the body of a baby.

A swelling of the skull, which is soft and compressible, may rarely persist for 1-2 months. This is called "cephal-haematoma" and is due to collection of some blood under the scalp. This regresses and disappears spontaneously, and doesn't require any intervention like taking out the collection of blood. Still, sadly, one sees some babies, whose such swellings have been incised by a knife or a needle was used to aspirate out the blood.

5. Eyes

The babies have a natural aversion to strong light called "photophobia." Therefore they keep their eyes closed under bright light and open it only in dimly lit areas. Sometimes they may open only one eye, which is normal. The babies don't usually spill tears while crying till the age of 3-4 months. So, if there is watering of the eyes, it may be abnormal (see below). The baby's eyes may deviate momentarily towards each other, giving the impression of cross-eyedness or squint. Such a phenomenon is normal. However, if there is persistent squinting, particularly after 6 months of age, you should definitely consult your child specialist.

A discreet red blotch may be seen on the conjunctiva of the baby on one side of the cornea, which is nothing else but a minor bleed called "subconjunctival haemorrhage." It requires no treatment and subsides of its own within a few days. If there is any discharge from the eyes, it is best to show it to your doctor.

6. Mouth

Sometimes the babies may have 1 or 2 teeth in the midline on the lower gums. These are called "natal teeth" and should not be pulled out unless they are loose. The tongue may be bound to the floor of the mouth with a short cord like structure called the frenulum, as a result of which it may not be able to protrude out fully. Popularly called as "tongue tie", nothing has to be done for it as long as it doesn't interfere with eating and speech (which usually it doesn't). A rule of thumb is that if the tongue is able to come out up to the lower lip's outer margin, it is normal and will not interfere with the speech of the baby (because when we speak we don't protrude our tongue!) If there is any hole or gap in the roof of the mouth (called cleft palate), it is abnormal and requires medical consultation.

7. Nose

The bridge of the baby's nose may be slightly depressed. The babies till the age of 3 months are obligatory nose breathers (i.e. they do not open their mouth to breathe, as adults do, if their nose is blocked). Thus a blocked nose makes breathing very difficult for them and they end up crying and getting irritated. Many babies have a "stuffy nose" right from birth till the age of 3-4 months. Some sound may come from the nose while breathing. This stuffiness of the nose, which doesn't interfere with the breathing (as compared to the blocked nose) usually doesn't require any treatment. Sneezing is a normal mechanism in the babies (as in adults) and is not indicative of a cold or a respiratory infection.

Some babies make an audible whistling sound (called stridor), which if you carefully listen doesn't come from the nose but rather appears to be coming from the throat of the baby. The sound comes when the baby is breathing in. A doctor should be consulted for such a sound. In most cases, such a sound is due to congenital weakness of the muscles of the "voice box (larynx)" and the condition is called as "laryngomalacia." It is benign and self-limiting. The muscles become stronger as the baby grows up and so the baby outgrows the sound, without any medicines, usually by the age of 1-2 years.

8. Skin

"Toxic erythema" is a flea bitten type of rash seen frequently in term babies on the 2nd day. It has to be differentiated from boils, which have a yellowish centre with surrounding redness. Most of the skin rashes are benign and self-limiting for which no medicines, lotions or creams are required. Do not apply cosmetics on the area of skin rashes.

Scaling and peeling of the skin is seen in some new-borns, particularly those who are post-term or are small for date. There may be numerous transverse creases on the abdomen. Hands and feet may also show peeling. Usually the skin is dry in these babies. An emollient like glycerine or paraffin or even oil is sufficient for the dryness and peeling of the skin.

Newborns and infants may sweat a lot, particularly in the area of the neck and head as a result of which parents complain that they have to change the clothes of the newborn often as it becomes wet due to sweating. This sweating is normal and not a sign of any underlying disease. However, if the baby sweats with some shortness of breath, show to the doctor as it may signify an underlying heart disease.

Slate blue spots may be present over the buttocks and back of the baby called "Mongolian spots." They are of no consequence and usually disappear by the age of 1 year.

Small red or bluish red well-demarcated blotches, which blanch on pressure and may be raised from the level of the skin, may be seen on the neck, back of the scalp, eyelids etc. Called hemangiomas, these do not require any therapy unless they are increasing in size.

Parents may find the hands and feet of the baby to be cold and the nails having a bluish hue. Called "acrocyanosis", this is usually due to exposure to cold. As long as the tongue is pink, there is nothing to worry. **If however, the tongue also is blue, it is very serious and immediate medical help should be sought**.

9. Jaundice

The skin of the baby and the eyes may show a yellowish hue. Parents consider it as jaundice (which it is) and are anxious about it. However, the yellowness in most babies is not due to a liver problem, but is what is called as "physiological jaundice". As the term "physiological" suggests, there is nothing to be alarmed about it. It requires no treatment and will subside spontaneously in 1-2 weeks. However, all babies with jaundice should be once shown to the doctor, who is the best judge of whether the jaundice is physiological or not.

10. Breasts

Some babies may have larger than normal breast nodules, out of which sometimes some milk may also be expressed. This is due to the influence of the maternal hormones. It is benign, self-limiting and doesn't require any treatment. **Do not squeeze or massage the enlarged breast tissue or try to express milk out of it.** However, if the skin around the breast tissue becomes red, consult your doctor.

11. Genitalia

Males: One or both testis may not be felt in the scrotum. In many cases, one of the testes is retractile, which means that it retracts into the abdomen and comes back into the scrotum off and on. This is a normal entity. So, absence of testis from the scrotum doesn't necessarily mean that there is something wrong with the baby, particularly if the testis were seen or felt in the scrotum even once anytime. Sometimes one testis may be actually absent. The parents need not be anxious as a single normally functioning testis is as good as two testes in carrying on the reproductive function i.e. your child will not be sterile. The skin over the tip of the penis is tight in the newborn and no attempt should be made to forcibly retract it. It is called "physiologic phimosis" and usually corrects itself by the age of 6 years. However, if there is a bulbous swelling of the skin at the tip of the penis while passing urine or the urinary stream is weak, a doctor should be consulted. In these cases, excision of the tight skin i.e. circumcision may be required.

Females: Sometimes, female babies bleed through the vagina (just like menstruation in the females) due to the influence of maternal hormones. Parents often interpret it as blood coming in the urine. It is benign for which no treatment is required. A slight whitish vaginal discharge in newborn female babies is also normal.

12. Limbs of the baby

The limbs of the baby, particularly the legs are a bit bowed and turn outwards. This condition is called bow legs and is normal till the age of 6 years. After that also if the legs are bowed, one should consult a doctor. Similarly the limbs of a baby are in a flexed (drawn together position). Attempts should not be made to extend them, e.g. the legs by swathing them in cloth wrap. Parents do so in the belief that the legs should be "straightened" so that they don't remain bent, which they feel may lead to problems like walking later on in life. However, no attempts should be made to extend the limbs. Babies may have hip dislocated from the time of birth (called CDH = congenital dislocation of the hip joint). It is difficult to pick up, but the doctor should make efforts to diagnose it as early treatment is better. If delayed for too long, beyond the age of 1 year, it may lead to a limp in the child.

Sometimes the ankle of the baby is twisted inwards. This is called CTEV = congenital talipes equino varus). If the ankle is stiff, it requires early physiotherapy and maybe even the application of a cast to keep the ankle straight so as to correct the twist.

13. Crying / sleeping

Parents are requested to refer to the chapters on "Crying and Sleeping" in this book. Newborn babies often jerk their limbs during sleep, but not while they are awake. This is called myoclonus and is a normal phenomenon.

14. Trembling

Babies often tremble or quiver momentarily in their sleep or while awake. They may appear jittery with momentary trembling of their extremities. All this is normal and as long as the baby is feeding and sucking well and is active; parents need not concern themselves.

COMMON NEWBORN PROBLEMS

Despite the old saying, "Don't take your troubles with you to bed, many men still sleep with their wives."

***A wife to her husband: "Can you tell me the difference between truth and belief?"*

*Husband replied after careful thought: "Look dear, Raju is your son is a truth. Raju is my son is a belief."***

1. Small Boils on the skin

They are broken by firmly rubbing them with a cotton swab soaked in gentian violet paint, which subsequently is applied over the raw areas till healing is there. As long as the baby is active and sucking well, there is no need for oral antibiotics or other medications.

2. Thrush

It is a fungal infection of the tongue seen mainly in bottle fed babies or those who are on antibiotics. It appears like a white coating on the tongue, which can be confused with a milk layer. The milk layer however, disappears if the tongue is cleaned. Thrush is common but benign. A 5-day local application over the tongue of an anti-fungal lotion cures it.

3. Jaundice

Most of the babies have a "physiological" jaundice for which no therapy is required. Some babies, however, may have jaundice which is more than normal (e.g. for term babies, the upper limit is 17 mg%. If the bilirubin is more than 17 mg%, the jaundice is not physiological and requires treatment). Putting the baby under light, called "phototherapy" is the treatment given to such babies. Rarely, jaundice may become severe enough to threaten damage to the baby's brain, in which case "exchange transfusion" is done. In this whole of the baby's blood is exchanged with an equal amount of adult blood.

Mothers of the "negative" blood group may have babies with severe jaundice if the baby's blood group is "positive". Usually, the first baby escapes and it is the 2nd baby onwards that is afflicted by severe jaundice. Excellent prevention against this is fortunately, available. It consists of giving "negative" mothers an injection of "Anti-D" during 24-28 weeks of pregnancy and again within 72 hours after delivery whenever they give birth to a "positive" baby. This prevents subsequent babies from developing severe jaundice.

4. Eye discharge

Many babies have discharge from their eyes. If the discharge is cloudy, pus like, with redness of the eyes, it is due to an infection of the eye called "conjunctivitis." It requires instillation of antibiotic eye drops. Often, a course of oral antibiotics is also required.

Commoner than this, however, is a condition in which the baby has a clear, watery discharge from the eyes without any redness. The eyes may appear sticky in the morning after sleep. This is a non-infective condition and is due to blockage of a thin tube called the nasolacrimal duct situated at the nose end of the eye, which drains the tears of the baby into the nose. When it gets blocked, the tears instead of going into the nose flow out of the eyes onto the cheeks. Many doctors recommend massaging the nose (near the eye). In most of the cases, the tube spontaneously opens by the end of 1-2 years; and so it is worth while for the parents to be patient and wait. If at the end of this period, the condition still persists, show your child to an eye specialist.

5. Navel problems

A slight discharge, whitish or yellowish in colour may come from the navel after the cord stump has fallen off. This is normal, usually lasts for a day or two and then stops. However, if the discharge is pus like or foul smelling, consult your doctor as it may signify an infection of the navel that may lead to dangerous complications. A slight amount of redness around the cord area is also normal.

Sometimes, there may be bleeding from the navel. If the blood is coming out because some clot or covering over the cord has been accidentally stripped off (e.g. during bathing or changing diapers), then there is no cause for alarm as the bleeding will usually stop by itself in 2-3 minutes. However, if there is spontaneous bleeding from the cord or the bleeding doesn't stop, then consult your doctor immediately.

In some babies, there is a swelling at the navel area, which is soft and compressible. This swelling can be made smaller and to subside into the abdomen by compressing it. However, it will re-appear. Called "Umbilical Hernia," this doesn't require any treatment as the swelling in most cases disappears permanently, as the child grows older. However, if the swelling is still present at the age of 4 years and above, show it to your doctor.

6. Blocked nose

It may be quite troublesome. The best treatment is to put normal saline drops in the nose and then clean the mucus in the nose by means of a cotton bud. Alternatively baby buds can be soaked in saline water and then gently inserted into the nose. After that the bud can be gently twirled in the nose and withdrawn. Any mucus that is present in the nose can thus be taken out along with the bud. Medicated drops (as opposed to normal saline drops) should be put only for 3-5 days at the maximum and that too under medical supervision.

Sometimes steroid nose drops may be required, particularly if the nose block is troublesome and not responding to the above treatments.

Oral decongestant drops may also be tried on the doctor's advice.

Putting oil or milk in nose, putting milk in eyes: It is often seen that mothers put oil in the nose as a means of relieving the nose block, a common complaint amongst newborns. It is dangerous as the oil having a low viscosity may trickle down into the throat and thence into the lungs. Chronic use of oil in the nose has resulted in damage to the lungs and difficulty in breathing. Oil should not be put in the nose. The best thing is to put normal saline in the nose. Similarly putting breast milk in the eyes can result in undesirable side effects for the eye and is mentioned here to be discouraged.

7. Fever

As opposed to fever in an older child, any fever in a newborn baby or the opposite, i.e. the baby appears cold and lethargic, should be shown to a doctor on an urgent basis.

8. Diarrhoea

If the baby is active, sucking well and the loose stools do not contain any pus or blood; there is no cause for alarm. Most of such diarrhoeas are self-limiting and don't require any medicines. If the mother is breast-feeding and is taking some medicines like antibiotics or laxatives, the baby can have diarrhoea due to that. In such a case it is advisable to stop or substitute the medicines that the mother is taking. Rarely, eating lots of onions, tomatoes, cabbages, chillies etc. by the breast-feeding mother can cause diarrhoea in the baby. A golden dictum is that breast-fed babies usually don't have infective diarrhoeas. So unless there is a compelling reason, a breast-fed baby having loose stools should not be prescribed any antibiotics, as the diarrhoea is usually non-infectious. Diarrhoea in a neonate may be harmless as mentioned above or a symptom of serious underlying disorders like sepsis. So if the baby doesn't look well, is apathetic and doesn't suck with the same vigour as before, immediately consult your doctor.

9. Upper limbs moving less

This is a complication of a difficult delivery, e.g. the baby is not coming out and so the doctor has to pull and manipulate the baby to make it deliver or apply forceps to pull out the baby. The above procedures adopted by the doctor to bring out the baby are medically fully justified. Rarely, as a result of this, there may be an injury to the bones of the upper limb (e.g. a break of the collarbone) or there may be an injury to the nerves supplying the upper limb (called "Erb's Paralysis"). Fortunately, in both types of injuries, i.e. to the bones or the nerves, the baby recovers well and usually doesn't have any residual problems. In case of a bone injury, the upper limb may be splinted for 1-2 weeks. In case of a nerve injury, it takes about 2-3 months for the injured nerves to recover. During this time, no particular therapy or positioning of the limbs is required. Making the limb immobile (as in the case of bone injuries) is not recommended. The parents, after a week or so, should start physiotherapy of the upper limb, by actively moving the joints of the upper limb so that the muscles of the arm don't go in a state of contracture.

CHAPTER 4

GROWTH AND DEVELOPMENT

KEY POINTS

- **Parental role**: A loving bond between parents and baby, a harmonious inter-spouse relationship and a congenial family atmosphere are the most important requirements for the healthy growth & development of a child. Accept your child as he is and forget about the qualities that he doesn't possess (no human being is perfect).
- **Comparisons and parental attitude:** Every individual is different and unique. Your child also is. Different children have different patterns of growth and development. Therefore it is superfluous to compare your child with others. The age of attainment of a milestone is an approximate average. If your child achieves a milestone early, it doesn't mean that he will be a prodigy and vice-versa. Parents use gross milestones like sitting, walking etc. as indicators of development. However they are least reliable. The most important indicators like alertness, responsiveness, concentration etc. are abstract and defy objective assessment.

Growth

- **Growth assessment:** Serial measurements of weight, height and head circumference are the most important indicators of the physical growth of a child. These are plotted on a "growth chart" periodically. Parents should try to keep a systemic record of them.
- **Weight**: Weight should be always measured on the same scales. The weight of a child may vary falsely, if different scales are used, creating anxiety in the parents.
- **Height:** The final height achieved by a child is determined strongly by genetic inheritance from parents. There is little medical intervention can do to alter the final height.
- **Head circumference:** 80% of the brain growth occurs during the 1st two years. Therefore measurement of HC has significance mainly up to 2 years. It should be measured every 1-2 months during the first year.

Development

- **Social smile:** It is a very important indicator of normal baby development. It is the baby's first way to show that he can also socially interact. If a baby doesn't smile by 2 months, one starts suspecting that the baby's development may be retarded in the future.
- **The 10-month milestone:** The child approaches an object kept in front by extending his index finger towards it. This "index finger" approach is a powerful evidence to show that the child is developing normally.
- **Separation anxiety:** It begins at 6-12 months when the child becomes wary of a stranger and clings to the mother for reassurance. Before this, the child goes to any stranger.
- **Mobility:** At 9-10 months, the child starts crawling on all fours. He can now rove from one spot to another and pull things from "hitherto protected areas".

- **Autonomy and Independence:** It starts at 1 year of age and leads to a lot of tension and struggle for control between the child and the parents. However, imagine if the child doesn't manifest this. This means that throughout his life, he will be dependant! Parents should understand this phase as a part of every child's growing up and make light of the "NO's" that the child says quite often in response to various parental requests and desires.
- **Language:** The first indication that the child will be able to speak in future comes at 2 months, when the baby coos (gurgling "throaty" sounds). The first meaningful word that pertains consistently to a specific object or person makes its appearance at the age of 1 year.
- **Dental development:** There is no fixed time when the first tooth erupts. In some children, it may erupt at 5 months, while in others it may not erupt till 1 year of age. Complaints at the time of teething like diarrhoea, fever etc. is attributed to it, which is not correct. Teething perse doesn't cause any illness.

Growth pertains to physical aspects like height, weight etc. which can be quantified and objectively measured. Development refers to the mental progress of the child like his intelligence etc. and therefore is qualitative. All parents are concerned and rightly so, about the growth and development of their child.

Unlike other species, the human development is the slowest with the child being dependent on parental care for a number of years. Therefore, the relationship between parents and the baby constitutes the most important requirement for the healthy development of a child. Fortunately, both parents and the baby are programmed by nature to form strong attachments towards each other. Even a few days old baby responds preferentially to the image of a human face and particularly to the mother's voice. Because of the love, affection and care of the parents, the young child experiences an early sense of security, warmth and positive self-worth. This early and secure bonding between the baby and the parents is essential for the healthy development of a child.

Parents feel joy and pride seeing their child growing. The day the baby smiles back in response to their social interaction is heart warming for the parents. Similarly as the child progresses and achieves other milestones like sitting, standing, saying "mama", "papa" etc., the parents feel proud and happy.

But, parents being parents (and it happens with all parents) subconsciously or consciously, monitor their child's progress. They are quick to worry if they feel that the progress of the child is not in keeping up with what they think should be. Or they may compare their child with other children and feel that he is not as quick as the other child was in achieving certain milestones, for example standing. This may make them not only anxious but also guilty as they may wonder whether there has been some fault in their upbringing. This is a natural feeling of the parents and this is the way that all good parents are made of.

Three important things regarding parenthood are:

*** (Alcoholism and good parenthood are not compatible): An alcoholic had "alcoholic liver disease" and was sternly asked to stop alcohol. Next day he went to the bar and asked for 1 peg instead of his normal 2. The bartender was* *astonished. He replied that he and his friend had taken an oath that they will drink one peg for themselves and one for each other's good health daily. The bartender asked, "Sir, has your friend died?" "No" replied the alcoholic, "he is fit and fine. It is just that I have given up drinking alcohol from today."* **

1. The way the parents care for their child and their love and affection for their baby is something that comes instinctively and naturally to all the parents without their having to attend any special classes for it. **And what is natural cannot be wrong.** So the development of the child cannot be slow or fast due to less or more love and affection of the parents, simply because all conscentitious parents love their children with all their hearts. So parents should not relate the growth and development of their child with the quality of their care because all good parents provide "quality care" to their child. Some rare exceptions where the child's development may suffer is when there is a broken home, strained marriage, divorce, mental stress between the spouses, the husband is a drunkard or drug addict, the mother or father suffers from mental illness etc. But if the relation between the spouses is harmonious and the family environment is blissful, then the child will develop to its full potential. The parents should not therefore hold themselves responsible and feel guilty for the "perceived" slow development of their child.

2. Every individual is different and unique. Your child also is. Because of this, they have different patterns of growth and development. Therefore it is superfluous to compare your child with others. There is no fixed time for reaching a certain milestone, which can be considered the gold standard against which comparisons can be made. For example, parents often "know" that the child should start walking by the age of 1 year. **What they don't know is that this "knowing" is not entirely correct.** For example, their child may not be walking by 15 months of age (though able to stand with support), while the relative's child was able to stand with support at the age of 10 months, and at 15 months, was walking freely around. The parents will immediately think that their child is a "slow" developer and blame themselves for it. What the parents should really know is that a child who walks at the age of 10 months and a child who walks at the age of 18 months, are both normal. A child who achieved walking earlier is certainly not going to be a super human or a prodigy just because he walked earlier; neither is a child who walked later be a mentally slow child and lag behind other children.

Milestones like sitting, standing, walking etc are evident and thus form an obvious way of comparison for the parents. On top of this is the "half knowledge" learned by the parents' e.g. the child should walk by 1 year of age. **In reality, the most easily scored items like walking are the least reliable indicators of the overall developmental potential of a child.** Some of the most important aspects of assessment like alertness, responsiveness, concentration, perseverance are abstract and defy an objective measurement or scoring.

3. The third and the most important point that I want to make is to enjoy and love your child for what it is (and not worry for what it is not). Appreciate them for what they can do, and forget about the qualities that they don't have (after all no human being is perfect and should not also be). The children who are reared positively, praised and liked by their parents for what they are, will grow up happy and with confidence in themselves. Even if by misfortune, they are clumsy or slow congenitally (by birth), they will have a spirit that will bring out the best in them and make the maximal use of all the capacities that they possess.

But a child, who otherwise was normal at birth, may grow up lacking confidence, if the parents are worried that their child is not one of the brightest children around. Such parents do not accept the child for what he is but want him to go on striving for perfection. Any shortcoming in him and the parents will quickly notice and point it out. Plus they will pressurise him to "iron" out the flaw. Such a child will not be able to make full use of his potential and skills firstly because he is under a constant pressure of parental expectations and secondly because his shortcomings are highlighted, leading to a feeling of inferiority in him.

GROWTH

*** Lecturer: "If a patient is able to understand, always tell him what is going to happen to him."*

Student nurse: "And if he doesn't".

*Lecturer: "It does not matter what you do to him." ***

The main criteria used for assessing growth are the weight, height and the head circumference of a child, which are measured periodically and plotted on a "growth chart." (A sample chart is given at the end of this book.)

1. Weight

The normal birth weight of a term baby ranges from 2.5 to 3.8 kilos. The baby loses some weight for the initial 3-4 days, and regains its birth weight by the end of 7-10 days (it may take 14 days in case of preterm babies). So if your baby is weighing the same as at birth even after 10 days, it is normal (and not an indicator of poor breast milk supply).

After this, the baby gains on an average, approximately 20 grams/day till the child becomes 5 months of age (initially the baby may gain even 30 grams/day for the first 1 or 2 months). A simple calculation shows that it translates to 20 x 140 days = 2.8 kilos. So the baby's birth weight doubles at 5 months.

After this, the child gains approximately 15 grams/day till the age of 1 year. It means a gain of 15 x 210 days = 3 kilos approximately. So the birth weight triples at 1 year.

It quadruples at the age of 2 years. After that it grows approximately 2 kilos/year till the age of 6 years and then 3-3.5 kilos/ year till adolescence.

Weight is ideally measured with the child in undergarments and always on the same weighing scales. I have found parents getting anxious about the weight of their child being static or even decreasing, which is not the real case because the previous weight was taken on a separate machine.

How frequently the weight of a child should be measured? There is no hard and fast rule about it, and as long as it doesn't become an obsession with the parents, they can measure it whenever they feel like it. I won't recommend parents to waste their time to take a healthy child to a clinic just for the sake of measuring weight. It can be done on the day of immunisation or on the day of a visit to the paediatrician.

2. Height

The final height attainable by a child is determined strongly by the genetic inheritance from the parents. After the age of 3 years, the child's height co-relates significantly with the parental stature. It also depends on the sex of the child, girls generally being shorter than boys are, even though both are offspring of the same parents. Based on genetic factors alone, a prediction of height can be done as follows:

Girls : (father's height - 13 cm) + (mother's height) / 2

Boys : (mother's height + 13 cm) + (father's height) / 2

N.B.: *A child's predicted adult height generally falls within 5 cm above or below the height calculated by the above formula.*

Since the height is so much genetically determined, there is little medical intervention can do to alter the final height. Nevertheless, parents who perceive their child as "short" want to make them taller. They will go to doctors, quacks, "height specialists" (who advertise a "guaranteed" increase in height) and try all sorts of medicines, tonics, etc along with exercises like stretching, hanging from a bar etc. to increase the height of their child. Though the intentions are noble, yet sadly, it speaks volumes of the lack of proper information amongst the parents, as also about their gullibility for "catchy" ads.

(Joke on quacks): Within a short time, 7 people arrived in heaven. Chitragupta (the secretary of God) went through his list and was exasperated to find not even a single name in it. He was thoroughly confused as to why people are arriving before their scheduled time on earth is over. On deeper probing, it was found out that all of them were clients of a particular doctor. Suddenly Chitragupta's face cleared up, "Oh! Now I understand. This doctor is known to send patients to me earlier than expected."

The stark and true fact is that there is no intervention that can increase the final attainable adult height of a child. (The word "final" is important here because unscrupulous and unethical use of anabolic steroids, hormones (commonly used is growth hormone) etc. can temporarily increase the height at the grave risk of reducing the final adult stature. There are also other potentially dangerous side effects associated with such modes of therapy in the hands of unqualified and untrained persons. So, unless there is a cause (e.g. a disease or a hormonal deficiency) that is causing short stature and can be treated, **the final adult stature cannot be altered.**

Certainly if the parents feel that their child is short, he should be taken to a doctor and be evaluated for it. Any treatment should only be given if some disease process is identified that is retarding growth and can be treated.

Normal height increment: A newborn (full term) has a length of approximately 50 cm. It becomes 1.5 times (i.e. 75 cm) at the age of 1 year, doubles (i.e. 100 cm) at the age of 4 years and triples (i.e. 150 cm) by 13 years.

Stating it in another way, the child gains approximately 4-5 inches (10 - 12 cm) during the second year and thereafter grows approximately 2 inches (5-6 cm)/ year till adolescence. Gain in height can be expected up to the age of 16 years in females and 18 years in males.

An absolute less height is less indicative of a problem than the annual increment in height. If the child is gaining 5-6 cm/year, it usually indicates no problems (even if the child is short as he may be a "late bloomer" i.e. may have a spurt at puberty). Serial measurements provide the most accurate indication of whether the physical growth of a child is progressing normally. Hence, parents should try to keep a serial and accurate record of the child's weight, height and head circumference.

3. Head circumference

It is the third indicator of the growth of a child (mainly brain growth). It doesn't mean that if a person has a large head, he will have more brain and thus more intelligence and vice-versa. In fact, the heads of Newton or Einstein were small (of course their head circumferences were within the normal range!).

It is usually measured a day or two after birth (to let the swelling of the scalp secondary to delivery subside, otherwise it will give a falsely higher HC). The normal HC at birth is 33-35 cm in a full term healthy baby. The HC should be measured at least every 1-2 months during the first year. A less or more than the normal increase in it is worrisome and should be investigated. The normal HC, length and weight will be much less for preterm babies.

During first 3 months, it increases 2 cm/month, so that at 3 months, it will be 39-41 cm.

During next 3 months, it increases 1 cm/month, so that at 6 months, it will be 42-44 cm.

During next 6 months, it increases 0.5 cm / month, so that at 1 year, it will be 45-47 cm.

It becomes 47-49 cm at the end of the second year and after that it gradually increases to the adult HC of 51-53 cm.

(About having brains): A Turkish brain surgeon removed half of the brain of an Iranian due to a brain tumour. On coming out of anaesthesia, the patient started conversing with the doctor in Turkish language, instead of Persian language. The anaesthetist who was an Indian and a good friend of the brain surgeon jokingly remarked, "See, after removal of half of his brain, he has started speaking in Turkish language." The surgeon, not to be outdone, said, "thank God, I didn't remove the whole brain, else he would have started speaking in Hindi."

As can be inferred from above, 80-90% of the brain development occurs during the 1st two years. Therefore the measurement of HC has significance mainly up to 2 years only.

It is amazing that what we learn after 2 years throughout our whole life constitutes just 10-20% of the total human learning, 80-90% being learned in the first two years of life. Readers will find it less amazing if they sit back and think deeply that a 2 year old child has already learned the most complex and difficult tasks of life, like co-ordination, walking, running, language (and they can easily learn 2-3 languages), eating without spilling etc. If still not convinced, ask an adult who has to learn a foreign language. Let me tell you it is a difficult task and for an adult to achieve the **sort of mastery** (over the foreign language) that a 2-year-old child has over the mother tongue is very, very difficult, if not impossible.

TABLE FOR CALCULATING WEIGHT AND HEIGHT

WEIGHT	KILOGRAMS
At birth	2.6-3.8 kilos
3-12 months	age (months) + 9 / 2
1-6 years	age (years) x 2 + 8
7-12 years	age (years) x 7 – 5 / 2

HEIGHT	CENTIMETRES
At birth	50 cms
At 1 year	75 cms
2-12 years	age (years) x 6 + 77

DEVELOPMENT

Development is the qualitative progress of a child, usually divided into 4 categories:

1. **Gross motor:** It refers to the gross motor activities like sitting, standing etc. As mentioned earlier, it is the least important and least reliable criteria to judge the overall development of a child, though the parents lay the most emphasis on it.
2. **Fine motor:** It refers to development of fine motor skills by the child that requires a fine co-ordination of his small muscles. Most of the things that the child learns to do with his hands in a dextrous fashion come under this category e.g. eating, grasping objects etc.
3. **Social:** It includes those milestones in which the child learns to interact with the parents and other human beings. Examples are smiling, laughing, playing etc.
4. **Language**: It refers to the development of the child by which he understands the mother tongue/other languages (called receptive language development) and also expresses his feelings in them (called expressive language development).

In human beings, like in animals, are there "critical periods" of development i.e. certain skills have to be learnt within a particular time frame, after which the "window of opportunity" is permanently and irrevocably lost? The answer fortunately is no. However the concept of "sensitive period" is there, according to which **some skills** are best-learnt and mastered during particular periods in the life cycle, although late emergence of them is not impossible. The establishment of basic trust in infancy and the development of language are 2 areas of competencies that have been postulated to be difficult to achieve beyond their sensitive periods.

Main milestones in each of the above mentioned 4 categories are discussed below:

1. GROSS MOTOR MILESTONES

A newborn baby is limp and floppy. His neck is like a ragged doll, and his head lolls forwards or backwards depending on gravity. Obviously, the first important milestone necessary in order to progress further (to sitting and standing) is neck control, which comes by 4 months age when his neck stays in the same plane as the body.

The child will roll from back to front at 4-5 months and from front to back at 5-6 months. During this time parents should be careful as their baby in sheer pleasure and excitement of doing something new may inadvertently roll to the edge of the bed or even beyond it, right from the centre of the bed. During the same time, the child in a prone (stomach down) position can rest his weight on the forearms first and later can lie with his body supported on his extended arms.

A child is usually able to sit unsupported by 7 months (he can sit with support 1-2 months earlier than this). If held standing, the child will start bouncing up and down with joy. But while sitting, he still cannot turn his body from side to side, which comes at 8-9 months.

At 9-10 months, the child starts creeping or crawling on all fours, just like an animal puppy. It is during this time that the mobility of the child truly increases as he can now go from one spot to another, a thing that he was unable to do so far. Thoroughly enjoying his recently achieved freedom, the child can pull things from their "hitherto protected areas", and thus break or damage objects, much to the anguish of the parents. Sometimes the child may hurt himself in the process. He may even "rummage" in dustbins etc. At this time, it appears to the hapless parents that nothing is safe from their "constantly on the prowl" child! They try to put things out of reach of the child, i.e. at a higher place; where also the child using his ingenuity can sometimes reach by climbing on chair etc.

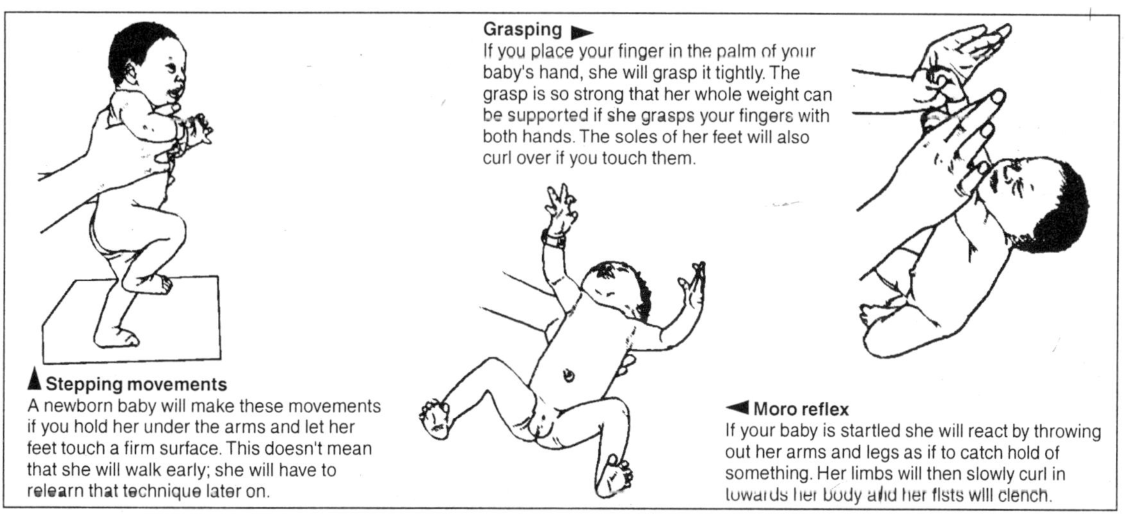

Newborn Reflexes

HOW A BABY DEVELOPS IN THE FIRST YEAR						
Step by step	MONTH 1	MONTH 2	MONTH 3	MONTH 4	MONTH 5	MONTH 6
Learning to sit	 When a newborn baby is lifted, the head drops. Always support it.		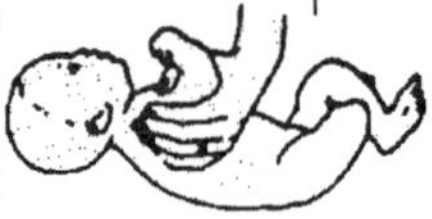 After 2 months the head is held up when in a sitting position.		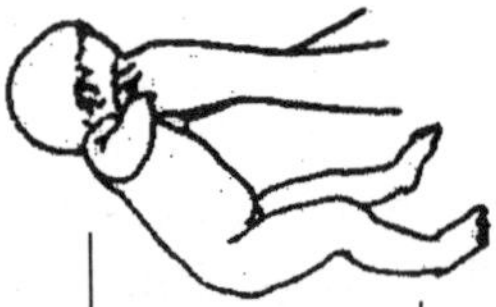 By 5 months the baby can lift chest and head while sitting.	 The baby can sit with support, but slips if support is removed.
Learning to crawl	 A newborn baby lies with pelvis higher than arms and legs.	 At 2 months the baby's pelvis is lower and legs are extended.		 By 4 months the baby is able to use the fore arms for support.		 By 6 months, weight is carried on arms which are extended.
Learning to stand				 At 4 months a baby can be held in a standing position.		
Learning use of hands	 When a newborn baby's palm is touched, the hand closes.		 During the 3rd month the baby starts sucking the fist.	 Between 3 and 4 months the baby is able to hold a rattle.		

HOW A BABY DEVELOPS IN THE FIRST YEAR

Step by step	MONTH 7	MONTH 8	MONTH 9	MONTH 10	MONTH 11	MONTH 12
Learning to sit	 Between 7 and 10 months the baby can sit unsupported.	 A baby begins by sitting with hands forward for support.	 At 9 months a baby can sit securely for about 10 minutes.	 By 10 months a baby can lean forward to pick up objects.	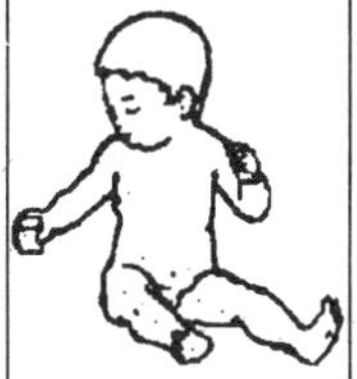 At 11 months a baby begins to pivot in sitting position.	 By the end of first year a baby twists around with ease.
Learning to crawl				The baby learns to crawl, pulling the body with the hands.	Within another month or so, the baby crawls on hands and knees.	By one year a baby may be able to move on hands and feet.
Learning to stand	 At 7 months a baby's legs can carry part of its weight if helped.	 At 8 months a baby's legs may carry all its weight, if helped.	 At 9 months a baby may stand briefly holding on to furniture.	 A baby learns to move about a room by holding on to furniture.	 Towards the end of the year a baby can stand upright if held.	 Before walking unaided a baby needs supporting by one hand.
Learning use of hands	 By 7 months the baby uses the hand like a scoop.	 By 8 months a baby is able to hold a mug in both hands.	 At 9 months the baby can bring small objects together.	 At 10 months a baby learns to clap hands together.	 Towards the end of the first year the baby prods with index finger.	 The baby begins picking up with index finger and thumb.

At the most, parents can do some "damage control exercises" because I am quite sure that in every household, some or the other thing is pulled down by the roving infant thus breaking or damaging it. More importantly, the parents should be careful during this stage that he doesn't injure himself.

Next comes the "cruising" stage i.e. the child first of all pulls himself to stand by grasping hold of some furniture like the table etc. and then starts cruising around it; moving hand by hand over it and foot by foot on the ground, i.e. he moves sideways. Gradually as his level of confidence increases, one fine day, he lets go off one hand and thus is able to cruise around with only one hand for support. Another fine day, while he is too engrossed in some absorbing act, so much so that he forgets that his one hand should be on the furniture for support, he may let go off it, thus freeing his other hand also. He may do so temporarily without realising what a daring act he has done! But this is the stage, when with his feet planted apart and he maintaining a "shaky" balance with both his hands off any support that he has become ready for walking as he has now acquired the fine sense of balance.

And so arrives the milestone, an important milestone that the parents were waiting for i.e. walking. It comes at about 1 year of age. It is an interesting act to watch. The infant will stand with his feet planted wide apart, knees slightly bent, both his arms flexed at the elbows in front of him. Then he will take a small and very cautious step forward and the entire torso rotates with it, the toes may point in or out and the foot strikes the floor flat. Then he will stop in order to regain his sense of balance. Once he again feels secure, he will take another small step forward. Gradually his sense of balance and confidence grows and he starts walking more freely with his feet apart and hands in front, aptly called the "waddling" gait. In the initial stages, when the baby has learned to stand and summons enough courage to put a step forward, the parents can encourage him by staying 2-3 steps away from the baby and then urging him to come to them. The baby secure in the presence of the proximity of the parents takes a step forward and ultimately, by trial and error learns that even if he falls, he won't get hurt as he is going to "crash land" in his parents' arms. After several weeks of practice and experience, the child's centre of gravity shifts back and the torso stays more stable, the knees extend and the arms stay at the side of the body and swings for the sake of balance.

During the initial stages of walking, all babies topple and fall down, and invariably all of them end up with some bruises, scratches etc. But all types of injuries sustained by the child during learning the art of walking are fortunately minor. So the baby forgets them soon and again starts his "practice" of learning to walk. It appears that the pleasure that the child derives from trying out new things and the feeling of pride and satisfaction that he derives out of mastering a new art far outweighs the minor unpleasant experiences like bruises and falls associated with mastering such an art.

A child usually starts to walk freely and with full confidence by 18 months of age. Toddlers are often described as being "intoxicated" with their newly acquired power to control the distance between themselves and the parents. They will "orbit" around the parents, moving further and then returning for a reassuring touch. In strange and non-familiar surroundings, this "orbit" might be small or non-existent i.e. the child simply clings on to the parents; in familiar surroundings, the child may "orbit" out of sight.

At round about 2 years, the child can run and also climb up and down the stairs. At 4 years, the child can hop and balance himself with one foot off the ground. The next important gross motor milestone, skipping, usually comes by the age of 6 years.

2. FINE MOTOR MILESTONES

These are more important than the gross motor milestones in assessing the development of a child because these milestones require fine co-ordination and use of the small muscles (e.g. of hand) to perform intricate and delicate tasks like eating, holding small objects etc. In gross motor milestones, big muscles like those of trunk, hips etc. are used.

At 3 months, the hands that in the newborn period were predominantly clenched, now remains predominantly open. It is an important thing because now only the child can grasp and manipulate things.

At 4 months, the child can bring his 2 hands together and thus grasps a red ring or a rattle dangling in front of him. Initially, he may overshoot it but with some practice, he manages to hold it in both his hands and then tries to manipulate it to his mouth. At the same time, the child does an interesting thing, called "hand regard." The child will take the hand in front of his eyes and regard it intently for several moments as though he is a palmist studying the various lines of "fate" of the hand.

At the age of 5 months, the child starts "foot play" i.e. starts kicking them at random; particularly when he is excited. He may also catch hold of one of his foot and manipulate it towards his mouth. At the same age "hand play" progresses further and the child instead of using both hands now tries to grasp things with one hand only, albeit crudely and that too from the little finger side of his palm; called the "ulnar grasp."

At 6 months, the baby can transfer objects like a cube from one hand to another and will even drop the object from his hand if another one is offered eager to take it also.

At about 8 months, the child starts grasping objects from the other side of his hand, i.e. the index finger side; called the "radial grasp", but in a crude and clumsy fashion.

At 9 months, the child can hit two objects grasped in each of his hands together and enjoys doing so.

The 10-month milestone is considered very important by doctors called an "index finger" approach to an object i.e. if an object is kept in front of the child; he approaches it by extending his index finger towards it. Second important thing is the thumb index finger oppositionality i.e. trying to hold objects in between his index finger and the thumb. God has blessed human beings with versatile use of the thumb; and once the child starts bringing it actively into play i.e. at the age of 10 months; it is considered that the child is developmentally normal.

At the age of 1 year, the child voluntarily releases objects from his grasp and gives it to the mother, if requested to do so. At about the same time, the child loves and enjoys putting things in and out of a box. At about 15 months, the child is able to insert a pellet in a bottle and at 18 months, can dump pellet out from a bottle. It heralds the beginning of true co-ordination, because to put in and then take out a thing from a small opening like that of a bottle really requires fine co-ordination of eyes and small muscles of the hand.

At about the same time, the child enjoys feeding himself with a spoon but in the process often rotates the spoon thereby spilling its contents. The child makes quite a mess, spilling food on his clothes, table ground etc. And while the parents inwardly or outwardly fume, the child, oblivious to the parental agony, enjoys by more spilling and dribbling. As mentioned earlier, it is not wise to curtail the child's sense of achievement and merriment. Parents should not mind much the mess being created but rather should use their common sense to do some "damage control" exercises to limit the mess being created by the child (refer to the chapter on "Feeding"). There are spoons available with a rotatory handle, so that even if the child rotates the spoon, the scoop of the spoon always stays straight and thus spilling is minimised. Fortunately for the parents, their agony is short lived (about 3 months) as after this the child becomes fairly adept in handling the spoon; so that more of the food goes *into the stomach rather than on to the stomach.*

Dressing and undressing: Undressing comes earlier than dressing because it is easier. At about 18 months, the child "helps" in undressing i.e. he makes appropriate limb adjustments so that the mother can undress him. By 2 years, the child helps in dressing also. At the same time he makes attempts, sometimes successful, sometimes ending up in a tangle, to take off his clothes. By the age of 3 years, however, the child has by and large mastered the art of both dressing and undressing and requires little parental help. He can often buckle his shoes at the same age but tying of shoelaces comes at about 5 years of age.

3. PERSONAL, SOCIAL AND COGNITIVE MILESTONES

The first milestone and a very important milestone that shows that your baby is a social being, is the "social smile" which comes at 1-2 months. The baby smiles "back" when the parents talk to him, smile at him or caress him. Actually this smile is more of a reflex smile, because the baby doesn't understand what the parents are saying. For all one knows the parents may be saying (out of pleasure) that he is the biggest idiot that they have ever come across! Their "truly idiotic" child acknowledges this and smiles back! Yet his smiling back proves to the world that he is not an idiot. For the social smile is a very powerful objective evidence that the baby's mental faculties are all right and he will develop into a normal human being without being mentally handicapped. In fact so much value is laid on the social smile by the doctors that if a baby doesn't smile "back" by the age of 2 months, one suspects that there is something seriously wrong with the baby's development and most likely he will lag behind developmentally. And why not to attach such importance to the social smile? For it is the first way of the baby to show objectively to the parents and to the world that he is also a social being like them capable of social interaction.

At about the same age i.e. 2 months, the baby stares intently at the person carrying him and talking to him. It appears as if the baby is trying hard to decipher what is being said and trying to make some sense out of it. In between he may give the hint of a smile. However for the parents, this eye contact and the smile give them the feeling of being loved back, which is very satisfying for them.

At about 3 months, the child recognises his mother and maybe the father (if he is also involved intimately in the care of the baby), as his primary caretakers and learns to differentiate them on a more intimate basis than other human beings.

The 4 month age is a very loveable age, maybe the most loveable one. The child becomes interested in a wider world and thus even if he is in his mother's lap and being fed, even a small noise can distract him so much that he may literally turn around to locate the source of distraction. At the same time, he also starts exploring his own body, which plays an important role in the emergence of "self" in the mind of a child as a concrete and objective thing. The baby starts showing the primary emotions of anger, joy, interest, fear, disgust and surprise as distinct facial expressions. Face to face with a trusted adult, the infant and adult match affective expressions about 30% of the time, the intensity of their smiling, eye widening and lip puckering rising and falling together in cadence. Every few seconds, as the excitement builds to a level that the infant cannot stomach, he will turn away, settle down and then again return back to the interaction, thoroughly enjoying it. While if the parents turn away, the infant leans forward, reaches, or in other ways tries to get the adult involved again. If it fails, the infant starts bawling, i.e. the child at this age shows an overt displeasure on a sustained and pleasurable social contact being broken. At the same time, the child learns to laugh out aloud and if for some reason, he thinks something as funny, he may burst out laughing aloud at times taking everyone by surprise, because in reality nothing funny was said or done! For most parents, this is a happy period. They are excited that they can hold "conversations" with their little ones, taking turns vocalising and then listening to the baby vocalise in response.

At about 5-6 months, the child enjoys seeing his own image in the mirror and smiles back at it, without understanding that what he is seeing is a "virtual image" and not a real thing. So he may thump the mirror to "catch" the image, without grasping anything concrete.

At about 7-8 months, comes another important concept in the overall development of the child called "object permanence." Earlier if an object like a ball rolls out of his sight, say under the table, the child is not bothered about it, as he doesn't understand that the ball is a permanent object. So if it has disappeared, fine! But at this age of about 7 months, the child knows that an object exists on a permanent basis. Therefore he will start looking for it by craning his neck or by going under the table and if by chance, he doesn't find it, he will bear a puzzled look on his face.

From the age of 6 to 12 months, (some children develop it earlier, some do so later), comes what is known as "separation anxiety." Before this, the child will go to any stranger and joyfully interact with him. For him at that stage, anyone who loves him can play with him, hours on together. But once this anxiety develops the child clings to the caretaker and views anybody who is a stranger with wariness and suspicion, anxiety writ on his face.

The child resists a toy or an object being pulled out of his hands at 7 months. At the same age, the child responds to changes in emotional context of the social contact. Therefore if the child commits some mischief, then an angry stare or a stern voice makes the child realise that the caretaker is not pleased with his deeds and thus quietens down.

At 9 months, when the child can crawl and hence is mobile, he makes determined efforts to reach and grasp a toy or an object kept out of his reach.

The child begins to show interest in interactive games at 10-12 months and "plays" with other human beings simple games like "peek-a-boo" or "pat-a cake." At about 10 months, the child responds to sound of name i.e. if you call out his name, he understands that he is being called and therefore responds to it. He also starts waving "bye-bye", something which all parents enjoy and urge him to repeat. At about 1 year, the child mimics any performance, which evokes appreciative laughter.

Alas for the parents, this is also the time when the issue of autonomy arises. The infant now no longer wants to be spoon fed, literally and figuratively. Now he wants to hold the spoon and to self-feed. In other day to day routines also, the infant starts challenging the parental control and wants to do things himself, in the way that he wants and not in the way that the parents want him to do. He may make a complete mess in doing so (which the parents were doing so far and the child was docilely letting it being done). The parents may react angrily to it and are often helpless as to why the child need to meddle so much and take matters in his own hands, when his abilities to accomplish the particular task are so limited. The parents should be aware that this is a part of growing up; it happens with all the children and is nothing else but a manifestation of the child's desire for autonomy and self-control. Therefore it is best for the parents to bear it with fortitude and patience. At the same time, tantrums make their first appearance. The child's drive for autonomy clashes with the parental controls and ideas as to how things should be done, leading to tantrums and sulkiness by the child.

The next important milestone comes at 18-24 months and that is "problem solving." For example, the child uses a stick to reach for a toy out of his reach or figures out how to wind a mechanical toy. These examples show that when faced with a problem, he is able to use his intellect to try to figure a way out.

At the same time, the child starts becoming self-conscious. The child who used to respond freely and without any inhibitions earlier now appears a bit embarrassed, particularly if too much attention is paid to him. If some familiar person calls the child and tries to have eye to eye contact with the child, the child may simply look askance and turn his head away, as if not interested, while actually he is most interested and curious! After some moments of your looking at him and he looking somewhere else, his level of embarrassment may become too much and he will suddenly break the silence by pointing with his fingers towards an object and naming it loudly (e.g. flower) or uttering something. You may say something like, "ah flower, very good" in response and the ice is broken between you two.

At the same time, toddlers looking in a mirror will, for the first time, reach for their own face rather than for the face in the mirror. If they see for example a "bindi" or a coloured dot on their face in the mirror image, they will reach out for the same on their face.

Internalised standards of evaluation also appear at the same time. When tempted to touch a forbidden object, they will say "no, no" to themselves, evidence of internalisation of the standards of behaviour. That finally they do reach out and touch the toy demonstrates the relative strength of the internalised inhibitions versus their curiosity and desire for autonomy.

At 2 years, the child narrates immediate experiences; e.g. he went to his friend's house where such and such thing happened. He may also do vice-versa i.e. start telling home secrets to others. So beware of this "Vibhishan" in your house at this age!

At 30 months, i.e. two and a half years, the child knows his full name and also refers to self by the pronoun "I". Before that he refers to his own self in the third person e.g. if the child's name is Astha, she will say "Astha plays with ball" rather than "I play with ball."

At 3 years, come 3 important things.

1. *He knows his age and sex.*
2. *He can count 3 objects and can also repeat 3 numbers or a sentence of 6 syllables.*
3. *Handedness is usually established by the age of 3 years and an attempt by parents to change it may result in frustration.*

"FANTASY LAND": Till the age of 5 years, the child is involved in "magical" thinking e.g. if it rains, the child may believe that it is the tears of the clouds; the sun goes down because it is "tired" etc. Fears, sometimes intense, like that of ghosts, monsters etc. can be generated during this time and parents should be aware of them. Attempts to demonstrate that there are no monsters in the closet often fail, as the fear is due to pre-rational thinking. Rather reassurances that the parents will use their "great power" (e.g. a mystic stick to beat and drive away the monster) to ensure the child's safety are more effective because they appeal to the child's magical thinking. Only after the age of 5 years is the child able to distinguish fantasy from reality.

PLAY: It is an integral & enjoyable part of development of a child. The child's earliest concept of play starts at 10 months, when he starts playing "peek-a-boo" or "pat-a-cake."

At 1 year, the child's "make-believe play" centres on himself, e.g. pretending to drink from an empty cup. At 18 months, symbolic transformations in play are no longer tied to one's own body, so that a doll (rather than itself) can be "fed" from an empty cup!

A type of play called "pretend or symbolic" play starts at about 18 months and lasts till the age of 5 years. In it, the child pretends to play with an inanimate object e.g. a doll. Thus she may dress it up, comb its hair, talk to it and even scold it as if the doll was a living baby.

A child of 1-2 years involves in "parallel play." The child plays parallel to older children but doesn't join them. Rather in a space of his own in a corner of the playground, the child will try to imitate what the older children are playing e.g. if they run, he will also run in parallel with them; if they laugh, he will also start laughing in concordance with them etc.

Copying Mother: The younger child loves to 'help' with dustpan and brush.

At 3-4 years of age, the children increasingly becomes involved in "co-operative play" like building a tower of cubes together or playing hide and seek, simple ball games etc. with the other children i.e. he now starts participating actively in the game with others.

A little later, comes the concept of "organised group play" that becomes increasingly rule governed, e.g. playing "house-house" with distinct role assignments to the various children and certain rules and norms to be followed.

4. LANGUAGE DEVELOPMENT

The development of language involves two distinct processes: **receptive** i.e. what the child hears and understands and **expressive** i.e. what the child speaks to express himself.

The first indication that the child will be able to speak in future comes at the age of 2 months, when the baby coos. Cooing is some gurgling "throaty" sounds made by the baby in response to a person "talking" to the baby.

At 3 months, the child listens to music and seemingly enjoys it (an example of receptive speech) while at the same time he starts to say "aah, gnah" (expressive speech).

At 6 months, the baby starts to babble. This is monosyllabic e.g. "ma" or "pa" or "da" etc. At 8-10 months the babbling becomes more complex with multiple syllables ("ba-da-ma") and the inflections mimic the native mother tongue. But whatever he speaks is not a true language or a meaningful word, which comes at the age of 1 year (see below). That's why it is called babbling.

At 7 months, the child follows one step command with gesture while at 10 months he follows one step spoken command without gesture (e.g. Give it to me; Go there etc.).

The first real word that is meaningful and pertains consistently to a specific object or person makes its appearance at the age of 1 year. This is the ideal age for verbal language acquisition, mainly through picture books. With a picture book as a common, shared focus of attention, the parent and the child can engage in pointing and labelling of pictures, with elaboration and feedback by the parents. This way the vocabulary of the child increase as he now knows names of specific things e.g. flower, moon, sun, star etc.

Receptive language precedes the development of expressive language (because the child has first to receive and understand words before being able to express it). Thus by the time that the first meaningful word makes its appearance, he already is following and responding appropriately to several simple commands like "no"; "give me" etc.

At 15 months, the child is able to point out to main body parts. At this time, he has a limited vocabulary of his own of 4-6 words that he can utter meaningfully. The way the child speaks at this age is "broken" and "fast" as if his mind wants to convey a lot of things, but his tongue is not able to keep pace with it because he doesn't have the required vocabulary at his command. So this speech is aptly termed as "jargon speech." At 18 months, the child has progressed a bit. His vocabulary consists of 10-15 words and he is also able to name pictures (if so trained).

Between 18-24 months, there is a dramatic development in his linguistic capabilities. The main reason for this is that now a child points towards an object, not with the purpose of having it, but rather to know its name. The child points towards an object and asks the adult "what is that?" i.e. tell me its name. The realisation that words can stand for things is a very important phase in the language development, so much so that his vocabulary increases dramatically from 10 words at the age of 18 months to 100 words at the age of 2 years. At 2 years comes another important linguistic milestone and that is putting words together to form a sentence. The child can usually put 3 words together (subject, verb, object) at this age to form a sentence.

At this stage, the child can follow 2 step commands (if you refer to this chapter earlier, you will find that he was able to follow one step command). Now he can carry out 2 separate commands joined by "and" e.g. "Give me the book **and** then go out to play."

IMPORTANT MILESTONES

(Tabulated for ready reference)

Caution: The age of attainment of a milestone is a gross average. If a child achieves a milestone before, it doesn't mean that he will be more advanced than other children and vice-versa. For e.g. a child may walk at 10 months, while another may walk at 18 months, even though both are normal. However if your child doesn't attain a particular milestone within the specified period, consult your doctor. In most of the cases, it will turn out to be a normal variant only. Parents can make a serial record in the column "age achieved" below.

GROSS MOTOR

MILESTONE	ACHIEVEMENT AGE	AGE ACHIEVED
1. Neck Control	4 Months	
2. Rolls (Front to Back, Vice Versa)	5-6 Months	
3. Sitting	6-7 Months	
4. Crawls/Creeps (on All Fours)	9-10 Months	
5. Stands And Walks	12-16 Months	
6. Runs	2 Years	
7. Up And Down Stairs	3 Years	
8. Rides Tricycle	3 Years	
9. Hops on One Foot	4 Years	
10. Skips Rope	5-6 Years	

FINE MOTOR

MILESTONE	ACHIEVEMENT AGE	AGE ACHIEVED
1. Hands Predominantly Open	3 Months	
2. Hands Grasp Objects / Hand Regard	4 Months	
3. Foot Play	5 Months	
4. Transfers Objects From Hand To Hand	6 Months	
5. Ulnar (Towards Little Finger) Grasp	5-6 Months	
6. Radial(Towards Thumb) Grasp	8-10 Months	
7. Index Finger Approach to Objects	10 Months	
8. Good Use of Cup And Spoon	18 Months	
9. Horizontal/Vertical Strokes With Pen	2 Years	
10. Undresses And Dresses Self	3 Years	

SOCIAL & COGNITIVE

MILESTONE	ACHIEVEMENT AGE	AGE ACHIEVED
1. Smiles On Social Interaction	1-2 Months	
2. Recognises Mother	3 Months	
3. Shows Emotions(Anger, Fear Etc)	4 Months	
4. Smiles at Image in Mirror	5 Months	
5. Object Permanence	7-8 Months	
6. Separation Anxiety	6-12 Months	
7. Waves bye-bye; Responds To Name	10 Months	
8. Autonomy (Struggle With Parents)	1.5-2 Years	
9. Narrates Immediate Experiences	2 Years	
10. Knows Age, Sex And Name	3 Years	

PLAY

MILESTONE	ACHIEVEMENT AGE	AGE ACHIEVED
1. Plays "Peek-A-Boo" ; "Pat-A-Cake"	10 Months	
2. Mimicry And Imitation of Others	12 Months	
3. Rolling Ball, Gathering Ball	15-18 Months	
4. "Pretend" Play With Doll	1.5-5 Years	
5. Parallel Play (Imitates Other's Play)	2-3 Years	
6. Co-operative Play (Takes Part)	3-4 Years	

SPEECH & LANGUAGE

MILESTONE	ACHIEVEMENT AGE	AGE ACHIEVED
1. Coos i.e. Vocalises	2 Months	
2. Says "Aah", "Gnah". Enjoys Music	3 Months	
3. Monosyllabic Babble (Pa, Da, Ma)	6 Months	
4. Polysyllabic Babble (Ba-Da-Ma, Mama)	8-10 Months	
5. Follows/Obeys 1 Step Command	10 Months	
6. First Real, Meaningful Word	12 Months	
7. Points Out to Major Body Parts	15 Months	
8. 10-15 Words Vocabulary	18 Months	
9. Forms Sentence, 100-Word Vocabulary	2 Years	
10. Follows/Obeys 2 Step Commands	2 Years	

DENTAL DEVELOPMENT

***Epitaph on a dentist's grave: "This is the last cavity he filled." ***

A common source of parental concern is regarding the teething of their child. They are worried as to when the child will cut his first tooth. As is true with all types of development, there is no fixed time when the first tooth should erupt. In some children, it may erupt as early as 5 months, while in others; it may not erupt up to the age of 1 year and even beyond. *There is nothing wrong with your child if his tooth doesn't come out by 1 year*. Most of the parents think that their child is deficient in calcium and/or vitamin-D, which is true only in a few cases. In majority of cases, it is just a normal variant and hence no intervention is required.

Some babies may be born with natal teeth i.e. teeth present at birth. These teeth are not taken out, unless they are loose or are sharp or causing some trauma to the tongue. Otherwise they are left alone and in due course of time, the milk teeth will take their place.

Parents attribute every complaint at the time of teething to it. Thus if the child has fever, irritability, diarrhoea etc., the parents feel it is due to teething. While the child may be a bit irritable due to the teeth causing discomfort while erupting out of the gums; things like fever, vomiting etc. are not due to teething. During the teething phase, there is irritation of the gums of the child, and to reduce it, he puts foreign objects in his mouth and chews on them. These foreign objects may be a source of infection in the child and cause diarrhoea.

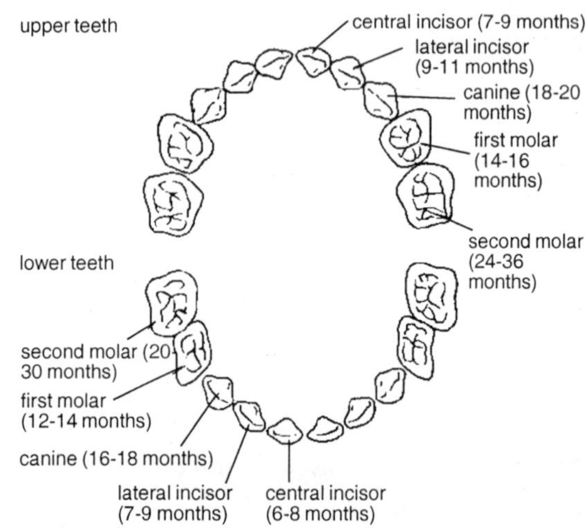

The milk (first)teeth, and the average ages at which they appear.

But per se, teething doesn't cause any problem, except a little irritability.

There are two types of teeth, deciduous or the milk teeth and the permanent teeth. There are 20 milk teeth and 32 permanent teeth. The milk teeth start erupting from the age of 5 months onwards and the first tooth to come is usually the lower central incisor.

A simple way to remember the eruption of milk teeth is that by 6 months there are 0 teeth; by 12 months, 6 teeth; by 18 months, 12 teeth; and by 24 months, 16 teeth. The last 4 teeth make their appearance by 2.5- 3 years.

The permanent teeth start erupting from the age of 6-7 years onwards. A little before that, the milk teeth are shed. This process continues on and by the age of 12-13 years, the child has 28 teeth. The last 4 teeth, popularly called as the wisdom teeth, erupt at a variable age, in the late teens or early twenties.

TABLE: Chronology of eruption of milk teeth and the permanent teeth

MILK TEETH

TEETH	AGE (Months)
2 lower central incisors	5-10 months
2 upper central incisors	8-12 months
2 upper lateral incisor	9-12 months
2 lower lateral incisors	10-14 months
2 lower anterior molars	13-16 months
2 upper anterior molars	13-17 months
4 canines	12-22 months
4 posterior molars	24-30 months

PERMANENT TEETH

TEETH	AGE (Years)
First molars	6-7 years
Incisors	7-9 years
Premolars	9-11 years
Canines	10-12 years
Second molars	12-16 years
Third molars	17-25 years

CHAPTER 5

FEEDING

KEY POINTS

- **Breast-feeding**: In the initial 4 months, the baby requires only milk (not even water). There is a fine balance by nature between the production of milk and its demand by the baby. More is the milk required by the baby, more it sucks, which is the most potent stimulus for more milk production. So more is the demand, more is the supply.
- **Milk tins**: The correct dilution for powdered milk is 1 scoop in 1ounce=30 cc of water. Due to economic reasons and ignorance, many babies are fed over diluted milk i.e. a "white water" diet, making them "skin and bones." This is a leading cause of infant deaths in India. No wonder, doctors call infant formulas as "white poison". Those who cannot afford infant formulas can go for undiluted cow's milk, as it is much cheaper.
- **Weaning:** The child is put on other foods besides milk, starting at 4 months of age. The child has to cultivate a liking for the texture and the taste of the new food. So, initially the volume of food consumed is less important than the experience of it.
- **Balanced diet:** Calculations for "balancing" the diet in terms of calories and the intake of proteins, fats etc. is not needed as what we eat daily tends to be balanced over a period of time by itself. Health tonics, multivitamins etc. are not recommended.
- **Feeding dictums:** Parents should be ready to accept some mess while the child is eating. Self-feeding should be encouraged. Mealtimes should be of a finite duration (20-30 minutes). The mealtime must not become a battleground (between the mother and child). Child's wishes regarding eating should be respected and he should not be pressurised to eat.
- **Poor eating**: Why do so many children eat poorly? Because parents force them to eat by threats, bribes etc. This problem is non-existent in the simple, uneducated people who live in villages, because the mothers in such populations are hardly bothered about the amount of food consumed by their children. They do not pressurise the child to eat and so they eat well. Pressure makes an activity unenjoyable. Almost all children eat better at neighbours than at home. Why? Because over there, there is no one monitoring their "eating performance" with "an eagle eye" on them. A golden dictum is that a child will never self-starve. Once you realise this fundamental fact, you will not force the child to eat more. If you leave the child completely free knowing that the child will not starve himself, the child will relish eating as he now enjoys it. Try to make the child eat well, he won't. Don't try and he will eat well.
- **Self-feeding:** A familiar scenario in many households is that of a hapless mother running around to feed the child with a spoon in her hand. The habit of "spoon feeding" makes the child dependent on you. It is O.K. to feed a child till 1 year, but after that self-feeding should be strongly inculcated in the child. You have to be firm with yourself (that you are not going to "spoon-feed").
- **Fooling at the table:** Some children indulge in meal time misbehaviours like getting up and down from the table, playing with the food etc. An effective management technique for such behaviour is to terminate the meal calmly when playing with the food exceeds the eating (regardless of how much the child has consumed).

❖ **Weight of a child:** There is a range of normalcy rather than a fixed "set point". For e.g. a 1 year child's normal range of weight is 8-12 kg. If you see a 8 kg baby and if you see a 12 kg baby (i.e. having 50% more weight), you may perceive a substantial difference in their built; but actually both of them are normal and neither of them is undernourished.

VARIOUS FOODS (An Introduction)

The baby's growth and good health depends on the quality of the food it is given:

- Most mothers have little knowledge of this subject, as you well know, and they would rather follow recipes handed down to them than simple, easy rules. This is why weaning is so important. The vast majority of breast-fed children actually grow without problems up to about 6 or 8 months.
- But the mother does not introduce the necessary foods to suplement breast-feeding until later, whereas human milk (though still an excellent food) is no longer sufficient to meet the baby's nutritional requirements after 4 to 6 months. Fresh or boxed cow's milk is similarly insufficient.
- Furthermore, in some regions or families, babies are weaned abruptly which is always harmful to them: changes in diet should always be gradual, not abrupt.
- The following advice is not at all revolutionary or miraculous; it is simply to help you cope with the nutritional problems you have to deal with everyday.
- We shall first consider the various types of food available, then the form in which they can be given to the baby before describing diets suitable for each age.

Warnings about weaning :

Avoid early and/or abrupt weaning.

From the age of 4 to 6 months human milk is insufficient food for a baby.

A varied diet is recommended between 4 and 6 months and is compulsory at 6 months to avoid malnutrition.

The diet should be altered gradually and minced fish, meat, eggs, fruit and vegetables introduced little by little.

The Various Foods

General Information About Food

The substances which form foods are:

- water
- proteins
- carbohydrates
- fats
- vitamins
- mineral salts

- Each of these substances has a different role in nutrition. Some are essential for growth, others for the functioning of the organism*.

*The organism functions thanks to the energy produced by food. Some foods produce more energy than others. This quantity of energy is counted in calories. A 6-month-old baby requires about 700 calories per day.

1. Water

Water is absolutely essential for life. Babies need a fairly large quantity of water, particularly when the weather is hot.

Up to 4 months, its mother's milk gives the baby all the water it needs, even in hot, dry climates, and water should not be given unless the baby is ill (fever, diarrhoea, vomiting, etc.) and on medical advice.

2. Proteins

These are substances necessary for the growth of the muscles and organs.

They can provide energy, but the organism usually prefers to save this energy and to use proteins as building materials.

Proteins are distinguished according to their origin:

- animal proteins : these are found in milk, meat, fish and eggs. They are rich proteins, absolutely essential for growth.
- vegetable proteins, by contrast, are of poorer quality; they are found in groundnuts, squash seeds, beans, soya, cereals (millet, sorghum, rice, corn and wheat) and cereal based products.

Animal proteins are absolutely essential for a child to grow.

A diet containing vegetable proteins only would be inadequate. Unless a mixture of 2 vegetable proteins (e.g. dal & wheat) is given.

3. Carbohydrates or sugars

Foods containing sugar provide energy to allow the organs and muscles to function. They are quite common and it is unusual for a baby to be short of them. Carbohydrates are found in milk, which contains everything the infant needs, and in many plants and fruits : wheat, corn, millet, sorghum, rice, pasta, yams, sweet potatoes, taro, manioc, potatoes, carrots, bananas and various fruits and vegetables.

4. Lipids or fats

Fats provide a lot of energy in a very small volume. They must form part of a balanced diet.

Fats are found in milk and in groundnut, palm, olive oil, butter and coconut.

A few reminders

- 100 g of meat or 100 g of fish or 3 eggs or ½ litre of cow's milk provide approximately the same quantity of proteins with good nutritional value.
- Sugar is composed exclusively of carbohydrates. I g of sugar provides 4 calories.
- A given quantity of fats provides twice as many calories as the same quantity of sugar or proteins.

5. Vitamins

These are substances acting in small doses to help the organism to function. Lack of vitamins causes particular diseases for each type of vitamin. The majority of essential vitamins are found in fruits (pineapples, bananas, papayas, melons, mangoes, lemons, oranges) and in vegetables (cucumbers, tomatoes, lettuce, onions, okra, avocados, courgettes, carrots) as well as in the green leaves used to prepare various dishes.

6. Mineral salts

Three mineral salts are very important:

- Salt : itself is essential for the organism; it is contained in milk but has to be aded to most other foods;
- Calcium : this is responsible for the strength of the bones. So, it is essential for growth. Calcium is found in milk and cheese.
- Iron : this is required for formation of blood. A deficiency o iron on lead to anemia.

Foods particularly rich in :

- Calcium : cheese, milk, green vegetables (spinach, letuce, sweet potato and manioc leaves).
- Iron : liver, dried caterpillars, meat, fish, egg yolk, dried beans.
- Phosphorus : cheese, liver, dried beans, cereals.
- Potassium : beans, lentils, avocado.

IN WHAT FORM SHOULD FOODS BE GIVEN TO THE CHILD?

Milk is the only food for babies

1. Breast-Feeding

- **Breast-feeding has nothing but benefits:**

- It provides the newborn baby with all the foods essential for its growth in a readily assimilable form*. It contains rich proteins, sugars, fats, mineral salts and antibodies which protet the baby against infection.
- This is the easiest and safest method of feeding a baby in all climates.
- The majority of women are able to feed their baby.

- So, human milk is the ideal food for any baby, but as it grows the baby will need new, more nutritious foods. We shall see how to introduce them to the baby little by little to avoid abrupt weaning.
- Women who are breast-feeding must have a balanced and varied diet. Drugs should only be taken on medical advice since some drugs pass into the milk and so can harm the baby.

2. Bottle-Feeding

- Bottle-feeding should only be used in very specific cases where it is absolutely impossible for the mother to breast-feed. Such cases are actually very rare : serious illness of the mother, complete absence of milk after several days.
- The mother will carry out mixed feeding if she works outside the home or is unable to produce sufficient milk, which is evident if the baby fails to gain weight as normal.

*A newborn baby's digestive system is physiologically incomplete. Some of its glands have not yet matured, which means that a newborn baby can only take milk. Later, as it grows, it will become progressively able to digest other foods. In all cases, however, the introduction of new foods must be very progressive.

The use of a bottle, as you know, involves two major risks:

- Infection due to lack of sterilization and poor hygiene.
- Incorrect dilution of concentrated milk or of powdered milk.

Consequently, if breast-feeding is really impossible, you must make sure that the young mother is adequately informed and has the necessary ability (not just to understand these risks, which you can explain to her individually and simply) but above all to avoid them by means of rigorous asepsis.

1. Microbes can infect a feeding bottle by 4 different routes. You will see how to guard against infection in each case :

- **Water**
  - Infected water contaminates the feeding bottle, then the baby.
  - Therefore use water from a clean source, filtered water, or mains water.
  - Boil the water for 10 minutes.
- **Milk**
  - Use powdered milk at the rate of one spoonful per 30 g of water; if it is very hot, the baby can be given water to drink other than in the bottle, but never reduce the proportion of water; insufficient dilution causes fever and digestive problems.
  - Warning : fresh cow's milk does not keep well and must be boiled; curds themselves are nutritional; condensed milk does not keep well after the can has been opened.

- **Equipment**
  - The bottle must be washed immediately after use then carefully dried.
  - The bottle and teats must be sterilized by boiling for 10 minutes before use. Make the mother understand that once sterilized, she must not touch the teat or inside of the bottle. Before preparing a bottle, the mother must always wash her hands thoroughly with soap.
- **The prepared bottle**

The prepared bottle must be given immmediately to the baby.

Mothers must not prepare bottles in advance, and they must not keep an unfinished bottle to give to the baby at the next meal. An unfinished bottle is an ideal place for microbes to find everything they need to grow.

3. Dilution errors

- Mothers who have not been adequately instructed often use too little milk in relation to the volume of water, or too little water.
  - In the first case, the baby will have an inadequate nutritional intake, it will stop growing and fail to thrive.
  - In the second case (too little water in relation to the quantity of powdered milk), the infant will have digestive problems and sometimes a slight fever. Remember that in tropical countries, particularly during the hot season, care must be taken to give babies who are not breast-fed enough to drink.
- Babies who are bottle-fed correctly, with the hygiene precautions listed above, can grow normally.

Milk is the food for a baby up to 4-6 months

1. Breast-feeding only should be the rule :

- It is entirely suitable for the infant.
- It can be carried out at any time and anywhere.
- It reaches the baby at the optimal temperature and without risk of infection.
- The nursing mother requires a rich and varied diet.

2. Bottle-feeding should be practised only by mothers who are unable to breast-feed :

- Take care with the water : use only boiled water.
- Take care with the milk : use only powdered milk; keep the box properly closed.
- Take care with the dilution.
- Take care with the equipment : sterilize the bottle and teat by boiling for 10 minutes.
- Take care with the prepared bottle : give it to the baby straightaway; do not keep left-overs.

4. Cereals

- Cereals can be given from the age of 4-6 months to supplement the milk diet. Cereals provide vegetable protein and mineral salts (calcium and a little iron).

- Cereal is included in the composition of baby food.

5. Fresh vegetables

- Fresh vegetables provide vegetable proteins, carbohydrates, vitamins and mineral salts. You should advise young mothers to use them as soon as the baby is 6 or 7 months old.
- The mother should boil the vegetables she can get in water for about 2 hours. She should try to vary the type of vegetable chosen fairly regularly.
- The cooking water forms the vegetable broth. Mixed with cereal, it should initially be given. The mother will then learn to make the food progressively thicker by adding mashed cooked vegetables to the broth to give a soup, then a vegetable puree. Or, the mother can take a few vegetables from dishes prepared for the whole family and mash them finely with a fork or vegetable mill before giving them to the baby.
- Well-cooked legumes (chickpeas, lentils, dried garden peas, haricot beans or broad beans) can be added to the vegetables.

6. Fruit

Fruit is essential for children. From the age of 4-6 months, regularly taking fruit juice or mashed fruit provides essential vitamins. Children can continue to eat mashed then whole fruit.

7. Meat, fish, eggs

These foods provide animal proteins which are absolutely essential for growth. Lack of these proteins causes malnutrition.

- Meat should initially be given very finely minced and well cooked. As the baby grows, it will be able to eat more coarsely minced meat, then normal meat.
- Fish should be very fresh, boiled then mashed. In regions where fish are scarce, the baby may receive its

requirement of animal proteins in the form of dried fish.

- Finally, eggs are a very good source of rich proteins.

For young children, half a very fresh, hard-boiled egg yolk is easily assimilable; a few months later they may be able to eat a whole egg.

8. Cheese

Yoghurt and curds, as well as cooked cheese, will provide the baby with the calcium it needs for its skeleton to grow.

DIET ACCORDING TO AGE

- There is no such thing as a standard diet for any child in any country. There are, however, simple rules to follow regarding local foods. Your experience will have taught you what needs to be given to each child for it to grow properly.

It is advisable to continue breast-feeding as long as possible, at the same time introducing from the age of 4-6 months new foods such as milk, fruit juice, vegetables, eggs, minced meat, fish, etc.

The baby can then be safely weaned very gradually.

FEEDING OF A NEONATE

There are three types of milk feeds for a newborn:

i) **Breast-feeds.**

ii) **Bottle-feeds** with powdered infant formulas (marketed in 2 forms; one for 0-6 months and the other for older infants more than 6 months. A third type is also available meant only for preterm babies).

iii) **Cow's milk.**

Feeling the ecstasy: Breast-feeding is ideal for your baby.

Breast milk is the ideal nutrition for a baby. It is the gold standard against which all infant formulas are compared. It is compulsory for all infant formulas to mention on the tin that breast milk is best for the baby. If for some reason, breast milk is not available for the baby there remains two options: a) Infant formulas b) Cow's milk.

Which is preferable? Medical evidence suggests that formulas are better as they are better tolerated and less allergenic. But there is nothing against cow's milk. In fact the Standard Textbook of Paediatrics clearly mentions that the rate of growth and development with cow's milk is comparable to that with the infant formulas.

*** (Purchasing power of an Indian): Once, President Bush, Garbachov and Rajiv Gandhi met God and asked when their country is going to be rich and prosperous so that all the people are happy. To Bush, God replied "50 years" and to Garbachov he replied "100 years." Both of them started crying, that they will not live that long to see their country become prosperous. When the turn of Rajiv Gandhi came and he asked the same question, there was a long pause after which God started crying! ***

The formulas are costly. A 1-month-old baby can finish a milk tin in 3-4 days and the cost translates to approximately Rs. 700-800/month (even more as the child gets older). In comparison, cow's milk costs only Rs. 200-250/month (⅓ to ¼ the cost of infant formulas). Can an average middle-class salaried person (who may be earning Rs. 4000-5000/month) afford to spend 20% of his income only on buying tins? The milk tins have become so popular in India because of our tendency to follow the western culture and also because of the commercial blitz. Thus today every layman knows about them and goes for them (I have encountered daily labourers, vegetable vendors, villagers i.e. the poor people who can hardly make their two ends meet, purchasing milk tins so as to give the best to their child). For such people, initially the cost may be low as the baby (few days old) may finish one tin in 15 days, but as it grows older and its demands increases, the baby may consume 1 tin in 3-4 days. That's the time when the person starts feeling the pinch and is no longer able to afford it. So they may over-dilute the milk (normal dilution for the formulas is 1 scoop in 1 ounce = 30 cc of water). I have seen parents putting 1 scoop or even less in 100 cc of water, which is not correct. The baby is made satisfied with a "white water" diet. Initially it may cry as it receives less nutrition to satisfy its hunger, but over a period of time, the child's metabolism and the body adjusts to the "over dilution" and the child becomes satisfied with whatever is offered to it. But this has disastrous consequences for the baby. It fails to gain weight (being fed only ⅓ to ¼ of its caloric requirements) and starts becoming "skin and bones." These babies are very vulnerable to infections, chronic diarrhoeas, vitamin deficiencies etc. and sadly, a large number of them succumb to malnutrition and die. In fact malnutrition is a leading cause of infant deaths in India and the infant formulas are much responsible for this malnutrition. In fact when one sees a case of infantile malnutrition in the paediatric ward, the doctors, even without asking the parents, have got a resigned feeling in their minds that the mother must have been giving diluted infant formula, which on asking, more often than not, is correct. This problem is so common, and the condition of the "skin and bones" infant looks so miserable and hopeless, that the infant formulas have been aptly termed as "white poison" by the doctors, particularly paediatricians. In fact there is a strong feeling amongst doctors that the infant formulas should be banned or at least OTC (over the counter) sale, without a doctor's prescription, should be prohibited.

One should also be aware of the danger in under-dilution (i.e. making concentrated feeds). Frequently it is due to ignorance about the "scoop of the powder." The scoop, which is included in the tin, should not be heaped but should be levelled off at the top by rubbing the scoop at the side of the tin so that the extra powder falls off and thus the scoop becomes levelled at the top. Another reason is that the mother may think that if she feeds the baby more powder (i.e. more concentrated milk); it will become stronger and gain weight faster. Whatever the reasons are, it is dangerous for the baby, so avoid it. The reason is that the child is getting more solid as compared to water. Thus his body becomes "water deficient" over a period of time. This leads to a combination of dehydration along with increased sodium levels of the blood, both of which are dangerous.

Parents who cannot afford infant formulas can give undiluted cow's milk to the baby. The cost is ⅓ to ¼ of milk tins and as stated above, over dilution of powdered milk is done so that the child gets ⅓ to ¼ of the calories. So if the parents give cow's milk, they can afford to give it undiluted. Thus the child gets the required calories making him grow at a normal pace. Fears that the cow's milk is hard to digest, child may suffer from diarrhoea or allergies are largely unfounded. An occasional child, who the parents feel is unable to tolerate the cow's milk, should seek a doctor's opinion.

Parents who can afford infant formulas can go for the infant tins, provided for some reason they are not having breast milk, which always is the nutrition of choice for all babies. They should follow the proper procedure in preparing milk from the powdered form (i.e. proper dilution is used, the bottles are properly washed and sterilised etc.)

What are the virtues of breast milk that it is so universally recommended?

ADVANTAGES OF BREAST MILK

1. **Nature's gift:** Breast milk is the nature's way of nourishing a child and what is natural cannot be wrong. Infant formulas have come into vogue recently, while breast milk exists from the very beginning of human race. When there were no infant formulas, all mothers used to breast-feed without giving it a second thought, but now with the presence of milk tins, the mother's motivation to breast feed has decreased.
2. **It is free:** Cost of breast milk is zero. If you exclusively breast-feed, you will save about Rs. 10,000/- per year (as the cost towards milk tins). If nothing else, save it and make a fixed deposit of it in your child's name!
3. **Sterile and hygienic**: A child who is exclusively breast-fed usually does not have infective diarrhoea, which speaks volumes of its hygienic and sterile nature. Bottle-fed infants are prone to have diarrhoea, unless the protocol for sterility is strictly maintained, which practically, is very difficult to maintain feed after feed and day after day.
4. **Ready made:** It is a pre-prepared ready to use food, available at the spur of the moment. Just ask those who go through all the trouble of sterilising bottles, boiling water, preparing the infant formula etc; and you will realise how much time, energy and headache you save for yourself.
5. **Anti-infective properties:** Breast milk contains certain protective elements like immunoglobulin, cells etc., which

help the body in protecting against infections. Thus, breast-fed infants fall sick less often than others do.

6. **Emotional bonding:** It is, arguably, the biggest advantage of breast-feeding. The neonate, such a delicate creature, like all human beings, has the innate desire to be loved and caressed. It derives much mental satisfaction out of it and blossoms better. The mother and child get deeply attached to each other via the medium of breast-feeding giving immense psychological satisfaction to both.

Despite so many advantages, the incidence of breast-feeding is declining and the use of commercial formulas increasing. Why?

1. **Figure consciousness**: In this modern age, the media hype and western norms have created a feeling of insecurity about a person's physical characteristics in the minds of both men and women. Breast-feeding being touted as the cause for breast sagging, women may prefer bottle feeding rather than running the risk of their figure being spoiled

If one rationally thinks about it, it is obvious that breast-feeding cannot affect any other part of the body. So one cannot become heavy at the hips or get a tummy bulge because of breast-feeding. Regarding breast sagging, the firmness and tone of the breasts depend largely on the chest muscles. Proper exercise of the chest wall muscles coupled with a firm brassiere for good support of breasts will not cause their sagging in a breast-feeding woman. In fact, breast-feeding makes the breasts heavier and larger (something many women crave for as is evident by the commercial success of silicon implants). So, breast-feeding has nothing to do with making the woman unattractive. What spoils the figure of the mother is a lack of post-delivery conditioning exercises and overeating (in India, mothers are fed *desi ghee* and other rich and high calorie diet post-delivery). On top of this is a sedentary life style, particularly for the first few months after delivery. All these factors contribute in making the mother plump and lead to the slumping of her figure. As coincidentally, this is also the time of breast-feeding; an erroneous association is made between breast-feeding and the sagging of the figure, while actually other factors are responsible for it. Realising this, western women are increasingly turning towards breast-feeding as the nutrition of choice for their baby and take pride in doing so.

2. **Lack of motivation**: The mothers give up easily if they feel that they are not able to breast-feed properly or they consider breast-feeding a bother. This "easy surrender" has a lot to do with the easy availability of infant milk tins. Because such an easy alternative is available, mothers don't try hard enough, nor do they have the patience to go on till a satisfactory pattern of breast-feeding is established. (Remember breast-feeding is an art and it does take some effort and time to establish a smooth pattern). So, unless the mothers are motivated enough and have a serious desire to breast-feed, they give up early. Motivation can come only if the mother understands the benefits of breast milk and takes pride in giving her baby her own milk.

3. **Career pressures**: Many mothers are working women who go to work from morning to evening. Such mothers should take full advantage of their maternity leave and breast-feed during this leave to foster a deep emotional bond between themselves and their babies. When the woman resumes her duties, before leaving for office, she can express her breast milk in a container and refrigerate it, so that the caretaker of the baby during her absence can feed the baby that milk.

Medical science strongly advises that mothers should breast-feed, so as not to deprive their baby of a nature's gift from the mother to the baby.

BREAST-FEEDING (Preparation & Technique)

The preparation for breast-feeding starts much before delivery i.e. during pregnancy. The mother should read about breast-feeding and any anticipated problems or doubts should be clarified with her obstetrician during her regular antenatal visits. For e.g., if there are retracted nipples, daily manual traction (i.e. catching the areola and the nipple area between the thumb and fingers and gently pulling it outwards) can correct it. Such measures will not lead to feeding problems when the baby is born.

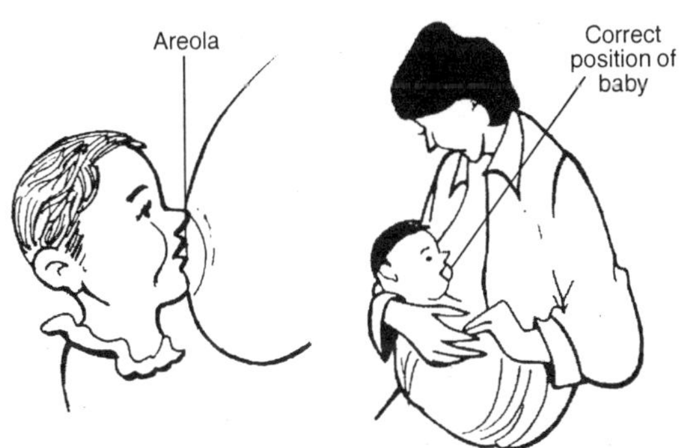

Wrong Position **Positioning your baby on the nipple**
When breast-feeding, the entire nipple and most of the areola (the darker area around the nipple) should be taken into the baby's mouth to avoid causing cracks in the skin of the nipple.

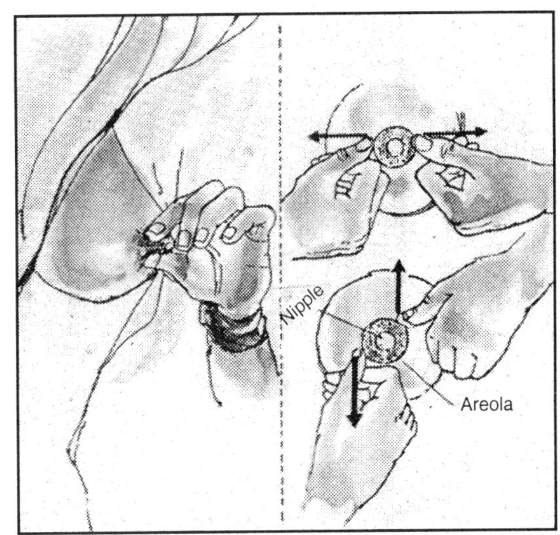

Preparing for the feed: Follow the above steps.

The position that the mother assumes for feeding is largely a matter of comfort and preference. She can nurse lying down

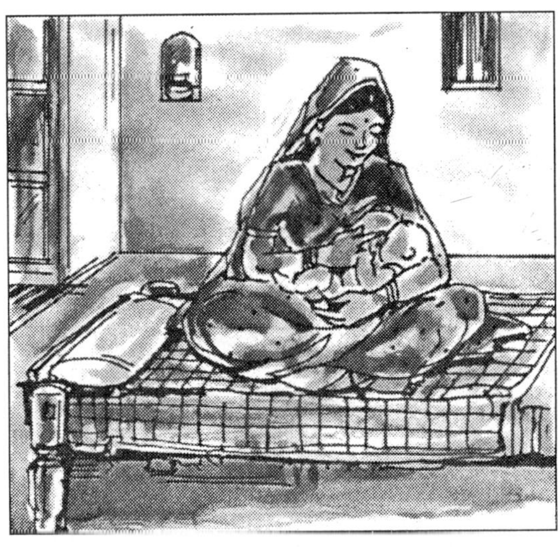

Position of breast-feeding while sitting.

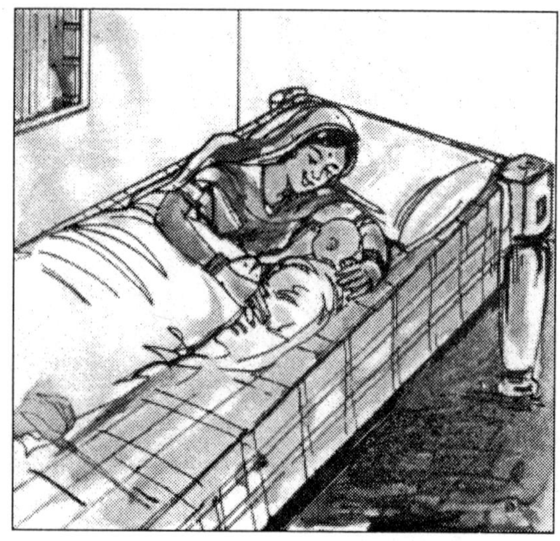

Position of breast-feeding while lying down.

on one side, or propped up with pillows underneath; or sitting comfortably in bed, chair etc. Breast-feeding can be started after delivery as soon as the mother and the baby are comfortable. Correct position and technique are necessary for optimal sucking with minimal nipple discomfort.

If the mother is sitting, the infant should be elevated to the height of the breast and turned so that he faces the mother. The mother's arm supporting the baby should bring the baby's mouth near to her breast. The other free arm should support the breast from below by the fingers, while the thumb and the index finger should grasp the nipple and compress it so as to make it more protractile. Ideally, the mother should touch the nipple at the corner of the baby's mouth and not directly put it into the baby's mouth. When the baby feels the nipple (or any stimulus including a finger touch at the corner of his mouth), it goes for it, the avidity depending upon his hunger. The baby tries to "catch" the stimulus (in this case the nipple) in his mouth, a natural reflex called rooting. When the baby, with its mouth open finds the nipple and tries to grasp it, the mother should gently but rapidly, push as much nipple and areola as possible in the baby's mouth.

The baby should apply rhythmic compressions on the areola (and not on the nipple, as it does in bottle-feeding) with its gums. Milk is stored in sinuses underneath the areola and these sinuses should be

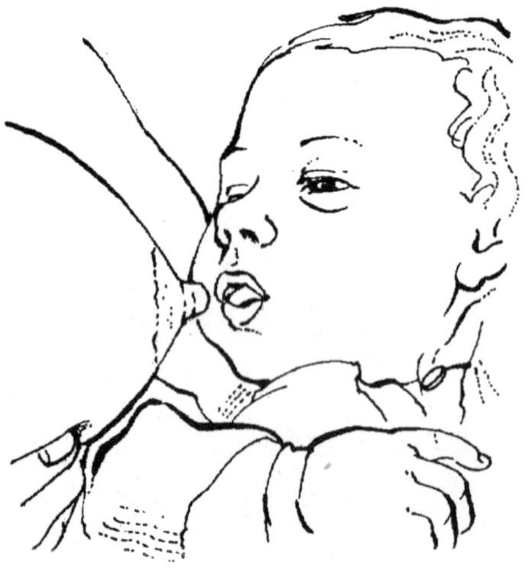

Rooting reflex

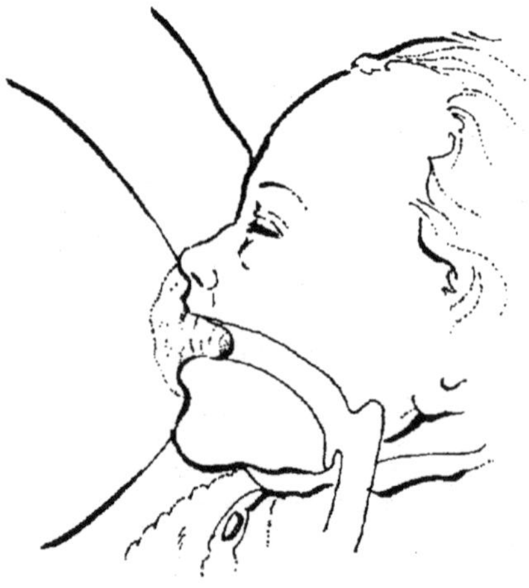

Latching on

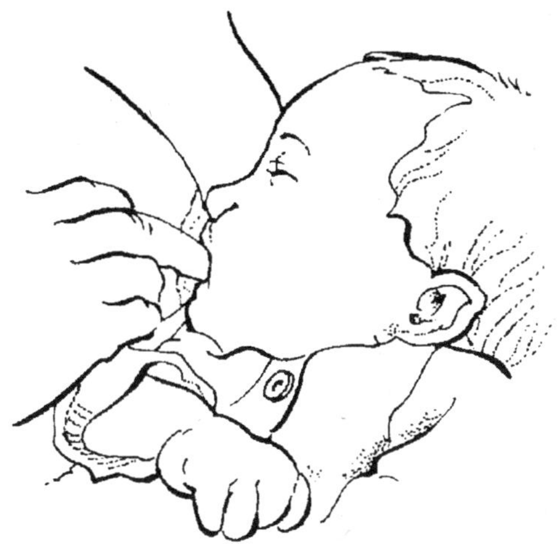

Breaking the suction

compressed rhythmically, so that the milk from them is squirted via the nipple into the baby's mouth. The nipple acts like a conduit for the passage of milk. Chewing on the nipple or rhythmic compression of the nipple by the gums is not helpful in getting the milk, because milk from the breast doesn't come from suction on the nipples, as in the case of bottle! Proper breast-feeding technique requires that the baby compress the areola (rather than the nipples) with its gums. In fact, improper technique and positioning is chiefly responsible for soreness and cracked nipples, a common complaint of nursing mothers.

Some useful advice and facts regarding breast-feeds are given below.

1. Express some milk from the breast before feeding. It makes the areolar area soft and compressible for the baby.
2. Both breasts should be offered to the baby at one feed. The breast offered first should be completely emptied (emptying is a potent stimulus for milk production.)
3. The breast to be offered first should be alternated with feeds, i.e. if the left breast was offered first during the previous feed, the right breast should be offered first now. This ensures complete emptying of at least one breast at each feeding, which is very necessary for adequate milk production.
4. A suitable time for suckling at each breast is about 15 minutes after the 3rd day. On the 1st day, it is 5 minutes and on the 2nd, 10 minutes. However, it depends more on the baby. Some babies finish their milk requirements fast in just 3-4 minutes and then doze off. Others may do it a leisurely pace. However, suckling for more than 15 minutes is not advised as it may lead to soreness and cracked nipples.
5. When the baby has finished feeding, don't pull it away from your breast. It will apply traction on the nipple and may make it sore. The best way to unlatch a baby is to insert your finger in the corner of the baby's mouth in between the gums. This will release the grasp of the gums and then you can take the baby off the breast.
6. If the baby dozes off while feeding, you can gently stimulate the baby by massaging behind the ears or rubbing the soles of the baby. If after 2-3 tries, the baby is still not feeding, stop and unlatch the baby.
7. There is no fixed time interval (say 3 hours or 4 hours) at which the baby has to be fed. Instead a flexible schedule is recommended, based chiefly on demand; i.e. to give the baby the milk when he starts demanding it. If more

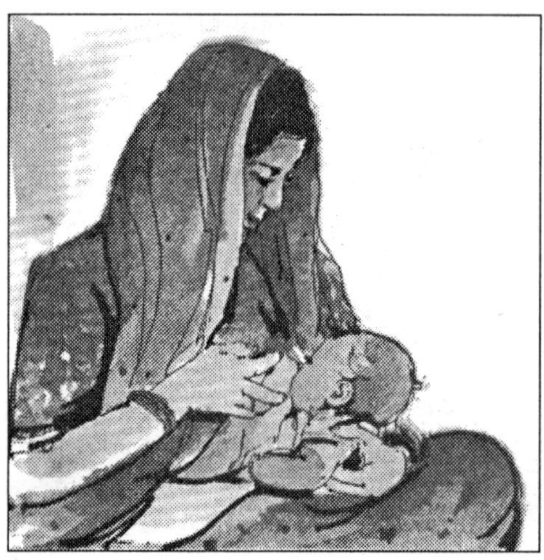

Feed the baby with both breasts.

than 4 hours elapse, and the baby is still sleepy, it is better to try to awaken him gently and see whether he will accept feeds.

8. The milk produced in the initial 3-4 days is fluidly, yellow and very less in amount. It is called "colostrum", which has a high content of nutrients and is invaluable to the child. It should always be given to the baby, without worrying about its quantity or quality.

9. During this phase, the mother starts doubting that she is not producing enough milk. All mothers produce colostrum (which as I have mentioned is physiologically less in amount) and all of them produce roughly the same amount in the initial 2-3 days. By the 4th day, the milk production starts increasing and adjusts itself to the baby's needs in another few days.

10. It is during this time also that the mother turns towards the bottle to supplement her "inadequate" breast milk (which actually is adequate for the baby). The baby's fluid and calorie requirements are less during the first 1-3 days, and so the "less" amount of milk i.e. the colostrum actually is sufficient for it. This is the critical point where all the trouble starts. Once the baby starts accepting bottle, the motivation of mother goes down. The baby finding the nipple of the bottle softer than the breast has to put less effort to suck milk from it, and so starts preferring it over the breast. The mother on seeing the baby prefer the bottle becomes discouraged and so it becomes difficult for her to breast-feed. Then there is an entity called "nipple confusion". The baby's gums compress the areola of the mother rather than the nipple, but with the bottle the baby compresses rhythmically the bottle's nipple. This may lead to confusion in the baby's mind and he may start chewing on the nipples of the mother's breasts, and on finding no milk coming may become irritated. Therefore if you want to breast-feed, no bottles, even for some feeds, until you are confident and have a well-established milk supply.

11. An important pre-requisite for a nursing mother is that she should be mentally and physically relaxed. Tension and fatigue has an inhibitory effect on milk production. After delivery, don't encourage long visits by well wishers. Instead try to rest, sleep or just relax with your baby by the side, thinking pleasurable thoughts about it.
12. The breast-feeding mother should consume adequate amounts of water and a wholesome diet. Wholesome diet doesn't mean eating lots of fattening things like ghee, chocolates, cakes etc. but to eat cereals, dals, vegetables, eggs, meat, curd etc. Eating lot of fruits is a good thing. Drinking a lot of milk in the belief that it will indirectly "come out" from the breasts and so replace the milk taken by the baby is an erroneous belief. By all means drink milk (and lots of it), if you really relish it. But drinking it for the reason mentioned above is not correct.
13. There is a fine-tuning by nature between the production of milk and its demand by the baby. The amount of milk produced is not a "static" quantity e.g. one mother will produce only 500 cc per day while another will produce only 700 cc per day. Milk production increases according to the baby's requirements. If the baby wants more, it sucks more, which empties the breast completely. This is the most potent stimulus to produce more milk. So more is the demand - more is the supply. However, if you supplement with bottle, the baby takes less milk from the breasts. The milk left behind in the breast sends a signal to produce

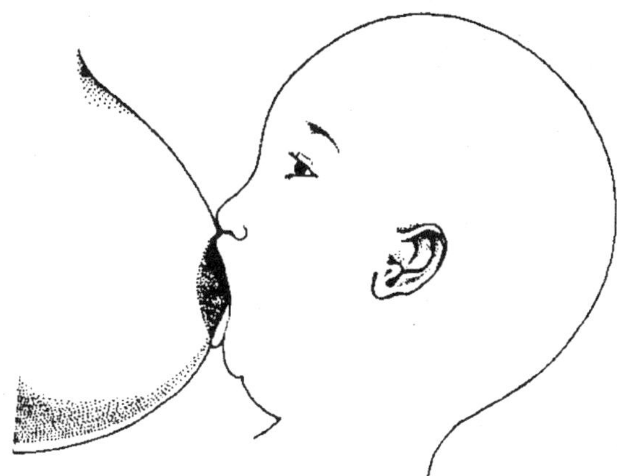

Putting the nipple and areola in the baby's mouth during breast-feeding.

less. Twins or even triplets can be wholly and successfully breast-fed. So don't be anxious that milk is not enough. Just leave it to nature.
14. There may be an increase in the appetite of the baby, sometimes dramatically, particularly at 3, 6 and 12 weeks. The nursing mother should anticipate this and not think that her breast milk is not enough for the baby during these times. Similarly when the mother is discharged from the hospital, her breast milk may temporarily decrease for 2-3 days as she adjusts and adapts herself to living with the baby at home.
15. Mothers worry a lot about the adequacy of milk. The best way to judge adequacy is by the behaviour of the child. If the child appears content and sleeps off for 2-3 hours, then the amount of milk is sufficient. However if the baby is fretful, demands feeds every 1 hour and doesn't seem satisfied, it is possible that the breast milk is less. Of course with time, the supply will increase (remember the

more you suckle, the more is the production of milk) but temporarily, one has to offer top feeds once in a while to satisfy the baby. This shouldn't worry the mother unduly because she knows that in due course of time; her supply will increase and be adequate for the child. Remember, more often than not, the child actually doesn't demand feeds every hour, but the mother only perceives so in her mind. So it is better to be objective in this rather than letting subjective feelings cloud the judgement. The best way is to take the help of a clock and note exactly after how much time the baby starts demanding another feed. Another excellent way of judging the adequacy of breast milk production is by weight gain of the child. But this should be done every 1-2 weeks. Weighing the baby after every feed or everyday is of no use and creates unnecessary anxiety in the minds of the parents.

16. A mother, particularly, one having her first child will face some problems off and on regarding breast-feeding. Some queries, doubts etc. will be in her mind. She requires help and support. Unfortunately, the doctors and nurses are too busy to individually explain to each mother the art of breast-feeding, and to reassure her off and on. Even if the mother says that her milk is not adequate, the doctors tend to take it lightly and the standard reply is, "Go on feeding, it will come." This doctor's attitude can easily be changed by the mother's attitude towards breast-feeding. If the mother says, "Doctor, I sincerely want to breast-feed my baby, but am facing few problems in doing so. Kindly help me;" I am sure the doctor will make extra efforts to help her.

17. Entail the help of the husband in the care of the baby including breast-feeding. The husband may help in positioning and supporting the baby while breast-feeding and give reassurance to the nursing mother. Most husbands want to contribute in the care of the baby. But, because they are not accustomed mentally (due to their upbringing) to do so, they feel embarrassed and confused. It appears that rather than making their own decisions, they need some directions in this regard. Here the wives can gently guide them. For e.g. tell them to fetch clothes for the baby, boil bottles, prepare milk and do so many other routine chores of the baby. They will do it happily and at the same time feel satisfied that they, too, are contributing in their own way in the rearing of the baby.

18. Some mothers feel that their milk is too dilute. Some even feel that their milk is harmful to the baby (particularly if the baby vomits or has loose stools). Some feel that what they eat affects the quality of the milk produced. All these are myths. Milk is milk containing 99% water and 1% solids in the form of proteins, lactose, minerals, vitamins etc. Your thinking cannot alter the quality of the breast milk. Only if the mother is taking some medicines, it is better to ask the doctor whether it will have any effect on the breast-fed baby.

BREAST-FEEDING

(Common Problems)

1. **Milk is not enough?** See the text before for guidance.
2. **Sore or cracked nipples**: It is usually due to a faulty technique where the gums of the baby apply undue traction on the nipples. The technique of feeding has to be modified. For cracked nipples, it is best to apply some milk over it and leave it open to air. Lanolin ointment can also be applied locally. But keep away from soap, boric acid and powders. The feeding should continue (for shorter periods and starting on the less sore side). If the problem is severe and causing excessive pain to the mother during suckling, then breast pumps should be used to empty the breast. If the breast is not emptied, not only will it lead to a decrease in the milk supply but will also lead to "breast engorgement" (discussed below). If the baby is not fed on time, in his "over-enthusiasm" he may suck vigorously on the nipples causing its soreness. Then again the baby may be latched on to the breast for more than 15 minutes or the mother may be using soap and antiseptics on the nipples (nipple cleaning is not required before feeds, only your hands should be washed). Milk overflows at the end of suckling cause the brassiere to stick to the nipple and may peel off the skin when the bra is removed. Therefore it is advisable that the mother dries the nipple and surrounding area before putting on the bra. Also advisable is to put a soft handkerchief between the nipple and the bra so that it absorbs the milk and hence the nipple doesn't stick to the bra as that milk dries off.
3. **Inverted or flat nipples:** This should be noted during pregnancy and measures to protrude it should begin in pregnancy itself. If still the nipples are not everted, then the mother can use a nipple shield or alternatively empty the milk in a bottle by a breast pump and then feed it to the baby.
4. **Breast engorgement:** The breast becomes heavy and painful due to the incomplete emptying of milk from it. The accumulation of milk causes it to become engorged. To relieve it one has to express out the milk manually. A hot shower or massaging the breast tissue with warm water will facilitate the milk expression by making the breast tissue softer. Breast pump may also help.

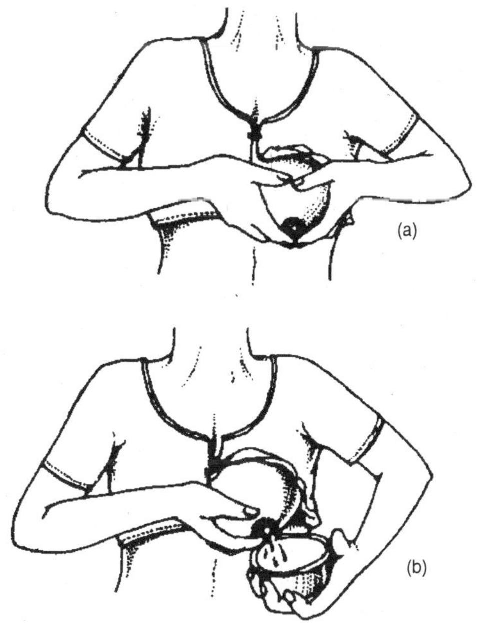

A mother manually exercising her breast milk (a, b).

BOTTLE-FEEDING

If for some reason the mother is unable to breast-feed; the obvious alternative is bottle-feeding. Some doctors recommend feeding by dropper or by cup and spoon, rather than the bottle (they are worried about the infection of the intestines by the bottle). I personally prefer bottle-feeding because:

- If you maintain cleanliness and follow the proper procedure in preparing the bottle milk, chances of infection are very less.

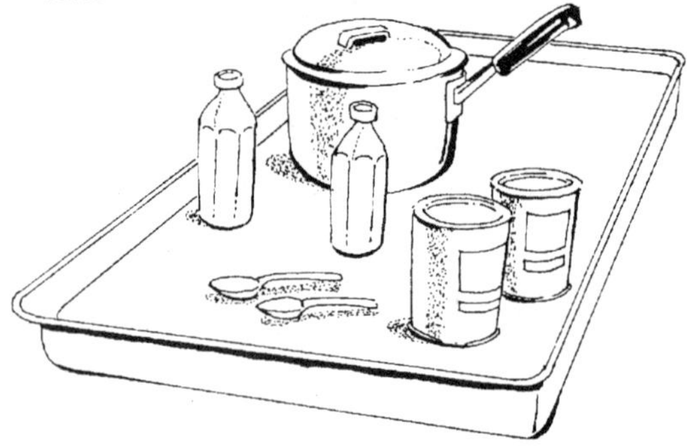

Equipment for bottle-feeding.

- Feeding by cups or droppers is time consuming and messy, requiring much patience.
- The biggest reason for which I advocate bottle is that for the baby, sucking is very soothing and satisfying. With cups and droppers, you eliminate this very basic instinct of the baby. Thus though the hunger may be satisfied, the craving for sucking remains unfulfilled. So the baby doesn't derive the psychological satisfaction of sucking, which is important.

Given below are some useful hints and advice regarding bottle- feeding:

1. **Choice of the tin:** There are 3 types of formulas available: preterm formula, 0-6 month formula (usually labelled number 1) and above 6 months formula (usually labelled number 2). Preterm formulas are usually given on the recommendation of the doctor. Give preterm formula only till the time that the baby is preterm (term baby is 37 weeks +). So if your baby was born premature (say at the gestational age of 32 weeks), it should be given the preterm formula for 5 weeks i.e. till it becomes 37 weeks (32 weeks + 5 weeks = 37 weeks). After that it should be shifted to the 0-6 month formula. There are many companies manufacturing powdered milk and there is little to choose one over the other.
2. **Choice of the bottle**: The bottle should be accurately calibrated in both ounces and ml (cc). It should be wide mouthed, so that cleaning is easier. One ounce is equal to 30 cc. Milk is preferably prepared taking into consideration the ounce markings. For one ounce of water (i.e. water till the level of the calibrated 1 ounce on the bottle), one scoop of the powdered milk is added. Preferably ask for a bottle that has an air inlet, so that as the baby empties the milk, it is automatically replaced by air and a vacuum is not created inside the bottle. In bottles, which don't have an air inlet, after some sucking, the nipple will become pinched and collapsed due to vacuum and the baby has to put more efforts to suck. Of course, babies are very smart and after sometime they learn to release the nipple periodically (when it becomes collapsed) so that air may enter through the nipple hole and replace the void.

While buying bottles, it is always a good idea to buy some extra nipples. Nowadays, nipples have readymade holes on them, so you are saved the bother of making a hole of the right size on it. The nipple hole is of the right size if, when you invert the bottle, the milk comes in the form of a fine spray for a second or two and then changes to drops. If the milk continues to come in the form of a spray, the hole is big and the baby may choke on the excess milk released at a faster rate through the big hole. If the milk comes in the form of drops right from beginning, the hole is small and the baby will require more effort to suck.

3. **Preparation of the formula:** Water should be taken to the appropriate mark in ounces (dictated by the baby's requirements), and the requisite number of scoops should be added to it. Remember, the scoop should be levelled at the top and not heaped (discussed earlier), as it may lead to dangerous under dilution i.e. the milk will become more concentrated than required. For e.g. if you take 90 cc (= 3 ounces) of water, then add 3 scoops of the milk powder to it. After capping the bottle and shaking it so that the powder dissolves in the water to form a homogeneous liquid, you will find that the mark has risen to maybe 100 cc. Don't worry about it. What you have done is correct. After preparing the formula, always test its hotness, by dropping a few drops of the milk at the back of your wrists. Accidental burns to the baby's mouth have resulted by omitting this step.

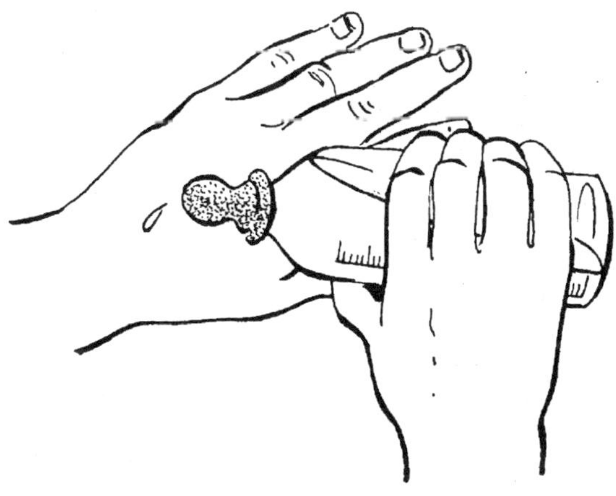

Testing Temperature: Test the temperature of the milk mixture by shaking a few drops on the wrist, or the back of the hand.

4. **Baby's requirements**: How much milk to prepare? If the baby finishes the bottle completely, then next time you should prepare ½ - 1 ounce more and so on till the baby leaves some milk in the bottle. That is the amount to be prepared as a routine (as the child grows up he will finish this also completely and you will have to prepare more). Mothers are sometimes worried that if there is more milk in the bottle than the baby's requirements, it may go on drinking it and land with some problem like vomiting or indigestion. Don't worry about it. The child (even a 1-day old neonate) knows when to stop. When satiated, the baby will start chewing on the nipple or pushing it out and even if you keep it in, he just won't suck. It is another strong evidence to prove that the babies and children know exactly how much to eat (just like adults) and therefore the parents should not be bothered about it.

5. **Sterilisation:** The bottle should be cleaned with washing powder and water. Put a scrubbing brush inside the bottle and scrub it thoroughly. Remove

the nipple from the screw lid of the bottle and wash both of them thoroughly. After washing, put the constituents of the bottle (i.e. the open bottle, nipple, the screw lid and the cap) in boiling water. The cap, the screw lid and the nipple should be boiled for 5 minutes while the bottle for 10 minutes (this time is considered after the water has started boiling). Remove the constituents from the water, fix them and then put the cap over the nipple. Ensure that your hands are washed clean before doing all this. The bottle is now ready to use. The water to be used for preparing the formula should be boiled and then put in a flask preferably (so that it stays warm and you needn't boil it for every feed). It is better to have 5-6 bottles and sterilise them together once or twice a day, rather than sterilising them after every feed, which will be quite cumbersome. Remember if the water is too hot, then the powder may "lump" and if it is cold, the powder may dissolve very slowly. So it should be just warm. Once the bottle is prepared and you have tested the temperature of the milk inside, it is ready to be fed to the baby.

6. **Technique of feeding:** While feeding, keep the bottle propped up so that the nipple is always filled with milk and not air. If it contains air (as is the case if the bottle is more horizontal than vertical), the baby will take this into the stomach and then may have gas or eructation problems. Never, never prop the bottle up by artificial means like pillows etc. and leave the baby unattended while feeding. The parents may consider holding the bottle till the baby finishes the milk a task, but it is worth it, as incidences of choking have occurred when the baby was left unattended. If the baby goes to sleep while feeding, you may rotate the bottle gently inside the mouth of the baby, whence it may again start sucking.

7. **Burping:** It is natural for the baby to swallow some air while feeding (whether breast or bottle). The process of trying to remove this air is called burping. For this, hold the baby upright on the shoulders and then massage and pat the back of the baby for a few minutes. An audible eructation signifies that the gas has been expelled. If there is no air expulsion also, do not worry; maybe the baby has swallowed less air.

8. **Practical tip**: Keep 4-5 sterilised bottles, a thermos flask of warm, boiled water and the milk tin near the bedside, so that milk can be prepared in a jiffy, if required.

Average milk requirements of a baby (according to age)

Age of Baby	Average No. of Feeds/Day	Average Amount Taken/Feed
0-2 weeks	6-10	2-3 oz
2 weeks-2 months	6-8	4-5 oz
2-3 months	5-6	5-6 oz
3-6 months	4-5	6-7 oz
6-9 months	3-4	7-8 oz
9-12 months	3	7-8 oz

1 Oz (ounce) = 30 ml

** The above mentioned requirements are just an average guideline and may vary from child to child. Parents are advised not to take it too rigidly. In case of doubts regarding your baby's intake of milk, kindly contact your paediatrician.

Interesting observations regarding behaviour of the baby while nursing is as follows:

"She wakes up because she is hungry, cries because she wants to be fed. She is so eager (when hungry) that when the nipple goes into her mouth, she almost shudders. When she nurses you can see that it is an intense experience. Perhaps she breaks into perspiration. If you stop her in the middle, she may cry furiously. When she has had as much as she wants, she is groggy with satisfaction and falls asleep. A look of bliss and contentment comes on her face when her hunger is satiated, as if she is thanking the person who has taken the effort to feed her. Even while she is asleep, it appears sometimes that she is dreaming of nursing. As she again gets hungry and starts coming out of her slumber, her mouth makes sucking motions and noises. Her fingers go near her mouth and she may start sucking on them, just for the soothing feeling that sucking gives. Her neck starts roving, searching for the nipple and her milk. After some vain attempts, when such manoeuvres of hers don't produce the desired effect (i.e. she doesn't get milk), she starts crying, signalling that she is hungry and someone should pay attention to it. All this adds to the fact that feeding is her great joy and satisfaction. She gets her early ideas about life from the way the feeding goes and she gets her first ideas about the world from the person who feeds her."

FEEDING OF A CHILD (4 Months and Above)

Weaning

It is the process by which the child is shifted from an exclusively milk diet to other foods. It is started at the age of 4 months when liquids other than milk (e.g. juices, soups) and semi-solid foods (e.g. dal, rice) are introduced in the baby's diet. Of course he still consumes milk, but as he starts consuming more and more of other foods, his milk consumption gradually decreases.

Caution: If there is a strong family history of allergy (e.g. skin allergies, urticaria, bronchial asthma, nasal allergy), it is prudent to exclusively breast-feed till the age of 6 months (no other milk should be given including milk tins). After that only the process of weaning should be started. This decreases the chances of allergy in the child.

In the initial 4 months, the baby requires only milk (not even water, let alone other things), as milk is the complete food for it till that time. If the climate is too hot, however, some water may be periodically offered to the baby. You will know that he is thirsty and not hungry by his rejection of the milk and avid sucking of the water. Adding glucose to water is of no

Weaning process: Increase the quantity of food and also its variety.

use and is mentioned only to be rejected because the child requires only plain water to quench his thirst. At 4 months, the baby is offered food that he can eat without having to chew it (a 4-month baby doesn't have any teeth). You can give dal, juices, soups, mashed rice, mashed potatoes, soft boiled egg yolk etc. that you routinely prepare at home and which is mashed and soft. *Egg white should be introduced at the age of 6 months as early introduction can lead to allergy.*

Preparation Instructions

There are a lot of commercial "baby foods" available like Cerelac, Nestum etc. Cerelac is a mixture of wheat and milk. You can prepare the same mixture at your house in the form of halwa (which constitutes wheat flour, milk, ghee and sugar). These commercial products have nothing special about them and giving them doesn't make the baby stronger and healthier (as compared to home made foods). If at all, halwa is more nutritious and richer in calories than Cerelac, as it contains ghee and sugar in addition to milk and wheat flour. So, commercial baby foods are not a must for your baby. The main advantage of them is that they are ready to prepare (e.g. add some water or milk to Cerelac powder and it is ready to be consumed), while making baby food at home is time consuming. Again it depends on the mother. Some mothers may take joy and pride in preparing different foods for their baby and find giving ready-made foods "dull". The main disadvantage of the commercial foods is their cost. Home-made food preparations are cheaper. Practically, however, what one often sees is that mothers give a combination of marketed baby foods and what she prepares in the kitchen.

Balanced diet

There is a lot of concern about a balanced diet. The diet consists of 6 main ingredients and these are proteins, carbohydrates, fats, minerals, vitamins and water. A balanced mixture of these six components is required for an optimum and healthy growth. The requirements of each of these constituents are specified (in nutritional textbooks) and

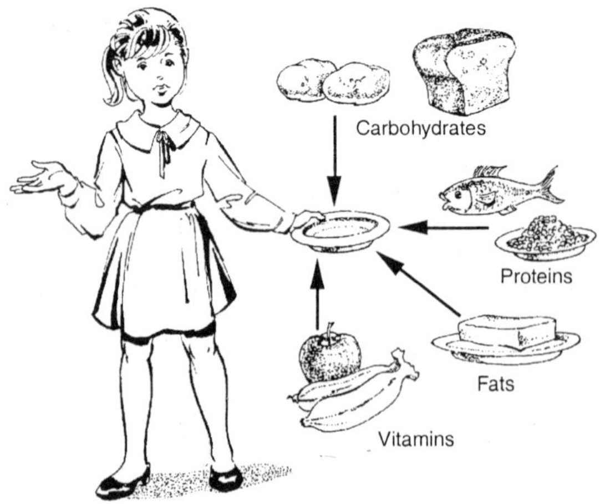

For good health: Give her a balanced diet.

they depend on the age. It appears to me that we are so enamoured by what modern science thinks we ought to eat, that we tend to forget that our bodies have known this for millions of years. Because of this, the mother wants her child to get a balanced diet. How can the mother be sure that the child is receiving a balanced proportion of the 6 "building blocks" of the body? After all, the child eats a variety of things. To calculate the quantity and the nutritional composition of each food item that the child takes and then compare them with standard nutritional tables is practically impossible on a day to day basis.

Fortunately calculations are not needed as what we eat daily tends to be balanced by itself over a period of time. Some people are vegetarians, some non-vegetarians. Some may be rice eaters, others' staple diet may be dal and roti. People in different parts of the world have culturally different food habits. Yet all of them are healthy, don't suffer from "imbalanced" diet and don't become deficient in one of the constituents of nutrition (e.g. Proteins or Vitamins). Why? Because, of the simple reason that the diet tends to balance itself. Our appetite is so geared by nature that we don't eat one constituent preferentially at the expense of other e.g., if there is too much fat in the food, you will find it heavy and disagreeable.

So what the parents should do is to offer the child a variety of foodstuff (like vegetables, fruits, cereals, meat, eggs, milk, legumes, dals etc), not necessarily all of them in one day but over a period of time, say a week. The child's instincts and appetite is sound enough to pick a well balanced diet in the long run. Therefore

Supplementary foods for infants–dal, chapati, curd and mashed vegetables, without spices.

mothers should not worry whether their child is getting a balanced diet or not, because he is!

Ideally, the baby's weaning should be started with some form of cereal (e.g. rice or wheat). By the age of 6 months, the baby can take strained or pureed vegetables and fruits. Fruit juices can be given by a cup. It is better to start with vegetables first to reduce a tendency to develop a taste for sweets. By 8-9 months, pureed meat, pureed beans and lentils can be given. At this time, they want to pick up the food article between their fingers and love to munch on them. The child may suck and chew at the food article with his bare gums even at the age of 5-6 months i.e. at the time of teething, because there is a lot of irritation of their gums and it soothes the irritated gums. As the food morsel softens gradually with their saliva, some of it goes into the stomach, enough to make them feel that they are getting somewhere. At a little older age, they will like to eat with the spoon. Initially they won't meet with much success and most of the food will spill. By 15 months, however, most of the children are adept enough to feed with the

Getting the feel of his food.

spoon without much spilling. Between 1-2 years, the child can usually take a mixed food diet and eats just like an adult member of the home. The only precaution to be taken is that foods which can cause choking should be avoided i.e. one should avoid large, round shaped, hard food items. The mother, by trial and error, can find out the likes and dislikes of the baby and thus know what to offer.

Some useful tips and advice regarding feeding of the children, is given below:

1. Putting an older infant (>5-6 months) to sleep with a bottle in his mouth is discouraged because it may lead to dental caries, as well as the potential for future sleep problems, because the child associates sleep with having the bottle in his mouth. Most parents can wean the child from a bottle to a cup at the age of 9-12 months of age.

New Adventure: A drink from a glass.

2. Routine supplementation of the food with "health tonics" and multivitamins is not recommended. The only exception is iron supplementation, which the child requires beginning at 4 months of age.
3. While the baby is being weaned and new foods introduced, it is but natural that the child has to develop a taste and liking for the texture and taste of the food. (It is also true in case of adults. If you are given a new thing to eat, say a dish of some foreign country, you will also take time and repeated eating of it to develop a taste for it). So, initially the volume of food consumed is less important than the experience of it. Because of this, it is recommended that parents give 1-2 spoons at a time of a new food daily and persist with the same food for 2 weeks before introducing another. This is done to give time and opportunity to the child to "acclimatise" and "savour" the new food. In the initial stages, while taking the spoonful of food, the child is not experienced in co-ordinating the action of catching hold of the piece of food with his tongue and then pushing it back to be swallowed ultimately. So what you may find is that the child just clacks his tongue against the roof of the mouth, and most of the food gets squeezed out onto his chin. Some

children initially have a strong tongue protrusion reflex and will push out the food offered with their tongue. All this is normal and the parents should be aware about it, so that they anticipate it and don't become discouraged. Children may even refuse the new food altogether initially, even on repeated offerings. In that case switch over to a new food item. However, foods previously refused can be periodically re-offered at a later time.

4. Parents should be mentally prepared and ready to accept (without getting irritated), some fun and mess while the child eats. They should allow the child freedom to explore food with his mouth and fingers or with the spoon. It is but natural that the child will spill some food on his clothes, table and the floor. You can use your ingenuity and common sense to lessen the mess (like putting bib on his neck, which covers and hence protects his clothes; putting newspapers on the floor on which the child can sit while eating etc.). But you should not prevent the child from having some fun. If you do that, the child may not find meal times pleasurable. Instead your constant worries about "messing" may adversely affect the child's mood and he may start resenting meal times. You, also, will be tense with the "dreaded" anticipation of spillage and mess. So your major attention will be focussed on this; and you won't be able to enjoy your child having fun experimenting with "novel ways" of eating.

Tips for introducing your baby to solids.

i. Introduce solids when your baby is most alert and happy.

ii. Be cheerful and relaxed. If your anxiety is obvious, your baby might refuse the new food.

iii. Don't force your baby to have the new food.

iv. Try a flat butter spreader to feed, so that the baby can easily scoop out the contents.

v. Try thinning the solid until your baby gets used to it and is more experienced in swallowing food.

vi. Try some variety by adding curd, fruit juice etc. to the solid food. Start with a spoonful and work up to a normal feed. Your baby will like the gradual changes.

vii. If your baby refuses solids inspite of variety, do not force-feed. Stop the solid for a couple of weeks and then try again. Meanwhile, consult your doctor.

viii. Introduce only one new food at a time. Stick with that food for a few days before starting another one. This way, you will know which food is the cause of any allergy.

ix. If your baby wants to feed himself, put a spoon in either of his hands and feed with a third spoon. Your baby will imitate what you are doing and will soon feed himself.

5. Children need consistent mealtime rules and routines. Parents should strive for the following during meal times:

i. The mealtime should be in a pleasant, interactive atmosphere. The family should sit together and avoid distracting activities such as T.V., magazine reading etc. during mealtimes. They should interact with each other and the child socially by conversation.

ii. The mealtime must not be a battleground between the child and the mother. Child's wishes regarding eating should be respected and he should not be forced or pressurised to eat.

Mealtime Problem: Do not fuss if he does not eat.

iii. Efforts should be made to include the child in the table conversation instead of having long and detailed discussions between the adults only.

iv. The family mealtime is an excellent opportunity to find opportunities to praise and encourage the child for appropriate meal time behaviour.

v. Self-feeding should be most encouraged, even though it may be lengthy and messy. Often, the mother feeds the child (to avoid messiness, finish the meals quicker or out of "greed" that the child will eat more this way). This is not correct, as the child gradually becomes dependent on the mother for his feeding and starts considering it as his "right to be fed." Later on he becomes so habituated to "spoon feeding" by the mother that it becomes very difficult to take him off this habit and to make him self-feed.

vi. Mealtimes should be of a finite duration (20-30 minutes). Leaving the table should not be contingent on "cleaning" the plate. Food not finished during the required time should be removed, sometimes firmly.

vii. It is better to give small servings to the child, starting with small amounts, and offering second servings rather than "piling" up the plate with lots of food.

viii. Excessive intake of liquids like milk, juices, beverages, cold drinks etc and continual "grazing" between meals should be avoided.

ix. Avoid pressure on the child related to either the type or the volume of intake.

x. Bribing the child to eat a particular food or to eat more is counter-productive and is best avoided. In fact, in the long run, it may increase the child's aversion to food.

6. Don't urge your child to take more than he wants as he is bound to resent it. He may try to escape from the "constant pressure" by rebelling or becoming balky. It is as though he gets the idea; "Eating is a struggle. The parents are constantly after me and so I have to fight to protect myself." So don't urge a child to take more than he wants. Let him enjoy his food, with you giving him the feeling that you are his friend, rather than his boss.

7. At the age of 1 year +, parents may find that the appetite of the child has

decreased and that he has become choosy in his diet. This is in contrast to what the child was at 7-8 months, when he usually used to accept whatever was offered without much fuss. The big change that has come now is a normal phenomenon and is due to the issue of "autonomy and independence." The child begins to realise that he is a separate person with a separate identity and mind of his own. He no longer wants the mother to control him; instead he wants to be autonomous. The parents should be aware of this and realise that this is a part of growing up. They should respect this feeling of "autonomy" (often perceived as rebellion by the parents). Otherwise at meal times, the mother may want the child to feed something, which he may reject to assert his control. The dining table may get converted into a battlefield, with the mother and the child "battling" for control, trying to show who the boss is. But if the mother is aware of this phenomenon, she will let the child choose and eat himself without imposing her own wishes. Also she won't be having the unpleasant feeling that the child is rebelling and "going out of control."

8. Another notion mothers have is that their child should consume a lot of milk (whatever the age) and more often than not, one finds that the child balks at it and doesn't want to drink milk. If at all he consumes milk, it is due to the "pressure" of the parents. I think the "over-stress" of the mothers on milk is due to the fact that they consider milk as a very nutritious and wholesome food. There is no doubt that milk is a wholesome and nutritious diet. But one should also realise that at the age of 1.5 - 2 years, when the child has started eating almost like an adult (i.e. he eats all the routine things prepared in the household), his milk consumption will naturally decrease. How much milk an adult takes? Some, practically nil; yet do they suffer from any malnutrition? The same applies to the child also. Even if he consumes less milk, he won't have any problems with his health as he is consuming other food items. Therefore the mother should not force the child to consume milk in the fear that without it, the child's health will suffer.

9. A golden dictum is that a child will never self-starve. You have just to keep within his reach different food items. Once you realise this fundamental fact, you will not "coerce" or "bribe" him to eat more. A sure way to lessen the appetite of the child and convert him into a "problem feeder" is the "pressure" being applied on the child by you to eat more; but what it actually does is just the opposite. Because the child doesn't consider this "pressure" as being pleasant, he loses the enjoyment of eating. On the other hand, if you leave the child free of pressures, knowing that the child will not starve himself; the child will relish eating as he now enjoys it. In this way, his wish to be autonomous is also maintained and he will not become balky.

***In a party, people were talking about their childhood dreams. A doctor said that his childhood dream was to become a swindler. One of the guests remarked, "You are lucky. Not everyone's childhood's dreams are fulfilled."* **

10. Supplementation of the child's diet with tonics or vitamins (e.g. B-complex syrups, vitamins A, C etc.) for otherwise healthy children is not recommended. Similarly, "appetisers", calcium and vitamin D (to make the bones strong), protein supplements (to make the muscles strong), liver tonics (to make the liver strong so that he is able to "better digest" the food), tonics to increase the height of the child etc. are not required. They do nothing else but burn a hole in the pockets of the parents without any objective benefit to the child. Unfortunately, selling medicines (e.g. children tonics) has become a big business where drug companies make a huge profit (at the expense of the parent's hard-earned money). Obviously, these "tonics" won't sell if the parents don't clamour for them. Unfortunately, the parents think that without tonics, their child's growth will not be optimal and so they unwittingly promote this "tonic selling business." I, in my day to day practice, hardly ever encounter a parent, who is not in "love" with the tonics. If the doctor prescribes a tonic, the parents are very pleased and eager to give their child that tonic. In fact, parents come to the doctor, bringing a perfectly healthy, active and smiling baby with no other complaints except that they want some tonic for their child. Imagine yourself in the doctor's shoes. The patient has paid the consultation fees to get a very good tonic prescribed. Can the doctor refuse this request? Practically, it is very hard. So the doctor writes some tonic, though in his heart, he knows that it may not be really beneficial and required.

A healthy child won't become deficient in calcium or vitamins or proteins. His liver and digestive capabilities cannot be improved by liver tonics. The height of a child is genetically determined and "tonics" do not increase it. Regarding the complaint that my child is malnourished (thin), in the majority of cases, it is only the subjective perception of the parents. Objectively it is not correct (as can be judged by the fact that the child is active and alert, has no anaemia or other signs of nutritional deficiencies, and his weight lies within the normal range). But still parents are not convinced. In fact I hardly meet a parent who is satisfied with the eating and appetite of his child. They always feel that the child is not eating properly. But this is not true, because to find a case of malnutrition in an educated middle or upper class family is very rare. Further the objective evidence (e.g. weight) proves beyond doubt that the child is not undernourished and thus it is only a parental anxiety. Agreed some children may appear thinner than others, but if you look at these "thin" children without a biased view, you will find that actually their growth is perfectly normal. As mentioned by me in one of the earlier chapters, there is always a range of normalcy rather than any fixed "set point". For e.g. a 1-year child's normal range of weight falls from 8-12 kg. So if you see an 8 kilo baby and if you see a 12 kg baby (i.e. having 50% more weight), you may perceive a substantial difference in their built; but actually both of them are growing normally and certainly neither of them can be termed as malnourished. Parents should also remember that the constitution and built of a child is to a large extent determined genetically (i.e. like father, like boy).

The appetisers and tonics toted to stimulate the appetite and weight gain of the child can at the most, do so temporarily i.e. the weight gained will be lost once the medicine is stopped (much like the anti-obesity drugs). Drugs (e.g. anabolic steroids etc.) have a temporary effect, cannot be continued for a prolonged period of time (due to undesirable side effects) and once they are stopped; the weight reduces back to the original.

Bottom line: Do not be obsessed with the appetite and weight of the child. Whatever he eats is enough for him to be fit and healthy.

WEIGHT AND APPETITE

Both (a slight built and a heavy built) are two ends of the spectrum of growth and development. Both ends are normal as long as they remain within the spectrum i.e. the weight is in a range, which is normal for that age. For example a child of 1 year is normal if he weighs 8-12 Kgs. Let us consider adults. Some adults may weigh 50 kilos; others may weigh 70 kilos. Some may be of slender constitution; others may have a heavy constitution. Some put on fat easily and so have a tendency towards obesity. These people struggle to keep their weight in check. There are others who just cannot put on weight despite all out efforts to increase it. Yet both types of adults are normal, as long as their weight remains within the normal, defined range. A similar analogy is true for children also.

Why are some children thin while others are chubby? There are many reasons; some of the important ones are as below:

i. **Genetics:** Hereditary plays a major role. Children born to parents of slender constitution are likely to be slender and vice-versa. What about those born to parents, where one is thin and the other is hefty? The child will take after one of them and not average both!

ii. **Physical activity:** Some children are not energetic and spend most of their time sitting, watching T.V., reading etc, i.e. like couch potatoes. On the other hand, some children involve in a lot of physical activities. Obviously the 2nd group of children will be thinner.

iii. **Mental temperament:** Some children are emotionally quiet. They appear relaxed with a smile on their faces and don't get tensed up easily. On the other hand, some children get tensed up and anxious over small matters. Therefore a lot of energy (nervous) is expended by thinking about something or the other and by being under chronic stress. Such children are apt to be on the thinner side. (It holds true for adults also).

iv. **Appetite:** Some children are born with a big appetite. They eat a lot and there is little in life that affects this. On the other hand, some children have a low appetite, which is also easily affected by their spirits (you can again compare with adults; some adults eat a lot, others eat less). But, as a golden rule of the thumb, every baby is born with enough appetite to keep him healthy and let him grow at a normal pace. In children, a major factor affecting the appetite is the "urging" or the "pressure" exerted by the parents on the child to eat more, which has a negative influence on the appetite of the child.

v. **Stress:** Stress takes appetite away. If a child is anxious or overburdened with work, he will eat less as happens when the child goes to school. Apart from the heavy burden of studies, the child is under a lot of mental stress. This leads to a low appetite. No wonder one finds that the child, who used to be of good weight during pre-school days, has now become thin. Parents should be aware of this.

FEEDING PROBLEMS

1. Child is thin

Check whether the child's weight is really below the expected for his age (e.g. is a 1-year-old child weighing only 6 kilos?). Don't be carried away by your subjective impressions or what others say. Don't compare your child with other children's built and weight. Parents, who harbour anxiety regarding the thinness of their child, invariably find some child amongst relatives or in the neighbourhood who is stouter than their child. Every child including yours is unique and comparisons are superfluous. As long as his weight is within the normal range, relax. A healthy child may stay thin in spite of a good appetite, and probably he is meant to be that way by nature. Such children prefer low caloric food like fruits and vegetables to rich food like desserts and cakes. Don't be worried if your child doesn't have a good layer of fat. Excess fat is harmful. The current concept is that it is better to be thin (even for children) rather than being plump. However, if the weight is below the expected range or the child is not gaining weight at the expected rates (a child gains 1.5-2 kilos/year after the age of 1 year), it is best to consult a doctor.

If you are still obsessed that the child is thin, you can do 2 things. Firstly, you can increase the caloric density (obviously the child will not increase the intake of food to a significant extent; so what you can do is to modify the quality of food and make it calorie rich). Some ways of doing so are by adding ghee in dal, rice etc; giving the child high energy and rich foods like ice-creams, chocolates, cakes, pastries, halwa, puddings, custards etc.

The second thing to do is to view, without prejudice, whether the child is really a poor eater. If it is so, try to find out what is leading to this poor appetite (most likely it is your urging and pressures). For more details, kindly see below.

2. Child is fat

***A doctor was lecturing on reduction of obesity by giving example: "Obesity is just like a savings account. If you deposit (eat) more, it swells, while if you spend (exercise) more, it dwindles." A fat fellow stood up and said, "but doctor, mine is a fixed deposit." ***

Definitely, it is a cause for more concern than being thin. Again, as mentioned before, if the weight is lying within the normal range, there is no need for worry or medical intervention. But if for example a 1-year-old child weighs 15 kilos, I will definitely be worried. Surprisingly, the parents seldom bring their child to the doctor complaining that their child is overweight. On the contrary, they may be proud of their child's health.

The reason for this lies in the way the society perceives the concept of plumpness in the child. As of today, the society views plump children with pleasure and find them attractive and desirable. The friends and relatives compliment the parents (as if it was evidence of their superior parental care, which it is not, as all parents care for their child to the best of their efforts). I don't think the society's way of looking at it will change in the near future because of the simple fact that a fat child (particularly till the age of 2-3 years) with chubby cheeks and dimple chins appear so cuddly. Plump children have smooth and rounded contours which people love to feel and caress. But, from the health point of view, what about the baby? Scientists are of the opinion that babies who become fat during the first two years create in themselves more fat cells, which persist for the rest of the life. These fat cells will swell up with fat whenever the diet goes out of control. Worse, an increased number of fat cells increase the craving for food. As a result, this becomes a harbinger of adulthood obesity.

The fat child needs exercise too.

An overweight child should be of concern to the parents and instead of basking in the glory of the compliments showered upon the child by the friends and relatives; they should make efforts to keep the weight in check. Remember a fat child isn't much interested in exercises, games and physical activities. This leads to more obesity and it becomes a vicious cycle. And finally, you should keep in mind that obesity may be due to a feeling of loneliness/depression in the child, where eating becomes a solace. So you should ensure that the child's social and home life is satisfying and happy.

One way to reduce weight is by dieting (you don't expect a 2-year-old child to do exercises to reduce obesity). Again, you can't prevent a child from eating whatever amounts of food he routinely eats (even adults require a strong will power to do so). What you can do is make the child eat more of fruits, salads and soups (don't make them rich). As children love these food items, they will satiate a major part of the appetite by eating them. Meanwhile you can gradually cut down on rich foods like cakes, pastries, ice creams, chocolates etc. You can also consult your doctor, who will tell the child what to eat and what not to eat. Children take such advice better from an outsider than the parents. No medicines should be given to the child to reduce weight.

3. Child is a poor eater

*** "Does your mother let you eat what she prepares at home?" asked a teacher of a young girl while taking a lecture in nutrition and importance of home made foods. "Let us?" she roared. "She makes us eat." ***

This is the commonest problem facing parents. Why do so many children eat poorly? Because parents try so hard to make them eat well, forcing them to feed by threats, cajoling, bribing, putting forth conditions like if you finish your plate, we will take you to zoo or tell you a story etc. You don't see these problems in animal babies (who eat whatever they like whenever they are hungry, without their parents bothering). Even in the human race, the simple, uneducated people who live in villages hardly face this problem, because the mothers in such populations are hardly bothered about the amount of food consumed by their children. They do not pressurise the child to eat more and so they eat well.

Pressure makes an activity unenjoyable. Supposing, you enjoy reading novels. Now suppose there is pressure on you to finish the novel in 2 days and after that you will be asked 10 questions pertaining to the novel. You will lose all the enjoyment in reading that novel, because now it becomes a "task". We cannot deny the fact that doing anything is pleasurable as long as there are no pressures. Same applies to the feeding of a child also. If he is urged to eat more, he is under pressure (i.e. eat what the parents expect of him). This takes the joy of eating away from the child who starts perceiving eating as a "task", which has to be done.

Consider yourself in the child's position. Suppose your stomach is full, but still someone forcibly puts more food onto your plate urging you to eat it (e.g. as happens in marriages and formal parties). Out of politeness and because you want to "finish" the plate so that it may not be considered indecent; you somehow eat it, though you don't feel like it. And finally imagine it becoming a daily task. Day after day and meal after meal, someone is forcing you to consume against your will. After some time you will become insolent and rebel against it by leaving the food unfinished. You will also start resenting "Mr. X", the person that daily forces you to eat more. You will not want Mr. "X" to be present while you are eating and instead long to eat peacefully in a restaurant or a friend's place or a neighbour's place, where you can eat whatever you like and stop whenever you want.

So parents should not be like Mr. X! Let the child eat whatever he likes, and stop acting like a "watch guard." Understandably it is difficult for the parents to do so. When the child doesn't eat well, the parents go through a lot of mental turmoil.

The first feeling is of anxiety that their child is not eating well and hence will become weak. They can take comfort from the fact that their problem is not an isolated one, but is a very common problem which most of the households face. The parents find it hard to relax as long as the child is eating poorly. Paradoxically, this concern is the main thing "shackling" the child's appetite.

The second feeling is that of guilt that they are not able to make the child eat well and thus they blame themselves for it.

The third feeling may be of shame (ashamed of their child's thin built in comparison to others and hence be obsessed to improve it). Parents are bothered by the comments of the relatives and friends "your child is thin." The parents should ignore these thoughtless comments.

The fourth and a very uncomfortable and nagging feeling, is that of frustration and powerlessness. It seems that whatever they do and however hard they try, it is all in vain because the "little insolent child" of theirs, with complete disdain, spurns all the parental efforts to somehow make him eat. It appears that the child has developed an attitude, that come what may, he will always do the opposite of what the parents want him to do.

Obviously parents will be much relieved if somehow their child eats nicely without fuss. The treatment of such a malady lies primarily in changing the parental attitude towards their child's eating (i.e. to resist the "irresistible" urge to make him eat). The main problem lies in the parent's minds (rather than with the child); so all parents faced with this problem should consider the following points carefully:

i. They are not the only ones facing this problem. In fact it is so common that practically every household faces this dilemma. So the parents can relax knowing that they are not alone and that there are many others who are sailing in the same boat with them.

ii. Almost all children (if not prohibited by their parents) eat better at the neighbours rather than at home. Why? For the simple reason that over there, there is no one standing with "an eagle eye" on them monitoring their "eating performance."

iii. The parents should keep on reminding themselves that all children have a remarkable natural mechanism that tells them how much food to eat for their normal growth and development. Parents should not tamper with it, because what is natural cannot be wrong. They should also imprint in their minds that no child will ever starve himself.

iv. Parents should bear in mind that all human beings including children are born with a natural instinct to get balky if pushed too hard. So a child will dislike food items if forced upon them, mainly due to parental urging.

v. Why the parental urging becomes an almost reflex, monotonous and perpetual routine? The reason is that there are some short-term gains initially, like the child accepting a little bit more of food when cajoled, threatened, bribed etc. The parents unwittingly accept the "small extra morsel of food" eaten by their child as a reward and result of their constant trying and perseverance. This positively reinforces their behaviour and it becomes a cycle. If parents are advised to change their behaviour and let the child be free from all "pressures", they may find it extremely hard to follow. This is because of their anxiety that the child is already eating less and if they stop urging him to eat, he will eat even less and thus starve. The parents also feel that their urging at least makes the child eat "a bit more."

I can understand the parent's dilemma and confusion. What the parents should understand is that their urging makes the child eat one or two spoons more and that too, not willingly, but because he is forced to do so by his parents. This extra one or two spoons hardly makes any positive difference to the child's health in the long run. On top of that, after sometime, this urging stops having any effect on the child and doesn't work. For e.g. if the mother says, "finish your plate, else I won't take you to the party", the child may reply, "I don't want to go to the party." In effect the child is indirectly saying that I don't want to eat more (and that none of your threats or bribes is going to induce me to do so).

So, these types of urgings are of no value in the long term and in fact are counter-productive. The parents should not go for short term "gains" (the child reluctantly eats one or two spoons more), but rather focus on the long term "losses" of such an approach. And the "losses" are very obvious. The child will become a chronic problem eater, his appetite may be reduced permanently, and the pleasure of the child for eating will go. The parents also suffer a lot of mental agony and in the end are reduced to a feeling of frustration and helplessness.

vi. Parents don't want their child to eat more because he has been "beaten" in a fight with them. There is really no satisfaction in this for them. The parents' real joy lies in the fact that they don't have to force the child to eat, but to let the natural appetite of the child surface, so that he eats of his own accord and with pleasure. Also remember that in the "feeding battle", initially the child may lose and eat a bit more; but in the long run a child can always outlast a parent when challenged to such a battle. And the child will feel joyous that at last he has "beaten" his parents and gains satisfaction out of it rather than out of eating. So ultimately you land up with a "poor eating child" whose attitude is just like the dog's tail. However much you try to straighten it, it will again bend back.

Why I am stressing so much on all this is because the parents should be absolutely convinced that it is their attitude, which has to be rectified. Once they accept this fact, the first step and the most important step has been achieved towards the remedy. What is this remedy? Though theoretically simple (i.e. the parents should stop forcing the child to eat), in practice, once a feeding problem is established, the cure of it takes time and patience. The parents should possess a strong will power and curb their natural habit to pressurise their child to eat more and to make a big fuss out of it. With patience, you will gradually stop paying attention to the feeding of the child and remove the pressure on him. This is real progress.

It may take weeks for the child's natural appetite to surface because he has to be given a genuine and long chance to forget the unpleasant associations with food. The appetite of the child is just like a mouse and the parents anxious urging just like a cat, which has been scaring it into its hole. And the cat must leave the mouse alone for a long time, before it becomes bold enough to venture out of its hiding. In between, parents may have the "itch" to urge the child to feed, as anxiety may gnaw at them (particularly if they perceive no real progress). In order to relieve this anxiety, they may feel "compelled" to go back to the old habits. But, under all circumstances, resist this impulse; otherwise you will be taking a step backward. The key words are patience and perseverance.

The ideal parental approach should be to put the food before the child (small portions that the child can take; let him ask for more if he wants), then say nothing and think nothing about the eating of the child. Take the plate away after 30 minutes, without bothering or fussing about the amount eaten. In no way indicate; even indirectly by your body language or eyes that you are worried about his feeding (though internally you may be anxious). Start with the foods that the child likes the best. Be patient and go on sticking to this routine. Your patience will surely be rewarded; and gradually as the child feels relieved of pressures, his appetite will come back, and he will start eating spontaneously to his optimal capacity.

Key summary line: Try to make the child eat more, he won't. Don't try and he will eat well.

4. Child is choosy about food

Parents complain that their child doesn't, for example, eat milk or green vegetables. This is of no concern, as everyone (including adults) has some food fads, some liking and disliking regarding food. As mentioned earlier, the child tends to eat a balanced diet over a period of time and being choosy about certain food items doesn't make it "imbalanced." The real problem is when the child eats only a few food items (like chocolates, toffees, ice creams, sweets etc.) and fills his stomach by them, so that he shuns the regular meals being prepared at home. In such cases, you have to be firm with the child and gradually cut down upon the excess sweets i.e. the marketed food items and offer him home made foods that he likes.

5. Child doesn't feed himself

Another common problem, it usually starts when the parents take the onus of feeding the children on themselves and consider it their solemn duty. Some parents feel joy in feeding their child; others think it to be their responsibility. Whatever the reasons are, the end result is that of a hapless mother running around to feed the child with a spoon in her hand. In between she has also to talk to the child and cajole, coax, urge or threaten him to eat.

It is reasonable to feed a child up to 1 year, but after that the habit of self-feeding should be strongly inculcated in the child. The child should sit at the table with the adults during meal times and encouraged eating food with his own hands. Don't worry about any mess he makes. Let him enjoy having fun with the food and trying out his own methods to "negotiate" the food into his mouth. The habit of "spoon feeding" makes the child dependent on you. He also starts taking it for granted his right to be fed by you, so much so that he won't eat by himself. You, out of sheer habit, and not wanting to turn down the plea of the child will feed him, thus perpetuating the cycle; ultimately ending up running after him, pleading him to eat.

For the child, this feeding becomes an important indicator of his parents' love and affection towards him and so if you suddenly stop it, he will feel hurt. So don't start this habit of spoonfeeding in the first place. If already established, you will have to be firm with yourself that you are not going to "spoonfeed" the child and also firm with the child that he has to feed himself. No child will wilfully starve himself! Maybe, he won't eat for a day or two and sulk. Just assure him that you love him a lot, and not feeding him doesn't mean that you are angry with him or that your love towards him has lessened.

Keep the plate in front of him and tell him that you want to see whether he can feed himself. Tell him that you want to judge whether he has grown up and can do things by himself. These are just examples. The basic idea is to throw a challenge to the child in a way that the child accepts it!

A direct statement that he has grown up and it is high time he feeds himself or a comparison with others of his age group is not desirable. Instead if you say, "let's see whether you have become big", the child may accept the challenge and to prove that he is big, he may start feeding. Once he does so, encourage and praise him. Gradually the child will relish eating food by his own hands. Once in a while, if he demands that you feed him, do it casually. Tell him that you are going to feed him only say 5 spoons and after that he has to feed himself. If after having 5 spoons he still insists, firmly tell him that this is not what was decided upon. You have kept up your part of the "contract", now the child should honour his part by self-feeding.

If the child wants to eat from the parent's hands only, it is very difficult for the parents to resist it. And supposing the child goes without meals and that too, 2 times in a row, just because the parents are not feeding him, it requires a supreme will power not to feed the child. The parents feel guilty that the child is going hungry because of them not feeding him, and may feel uncomfortable.

Firstly, the parents have to decide firmly that the child has to be independently feeding. Remember self-reliance and independence are very important gifts that you, as parents, give to the child. The sooner the child is made independent, the better it is for him in the long run.

Secondly, parents must keep in mind that if they are not feeding the child, in spite of his asking for it, it is not because they don't want to feed him, or that they are punishing him or have stopped loving him. It is because of a much greater and sublime love towards him (i.e. they want him not to be dependent on others). This type of thinking, which is rational, instead of being prejudiced by their emotions, strengthens their resolve to resist the urge to feed the child.

Finally once the child has started feeding himself, let it not relapse. Often what happens is that the parents feel tempted to feed him when he loses his appetite or falls sick. This should be resisted as the child may again start becoming dependent.

6. Fooling at the table

Some children indulge in mealtime misbehaviours like getting up and down from the table, playing with the food, fighting with the sibling etc. An effective management technique for such behaviour is to terminate the meal calmly when playing with the food exceeds the eating (regardless of how much the child has consumed). One hour later when the child becomes more agreeable and also hungry, food may be re-offered to him.

❖❖❖

CHAPTER 6

IMMUNISATION

KEY POINTS

- Amongst all vaccines, BCG is the least efficacious. It does, however, protect against the severity of the disease. The formation of the BCG scar may take 8-12 weeks.
- Polio: More doses than recommended can be safely given. Therefore, children can receive polio doses as a part of Pulse Polio immunisation, even if recently vaccinated.
- Hepatitis-B vaccine is given in the muscle of the arm (after the age of 1 year) and in the thighs (before the age of 1 year).
- Immunisation can be safely given in the presence of minor illnesses like cough, cold, diarrhoea & low- grade fever.
- Anyone at any age can be immunised, if not immunised before or partially immunised. The same immunisation schedule is followed.
- It is not necessary to restart an interrupted schedule from the beginning or give extra doses. Instead, Immunisation is continued as if no interruption has occurred.
- Multiple vaccines can be given together on the same visit without any problem.
- As the efficacy of a vaccine is never 100%, vaccinating the child doesn't mean that he cannot get the disease. Most vaccines have efficacy of over 95%, except BCG (efficacy 50%).
- Rubella vaccine is primarily used not to protect the recipient (as other vaccines are), but to protect the baby of a pregnant woman from congenital rubella, a devastating disease.
- Vaccines rarely have side effects, like allergic reaction, pain, fever etc. It is prudent to ask your doctor about these side effects.

The doctor took the patient to a separate room and said, "Well I have both good news and bad news."

Patient: "Give me the good news first."

"Well, we are going to name a disease after you!"

Vaccines are made of dead/live attenuated viral or bacterial products called "antigens." They stimulate the defence mechanisms of the body and lead to the formation of certain protective proteins called "antibodies" in the body. For example when your child receives Polio drops (containing attenuated live Polio viral antigen); the body produces antibodies against it. Later on in life, supposing your child comes into contact with the Polio virus, because of the wise step taken by you in getting your child immunised, the child has the capacity to resist this infection because of the protective antibodies formed in his body earlier due to the vaccination. Hence the child doesn't suffer from Polio. This holds true for all diseases against which vaccines are available. What are the different types of vaccines?

1. **BCG:** It is a vaccine given to protect against tuberculosis (T.B.). Usually given at birth intra-dermally in the upper arm, it causes a swelling at the injection site that ulcerates and ultimately heals to leave a scar. The whole process from the time of injection to the formation of the scar may take 8-12 weeks. I often encounter anxious parents with the complaint that the injection has 'reacted' and there is a swelling at the local site. As mentioned above, this is normal. A child may get T.B. in spite of being vaccinated as amongst all vaccines, BCG is the least efficacious. It has got a protection rate of about 50% (as compared to other vaccines whose efficacy is 90-95%). BCG does protect against the severity of the disease. So until a better vaccine is available, BCG is recommended, particularly in a country like India where T.B. is rampant. Another rare side effect of the vaccine is that few children may develop a swelling in the armpit, which is nothing else but lymph glands. It is benign and over a period of time subsides. However if it doesn't subside, consult your paediatrician who will prescribe medicines for it. A 2nd dose (called the "booster dose") is generally not recommended.

2. **Polio:** It is given at birth along with BCG (2 drops orally). Booster doses are given along with DTP (diphtheria, pertussis and tetanus), at 1.5, 2.5, 3.5, 18 months and finally at the age of 5 years. It protects against a disease called Polio, which can have devastating effects like paralysis of one or more limbs. Up to ½ hour after giving Polio, do not administer warm liquids to the

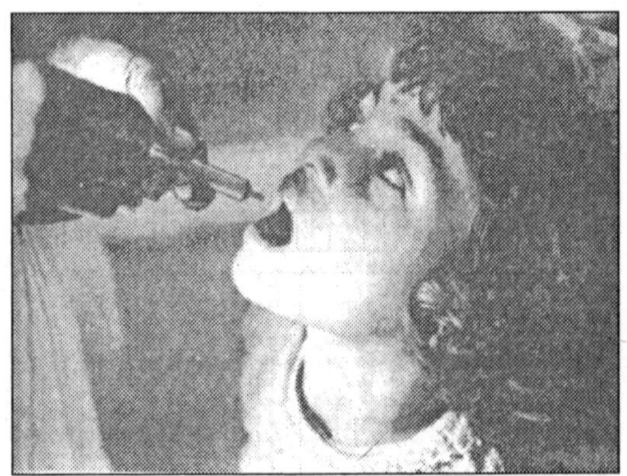

Preventive Measure: Administering the polio vaccine.

child. However, breast milk can be given immediately.

3. **DTP vaccine:** It is a triple vaccine protecting against three diseases namely diphtheria, pertussis and tetanus. It is given intramuscularly in the anterolateral aspect of the thigh. The schedule is similar to that of Polio except that it is not given at birth. It can cause local pain at the injection site and also fever and irritability in the child. The treatment is to do cold compresses at the local site and the administration of paracetamol drops/syrup (10-15 mg/kg/dose) which can be repeated every 6 hours. Sometimes a few days after giving the DTP injection, the parents may feel a small, firm nodule at the site of injection. It doesn't require any treatment and will spontaneously regress with time.

4. **Measles vaccine:** It is a live attenuated viral vaccine given at the age of 9 months in India (in western countries it is given at the age of 15 months as a triple vaccine, MMR). In India it is given earlier because of the common prevalence of this disease. The administration of this vaccine can also cause fever and a mild rash (5-7 days post vaccination). The treatment is same as for DPT injection.

These 4 vaccines are recommended by the National Health Policy of India and also form a part of the WHO schedule of Immunisation for the developing countries to protect against the 6 major killer diseases considered to be common and associated with a lot of deaths. These vaccines are supplied free of cost at all government dispensaries.

Other vaccines that are recommended but have to be purchased, i.e. they are not supplied free of cost, are described below.

1. **Hepatitis-B vaccine:** It is a killed viral vaccine having excellent protection against Hepatitis-B virus. There are 5 common hepatitis viruses; A to E. Out of these, at present, vaccines are only available against Hepatitis A & B. Hepatitis-A causes only acute (lasting for a brief time say 1-2 weeks) liver disease while Hepatitis-B may cause a chronic liver disease which may ultimately lead to liver failure. It has also been known to cause liver cancer. That's why one should get oneself immunised against it.

- *In an infant (i.e. till the age of 1 year), it is given as 3 doses at 1 month interval and the injection is given in the thigh. Ideally the first dose should be given at birth, the second dose at the age of 1.5 months and the 3rd dose at the age of 2.5 months.*
- *In older children including adults it is given as a 3 dose schedule at 0, 1 and 6 months and the injection is given in the arm. No booster doses are recommended.*
- *The dose after the age of 10 years is considered as adult dose and is 1 cc. below the age of 1 year, the dose is 0.5 cc.*
- *You should also get your child immunised against Hepatitis-A.*

2. **MMR vaccine:** This is a triple vaccine, which affords protection against Measles, Mumps and Rubella. It is given as a single dose intramuscularly at the age of 15 months. Even if your child has got Measles vaccine at the age of 9 months, it should be given.

3. **Typhoid vaccine:** It is available in two forms. One is injectable, given i.m. to children above the age of 2 years and repeated every 3 years thereafter. The second one is in the form of capsules (3 capsules given as a single capsule every alternate day). The oral form is recommended only for children above 6 years; so initially you have to vaccinate them with the injectable form. Due to the poor sanitation and water supply, Typhoid is quite common in India and therefore it is better to vaccinate your child against this disease.

4. **H.Influenza vaccine:** H.Influenza is a bacterium that may cause serious disease in the child including meningitis (brain fever) and pneumonia. It is given i.m. The vaccination schedule parallels that of DTP; excepting that the 5-year dose is not given. It is the only vaccine in which the number of doses is reduced depending upon the age.

- *Below 6 months: 3 doses at 1 month interval + 1 booster at 18 months.*
- *6-12 months: 2 doses at 1 month interval + booster at the age of 15-18 months.*
- *12-15 months: 1 dose +1 booster.*
- *Above 15 months-5 years: only single dose.*
- *Above the age of 5 years: not required.*

It is a relatively costly vaccine, 1 dose being priced approximately Rs. 450/-, though highly recommended due to the serious nature of the disease.

5. **Hepatitis-A vaccine**: It is a killed vaccine given as a 2 dose schedule 6 months apart. The adult dose (i.e. above the age of 19 years is double that of child's dose). It can be started above the age of 1 year, though some manufacturers recommend it to be given after the age of 2 years. It is a costly vaccine, the cost of 1 injection being approximately Rs.1000. It protects against the water-borne type of jaundice and is much commoner than Hepatitis-B. In India, it is estimated that adults usually don't require the vaccine as they are already immunised due to this infection being contracted by them during childhood.

6. **Chickenpox vaccine:** This is a live attenuated vaccine. A single dose is recommended below the age of 13 years and after that 2 doses at 1 month interval is recommended. It protects against chickenpox, a viral rash associated with fever, pain and itching at the site of the rash. It is a costly vaccine, priced at approximately Rs. 1500.

7. **Pneumococcal vaccine:** It is recommended above the age of 2 years as a single dose. The protection lasts for 5 years after which it has to be given again. It prevents against infection due to Pneumococcal bacteria, serious infections being pneumonia and meningitis. Pneumococcus along with H.Influenza-B (and staphylococcal aureus against which no vaccine is available presently) are 3 bacteria which are common causes of infection in childhood and all 3 of them can cause serious, life threatening infections. Therefore it is strongly recommended that one should protect the child

against these infections. H-Influenza-B is dangerous till the age of 5 years only and thus is not given above the age of 5 years. Pneumococcal infections are common even in adults and therefore can be given at any age. It is currently recommended for patients with underlying diseases, which weaken the immune (defence) system of the body.

Apart from the 4 vaccines (BCG, Measles, DPT and Polio) given to protect against the 6 major killer diseases, as per the national health policy of Govt. of India, parents should also get the child immunised with the other seven vaccines mentioned above.

Influenza vaccine: This is a special vaccine which is not given as a routine but only to high risk cases. It protects against influenza, a viral infection chiefly affecting the respiratory system. It is recommended in asthmatics, those with heart diseases, diabetes, chronic lung diseases, chronic renal disease etc. For the use of this vaccine, consult your doctor. Just remember that it is not given to healthy children, but to children who are having an underlying disease, e.g. asthma which can become severe due to the child getting influenza.

IMMUNISATION GUIDELINES

1. Live vaccines (BCG, Polio, MMR, Measles, and Oral Typhoid) are contraindicated in malignancies, immunosuppressed patients, patients on chronic steroid therapy or on chemotherapeutic agents. In AIDS, BCG & Measles are recommended, as the benefits outweigh the risk, but not oral polio drops. Instead dead polio vaccine (i.m.) can be given.
2. BCG: A nodule appears 3-4 weeks after the injection, which softens and ulcerates, in another 2-4 weeks. This heals, leaving behind a scar, indicating successful Immunisation. If this does not happen, the child should be re-vaccinated.
3. Oral polio can be given in cases of mild diarrhoea. Breast feeds can be given immediately after oral polio vaccine, though warm liquids should be withheld for half- hour.
4. DTP: This causes pain and swelling at the local site with fever. Give Crocin drops (2 drops/kg) stat and prn (dose should be at least 4 hours apart) and cold fomentation at the local site. A small, painless lump may remain for a few weeks, which is of no concern.
5. Measles/MMR may also cause fever but 5-7 days after the vaccine and may be associated with a mild rash. Treatment is same as above.
6. Immunisation can be safely given in the presence of minor illnesses like cough, cold, diarrhoea & low- grade fever.
7. After 6 years of age, the child can be given oral typhoid vaccine (1 capsule every alternate day for 3 days with booster dose every 5 years). For 2-6 years, i.m. vaccine is recommended with boosters every 3 years.
8. After the age of 5 years, only DT is given, i.e. P (pertusssis) is not required. DT is again recommended at the age of 10 year, then at 16 years and thereafter every 10 years. Practically, however, it

is seen that the vast majority of children are regularly and routinely immunized till the age of 5 years. After that the recommendation of DT is hardly followed. Not much emphasis is given because DT chiefly prevents against tetanus, and a person is given a tetanus shot whenever he / she gets any injury, so the protection against tetanus is by and large ensured anyhow.

9. Anyone at any age can be immunised, if not immunised before. The same schedule is followed. However after the age of 5 years, only DT and not DTP should be given. HiB is not required after 5 years and if the patient is > 15 months, a single dose only is required.

10. It is not necessary to restart an interrupted schedule from the beginning or give extra doses. Instead, continue as if no interruption has occurred.

11. Multiple vaccines can be given together on the same visit without any problem.

12. Measles vaccine can interfere with tuberculin testing. Therefore the test should be done on the day of immunisation or 6 weeks later. Measles vaccine can also flare up T.B. and so if the child is having active T.B., he/she should be on Anti-T.B. drugs while receiving it.

13. For preterm babies, the exact schedule and dosage as for term babies is followed and no adjustments for prematurity are made.

14. ROUTE OF ADMINISTRATION

- *Intradermal* : *BCG (in deltoid area).*
- *Subcutaneous* : *Measles, MMR and chickenpox.*
- *Orally* : *Polio and Oral Typhoid.*
- *Intramuscular* : *Rest all vaccines.*

15. Efficacy of no vaccine is 100%. Vaccinating the child doesn't mean that he cannot get the disease. Most vaccines have efficacy of over 95%, except BCG (efficacy 50%).

16. Though vaccines are very safe, yet very rarely there may be a serious allergic reaction called anaphylaxis which if not treated in time may sometimes cause even death. A previous hypersensitivity reaction to a particular vaccine is an absolute contraindication for further doses of the same vaccine.

17. Rubella vaccine is used primarily not to protect the recipient (as other vaccines are), but to protect the baby of a pregnant woman from congenital rubella. Ideally all women of child-bearing age should be immunised by it pre-pregnancy (rubella vaccination is contraindicated during pregnancy). As it is practical difficult to achieve this goal, both males & females are normally vaccinated at the age of 15 months, males are vaccinated to decrease them as being the reservoir of infection.

18. Rabies and Hepatitis - B are perhaps the only vaccines, which are effective post-exposure and recommended urgently along with the respective immune globulin on exposure. They can also, of course, be used pre-exposure i.e. like other vaccines. Hepatitis-B is nowadays routinely given pre-exposure, though not so rabies.

19. For persons at high risk of rabies, the vaccine is recommended pre-exposure

as a 3-dose schedule (1-ml i.m. at 0, 7 and 28 days) with boosters every 3 years. If exposure to rabies occurs, then he/she has to take only 2 doses of the vaccine at 0 and 3 days + RIG (rabies immunoglobulin) with the 1st dose. For others, it is recommended only post-exposure as 5 doses at 0, 3, 7, 14 and 28 days (6th dose at 90 days being optional) + RIG with the 1st dose (20U/kg, half at the site of bite and half i.m. in the gluteal region).

20. DTP vaccine (due to the pertussis component) can rarely cause neurological side effects like encephalopathy, convulsions, prolonged inconsolable crying or prolonged somnolescence. It may also cause fever >105°F and sometimes may result in a collapsed, hypotensive shock like state. If such adverse reactions are observed, consult the doctor, who will usually advise to give only DT instead of DTP in future.

CAUTION

Before immunising, always ask for:

- *Any previous hypersensitive reaction to a vaccine?*
- *Any side effects of previous DTP, particularly CNS?*
- *H/O T.B. (before giving measles)?*

Only if the answers to them are negative, vaccinate. If in doubt, seek expert opinion.

IMMUNISATION SCHEDULE

AGE :			VACCINE		
Time of Birth	Polio - 1 ;	BCG ;	Hepatitis B - 1;		
1.5 months	Polio - 2 ;	DTP - 1 ;	Hepatitis B - 2 ;	HiB - 1	
2.5 months	Polio - 3 ;	DTP - 2 ;	Hepatitis B - 3;	HiB - 2	
3.5 months	Polio - 4 ;	DTP - 3 ;		HiB - 3	
9 months					Measles
1 year	Chickenpox		Hepatitis – A - 1		
5-18 months	Polio - 6 ;	DTP - 4 ;	Hepatitis – A - 2	HiB - 4	MMR
2 years	Pneumococcal vaccine		Typhoid - 1		
5 years	Polio - 7 ;	DTP - 5 ;	Typhoid - 2		

- *BCG = Vaccine against tuberculosis. DTP = Diphtheria, pertussis and tetanus.*
- *HiB = Hemophilus influenza type B. MMR = Measles, mumps and rubella.*

** *1) after 5 years, DT is given at 10 and 16 years and then every 10 years.*

** *2) After the age of 6 years, typhoid can be given orally with boosters every 5 years.*

Are there situations where the child should not be vaccinated? Yes, there are and if your child fits into any of the following categories, be sure to tell your doctor.

- *If there is any previous hypersensitivity/ allergic reaction to a vaccine.*
- *If a person is profoundly immunosuppressed (e.g. the person is on chemotherapy for cancer, is having some malignancy, is congenitally immunodeficient or is taking steroids chronically), then live vaccines are not to be given (BCG, Polio, Measles, MMR).*
- *Following DTP injection, if the child goes into a state of coma or abnormal behaviour, gets fever > 105° F; has inconsolable crying for more than 3 hours or has excessive sleepiness for more than 4 hours or goes into a shock like state, then further doses of DTP are not given. Also if the child is having any progressive neurological disease, DTP is not given. Since the culprit is "P" i.e. Pertussis component, hence in future only DT is given.*
- *Insist on the use of a sterile, disposable syringe for the immunisation of your child even if it means shelling out some money for the purchase of syringe and needle. Reused needles and syringes may be a source of infection to your child. Always buy syringes of reputed companies, even though they are costlier than the local brands. There is concern that local brands may be used syringes, recycled and sold in a fresh packaging.*

CHAPTER 7

COMMON CHILDHOOD DISEASES

KEY POINTS

- **T.B.:** It is completely treatable. T.B. is over-diagnosed frequently, when any child having chronic cough or recurrent chest infections is "empirically" put on T.B. drugs.
- **Polio:** It can cause paralysis and the child may be left with permanent disability. Once a child gets Polio, there is no cure. So best is prevention through vaccination.
- **Rabies:** Alteration in the behaviour of the dog under observation for 10 days is as important as is the death of the animal to give rabies vaccination. The vaccine is given on days 0,3,7,14,28 and 90. Rabies immunoglobulin is as important as the vaccine.
- **Parental attitude:** Most of the symptoms (e.g. fever, diarrhoea, coughs and colds) are viral, benign and self-limiting. It may take a week for the illness to subside. So if the child doesn't become OK in 2 days, don't panic and go "doctor-shopping". Many parents pressurise the doctors for a rapid and "magic" cure. My request is, be patient, else it leads to "shot gun" type of multi-drug prescription, e.g. an antibiotic, ant malarial, anti-typhoid, steroids etc. simultaneously, in the hope that one of them will hit the target and cure the disease. This is not rational. Sadly, this happens quite often because the doctor does not want to lose the patient as his client. The most commonly over prescribed medicines are antibiotics and tonics.
- **Fever:** It is the body's response to infections, and plays a role in fighting them. In some cases, the cause of fever may not be immediately apparent and the doctor may follow a "wait and watch" policy (if the condition of the child is not serious) till the diagnosis is clearer. This is correct rather than a multi- drug prescription. Parents often clothe their child excessively when they have fever. In fact the child should be dressed lightly, so that excessive heat from the body can dissipate. Sponging for fever should be done with tepid (lukewarm) water over as much area of the body as possible, followed by light fanning. Cold water should not be used. Whole body should be sponged and not just a strip of wet cloth kept on the forehead, which is of no benefit.
- **Diarrhoea:** It is usually due to a viral infection of the intestines. Benign and self-limiting, its therapy is mainly ORS solution for dehydration. "Over vigorous" therapy like antibiotics may worsen it because antibiotics kill the "good" bacteria in the intestines.
- **Constipation:** Constipation may be part of an acute febrile illness. Some parents believe that unless a child has normal stools, his disease won't get better, which is erroneous.
- **Respiratory infections:** Children may have 10-12 attacks per year. The role of steam inhalation is questionable. Neither Vitamin-C nor swathing the child from head to toe in multiple wrappings of warm clothing prevents colds. Colds are due to viruses, which are ubiquitously present in the air. And how can one prevent the child from inhaling that air and thus the viruses?
- **Use of steroids:** Doctors use steroids as a "magic bullet" to maintain their clientele, as steroids can provide quick and dramatic relief from fever, colds, cough etc., which the parents want. Actually steroids lull the parents into a false sense of relief as the symptoms are being suppressed and not

cured. This may sometimes be dangerous, as the disease is still silently smouldering inside. But in some diseases, steroids are really beneficial (like asthma, allergic cough, meningitis etc).

- **Tonsils:** Tonsils may be enlarged normally. Parents believe that removal of tonsils will cure frequently occurring cough, cold, sinusitis, chronic nose block etc. It is not true in the vast majority of cases.
- **Asthma:** It is a chronic recurrent disorder with negative psychological consequences for parents & child. The treatment is bronchodilators (preferably inhaled) and steroids.
- **Heart problems:** If your doctor detects some murmur in the heart of the child and tells you that it is innocent, don't worry. The heart is normal in such cases.
- **Convulsions:** "Febrile Convulsions" (associated with fever and occurring in an otherwise normal child) are benign and the child outgrows them by 5 years of age. These fits have no ill effects on the long-term development of the child. Recurrent convulsions are termed "Epilepsy". Fortunately, excellent anti-convulsants are available to control epilepsy. They are given for a period of 3 years. An epileptic and an asthmatic should lead as normal a life as possible. Some of the greatest personalities like Caesar, Napoleon, and Einstein etc. suffered from epilepsy, which proves that greatness has no relation with epilepsy.
- **Hernias:** The only treatment is surgery. There is no medical cure. Wearing trusses and belts in order to keep the hernia in check may do more harm than good.
- **Undescended testis:** Testes that have been seen or felt in the scrotum at any time are retractile and normal. On the other hand, truly undescended testes lie in the abdomen and should be brought into the scrotum by operation before the child is 3-4 years old, as the testis after that may atrophy and lose its function. Some children are born with one testis only. A single testis can carry on the function of reproduction and the person won't be sterile.
- **Squint:** A condition in which the child appears cross eyed is not to be taken lightly, particularly if the child is older than 6 months, as one eye can become "functionally" blind.
- **Myopia (short-sightedness):** The first inkling often comes during school going when the child may not be able to see the blackboard clearly. The child may not complain because of shyness. So all parents should check periodically whether the child's vision is good.

Simple measures to prevent loose motions, maintain a healthy bowel & keep the child cheerful:

Clean & healthy food habits can prevent loose motions.
Infants should be only on breast milk for the first 4 to 6 months & breast feeding should be Continued along with other foods until the child is 2 years of age.

When you start the child on solid foods, give cereals or starchy foods mixed with pulses, vegetables & meat or fish.
Fresh fruit juice or bananas also help.
This prevents loose motions caused by malnutrition.

Give the child freshly prepared food.
The water given for drinking should be boiled & cooled. This prevents infection from food & water.

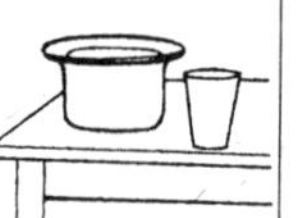

Give milk & other fluids by cup & spoon instead of a feeding bottle to prevent infection arising due to unclean bottles.

Maintaining cleanliness at home can prevent infections and thereby prevent loose motions.
Have all the family members wash their hands after passing stools & before preparing or eating food to maintain cleanliness.

Have all the family members use a latrine to control the spread of infection.
Put a young child's stool in the latrine or bury them.

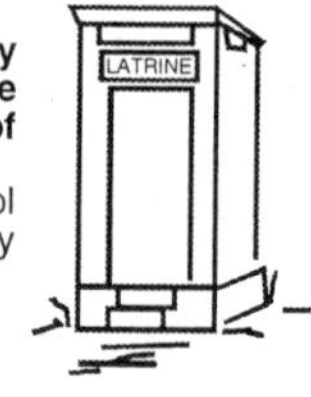

Following the immunization schedule can prevent loose motions.
Have your child immunized against measles at 9 months to improve the ability to resist infections.

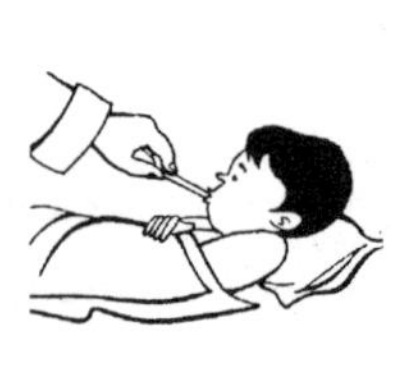

INFECTIOUS DISEASES

***There are many diseases, which are labelled idiopathic by the medical science i.e. whose cause is not known. The term actually should mean a condition where the doctor is an idiot and the patient's condition is pathetic. Combine idiot and pathetic, it becomes "idiopathic." ***

1. Tuberculosis (T.B.)

The child may present with fever, cough, weight loss, decreased appetite and a general feeling of ill being, listlessness and apathy. The most important fact to determine is whether the child had a close contact with an adult T.B. patient, as it is an infectious disease that spreads through airborne bacteria. T.B. usually does not spread from a child to another child, as the child does not release many T.B. bacteria in the air due to lack of a forceful cough and absence of a cavity in the lungs (which adults have). The adult, with coughing releases T.B. bacteria in the air, which the child inhales, thus infecting him. Don't feel embarrassed in telling the doctor that there is an adult in the family suffering from T.B., because this helps the doctor in arriving at a diagnosis. Since the diagnosis of T.B. often is based on exposure to a positive contact, the reluctance of the parents to come out with the truth leads to a delay in the diagnosis of the disease, to the detriment of the child. T.B. is a disease that is completely treatable, provided the patient takes the medicines regularly and also completes the whole course, which nowadays is usually of 6 months. A not so uncommon scenario is the patient stopping the medicines after 1 or 2 months when he/she feels all right, a nightmare for the doctors because this may lead to drug resistance for T.B. and then becomes very difficult to cure.

I have seen T.B. being over-diagnosed frequently, particularly in children, when any child having a chronic cough or recurrent respiratory infections is "empirically" put on T.B. treatment. If the child becomes well after 1-2 weeks of treatment, the parents and the treating doctor think that the child had T.B. and thus has responded to the drugs against T.B. But it is quite possible that the child had some other disease (e.g. a prolonged viral illness or a respiratory allergy or pertussis, described below), which by now has completed its disease cycle and thus would have got cured of its own accord without any medications! This is what I mean by over diagnosis and the parents should be wary and aware of this pitfall. So if the parents have doubts in their minds regarding the diagnosis, don't hesitate to seek a second opinion preferably of a specialist in the field.

*** A doctor and his wife were having a big argument at breakfast. "You are not good in bed either!" he shouted and stormed off to work.*

By afternoon he decided to make amends and phoned home. After many rings, his wife finally picked up the phone. "What took you so long", asked the doctor.

"I was in bed", replied the wife.

"What are you doing in bed this late?"

"Getting a second opinion."

A new blood test called as ELISA test for T.B. has nowadays become very popular and even educated parents ask the doctor for it, as if it is the definitive diagnostic test that will once and forever decide whether the child is having T.B. or not. In fact the test is of dubious value and cannot prove that a person is having active T.B. So going for this expensive test is burning a hole in your pockets. The same information can be obtained by a relatively simpler and non-expensive skin test called "Mantoux test."

2. Polio

The Polio virus is excreted in the stools of an infected patient from where it can infect others via the oral route. A dreaded disease of childhood, contracted usually due to the negligence of the parents in not getting their child properly immunised, it may cause paralysis of one or more extremities which may be devastating as the child may be left with permanent disability. Unfortunately once a child gets Polio there is no cure. So the only hope lies in prevention through vaccination. Polio is now on the agenda of the WHO (World Health Organisation) to be eradicated from the world (like smallpox was eradicated) through a program called "Pulse Polio Program." In this program, every child below the age of 5 years is immunised simultaneously every year by 2 doses given at 1 month interval. Parents should give their child these Polio drops, even if they have received Polio drops from their child specialist 1 day back. More than necessary doses of Polio do not do any harm to the child.

3. Diphtheria

The typical presentation is that of a whitish-grey membrane in the throat, which may cause coughing, sore throat and fever plus a swelling of the neck due to enlarged lymph nodes (often called "bull neck"). If the membrane progresses to involve the voice box (larynx), it may lead to breathing difficulty in the child often with a noisy and laboured breathing. In some cases it may even be fatal. The toxin of diphtheria can lead to many complications like heart failure and paralysis of the muscles by damaging their nerve supply. Though a cure is available in the form of anti-toxin and antibiotics, considering its serious nature, one must go for prevention by DTP vaccine than cure.

4. Pertussis

It is a bacterium which clogs the lungs with mucus. This leads to a severe and prolonged cough. Also called whooping cough or a 99-day cough because of its prolonged nature, it is characterised by severe spasmodic coughing, lasting for weeks. The child goes on coughing many times during a single breath and at the end takes a deep breath to fill his lungs again with air. This deep breath sometimes produces a crowing sound called as whoop. Sometimes the child may gag and vomit at the end of one of these long spells of coughing. An airborne disease, it is contracted by close contact with a person suffering from pertussis, who while coughing releases the pertussis bacteria in the air. The cough is very distressing and can be initiated by even a mild stimulus like feeding or a sudden noise. Though the drug, erythromycin, is prescribed for it and it does kill the bacteria and limits further spread of the disease, it is not of much help for the coughing episodes, which becomes less severe in intensity with time only.

5. Tetanus

It is an infection caused by the bacteria found in dirt, gravy and rusty metals. It usually enters the body through a cut. It is characterised chiefly by spasms, which may be precipitated by even a mild stimulus like light or sound. Another distinctive feature is "lock- jaw" where the jaws are tightly clenched together due to the spasm of the muscles of the cheeks, causing a peculiar grin on the face called as "risus sardonicus." (Try smiling in front of a mirror with your cheeks tightly clenched and you will know what risus sardonicus looks like). The treatment lies in giving anti-toxin, penicillin and control of the recurrent spasms. Though completely curable, many deaths also result due to tetanus and so it is very important to get oneself immunised against it. A notion that tetanus is caused by injury due to rusted nails is incorrect. In fact any wound has the potential to cause tetanus. That's why your doctor prescribes tetanus toxoid in case of any injury.

6. Measles

An airborne viral disease, the chief features are red eyes, nasal discharge, fever, cough and a rash that begins on the face and progresses downwards. Being a viral disease there is no specific drug for it and the treatment is limited to control of the symptoms i.e. control of fever, cough etc. It is quite common in India and its complications may be serious. So best is to prevent it by Measles/MMR vaccine.

7. Mumps

An airborne disease, the distinctive feature is swelling of the parotid glands that appear as if the sides of the jaws and cheeks are swollen. Chewing is painful and so mashed food and liquids should be given to the child. Being a viral disease, there is no specific drug for it, and at the most your doctor may prescribe some analgesics for the pain. It can rarely lead to complications like sterility. Prevention is by MMR vaccine.

8. Rubella

Also called German measles, it is a benign disease characterised by a generalised, self limiting rash, swelling of lymph glands of the neck and fever. Its danger lies in the fact that if an unimmunised pregnant mother gets rubella, the virus may infect the baby inside and it may be born with congenital rubella, a devastating disease. In fact so bad is the disease for the new-born, who may suffer permanent handicap(s) for the rest of his life, that if an unimmunised mother gets rubella during pregnancy, doctors offer the choice of therapeutic abortion to the mother. Thus every girl of childbearing age should ensure that she is immunised against it. Rubella vaccine is contraindicated during pregnancy and so if you have to receive this vaccine, make sure that you are not pregnant.

9. Hepatitis-A

Hepatitis A is one of the most widespread infectious diseases worldwide. It is caused by the hepatitis-A virus and is common in places with poor standards of hygiene and sanitation. The virus attacks the liver and causes varying degrees of illness in patients.

The hepatitis-A virus is excreted in the faeces, and spreads primarily by the faecal-oral route. The virus has a relatively long and infectious incubation period. Hence, the infected individual can pass on the disease to others even before the symptoms develop. Hepatitis-A in children under 2 years is often unrecognized; thus they can be a potential source of infection. Direct contact with an infected person's faeces or indirect contamination of food, water, hands and cooking utensils may result in the virus being ingested, causing infection.

A common source of infection is contaminated water or food, especially raw or insufficiently cooked food (fruits, salad, vegetables, seafood, etc.) Food which is well cooked but handled by infected individuals can also be a source of infection. The infection may also be acquired through close contact with infected individuals within families, schools, day-care centres and hostels.

Symptoms include nausea/vomiting, Jaundice (yellowness of eyes, skin & urine), diarrhoea, pale stools, abdominal pain, malaise/fatigue, fever/chills, lack of appetite, sore throat, etc. The frequency/ severity with which these symptoms occur, vary depending on the age of the person.

Though hepatitis A is considered to be a relatively benign disease in young children, this may not always be the case. Acute symptoms last for 4 weeks to 3 months and may be debilitating requiring total rest and occasionally hospitalization. This causes disruption of daily activities and often leads to absence from work / school. Complete recovery can take as long as 6-12 months, with serious and occasionally fatal complications occurring in minority of patients. Hepatitis-A can relapse in 20% of cases who acquire the disease, and the symptoms may, persist for up to 6 months.

It is water borne disease, which is common in India due to poor hygiene and sanitary conditions. In most of the cases, the child may not even have jaundice! It is called "anicteric hepatitis" i.e. hepatitis without icterus (jaundice). The child will suffer from fever, pain in the upper part of abdomen, deep yellow urine, loss of appetite and nausea/vomiting. Being a viral disease there is no drug to cure it. Fortunately no medicine is required because by and large not serious and self cures by 1- 2 weeks. During the sickness, however the child may suffer a lot.

10. Hepatitis-B

A viral infection of the liver, it is transmitted by close sexual contact, contaminated needles and blood transfusions. It can also be transmitted from the pregnant mother to her baby. AIDS is also transmitted by the same modes of transmission. The chief complaints are jaundice and fever with vomiting. Urine becomes dark yellow. The infection may become chronic and lead to liver failure and sometimes to liver cancer. As treatment of it is disappointing, prevention by vaccination is the best course.

11. Typhoid

A disease characterised by high fever, abdominal pain and diarrhoea or constipation; it is mainly a water borne disease. Because of lack of safe drinking water, poor hygiene and sanitation, it is very common in India. The disease, though having an effective cure, may sometimes lead to serious complications and so vaccination is recommended.

12. Chickenpox

It is characterized mainly by fever and a vesicular (clear fluid filled, like a blister) rash, which is painful and itchy. It is air borne and it is very infectious to others. School going children or those who are in crèches etc. are more likely to get it. It is not serious and is self-curing. Being a viral disease, medicine are not usually required (though available) for it. It takes about a week to cure.

CHICKENPOX RASH

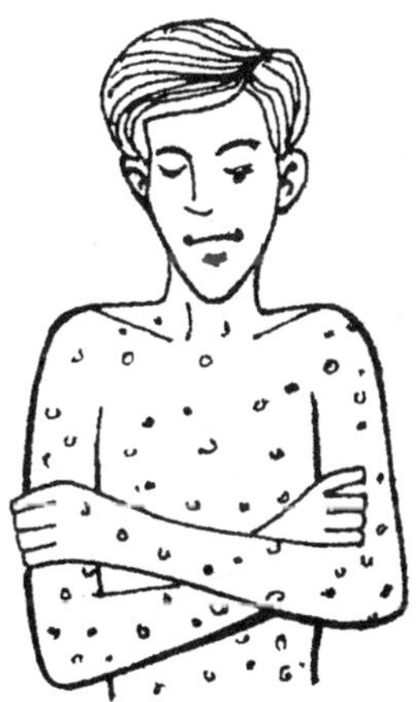

13. Rabies

Bites and scratches by rabid animals (commonly dogs) have the potential of causing a uniformly fatal disease called Rabies for which there is no cure. It can only be prevented by immunisation. Whenever any person is bitten or scratched by animals like dogs, cats, monkeys etc., the local wound should immediately be washed copiously with soap and water for 30 minutes. After that apply some antiseptic solution on it and rush to your doctor. If the animal is a pet or someone who can be observed for at least 10 days, then nothing more is to be done on an immediate basis. However during the period of observation, if the animal shows any change in its behaviour or dies, report immediately to your doctor. Remember that alteration in the behaviour of the animal under observation is as valid a sign as is the death of the animal for you to start taking urgent steps. If the animal cannot be observed or is a proved rabid one, then immediately rabies immunoglobulin is given (half the dose at the local wound and half intramuscularly) plus the 1st dose of anti-rabies vaccine is given. The vaccine is again repeated on days 3, 7, 14, 28 and 90. Rabies immunoglobulin is as important as the vaccine and so make sure that the child receives both.

COMMON CHILDHOOD COMPLAINTS

***Doctors and lawyers are famous for their greed for money. A doctor and a lawyer were sitted next to each other in a dinner party when an urgent call came for the doctor. Piqued at this, he asked the lawyer, "Don't you think people should not disturb me at least here." The lawyer coolly replied, "Yours is a noble profession. You should go." Reluctantly the doctor left. The next day lying on his table was a bill from the lawyer for his timely advice.* **

Some of the common day to day complaints afflicting a child, which often bother the parents, are discussed below. I hope that after reading it, the parents will feel more relaxed and as a result not pressurise themselves and their doctors for a rapid and "magic" cure. Some parents get so anxious that they go from pillar to post every 2nd or 3rd day changing doctors, in quest of a "magic cure". Unfortunately no doctor is a magician. He has to treat logically and not magically and it takes time. So my sincere request is, be patient. Most of the symptoms that your child suffers from are benign and self-limiting. Only thing is that it might take some days for the illness to subside. If there is something serious, your doctor will not dismiss your child by just writing some medicines. So by and large, as a rule of thumb, if your doctor is not worried, you should also be not worried. Please don't pressurise your doctor for it leads to detailed, shot gun type of prescriptions. As a result not only your child is subjected to a lot of unnecessary medications, but you also waste money in buying so many medicines which really were not required in the first place. You will realise this more as you read below. The most commonly over prescribed medicine is antibiotics and tonics.

** *"I hope I am ill," said the unhappy man to the doctor. "I hate to feel like this if I am well."***

1. Fever

The majority of childhood fevers are viral, for which antibiotics are not required. So if your doctor thinks the fever to be viral and prescribes at the most some antipyretic (e.g. Paracetamol), don't think that "less" medicines are being given to your child and so how it will cure the sickness? Since most viral fevers are benign and self-limiting, they don't require much drug therapy. Do not take aspirin for childhood fevers, as it can, in some diseases like chickenpox and influenza, cause a serious illness to the liver and brain. The viral illness can last as long as 5-7 days. So if the child doesn't become OK in 2-3 days, don't panic and go "doctor-shopping". I can understand the parents getting worried if the baby is not all right soon. It starts taxing their patience. But if the parents are reassured that the illness is self-limiting, not serious and will get all right in another 2-3 days, they will be relaxed. Parents can always seek reassurance from their doctor, (visit him again or telephone to him) who will reiterate that the child is having nothing else but a benign viral illness.

Many parents have a "fever phobia." They think that fever should be energetically treated and brought down urgently; else it will go on rising and cause brain damage and other serious problems to the child. This is not true. In fact fever is the body's response to infection, and plays a role in fighting it. Scientists even say that fever is useful, both as a clue to the ongoing disease process, and also because it enhances the immunity of the body.

In some cases of fever, the cause of the fever may not be immediately apparent and so the doctor may follow a "wait and watch" policy (if the condition of the child is not serious) till the diagnosis becomes clearer. In the meantime he may not prescribe any medicines except paracetamol s.o.s. (Paracetamol is usually given when the fever is higher than 102° F; it will reduce the temperature but may not bring it completely to normal.) The effect of paracetamol lasts for 3-4 hours after which the fever will again start rising unless the underlying infection is taken care of. In my opinion, this is the correct approach. Every doctor must strive to reach a diagnosis (i.e. try to find out the underlying disease responsible for fever or any other complaints). Prescribing an antibiotic, anti- malarial, anti-typhoid and other medicines as a "shotgun" therapy in the hope that one of them will hit the target and cure the disease is not correct and rational. Sadly this happens often because the doctor wants to satisfy the parents so that he may not lose their confidence and hence the patient as his client. It is only when the parental attitudes will change and they will question the need for a concoction of 6-8 medicines together for a simple disease like viral fever that the doctor's attitude will also change. Till that time, I am afraid; this "magic bullet" therapy will go on.

Parents often bundle their child with excessive clothing whenever they have fever, which is not a good idea (unless the child is shivering and feeling cold.) Infact the child should be dressed lightly, so that excessive heat from the body can dissipate. If sponging is to be done to bring down the fever, it should be done with tepid (lukewarm) water over as much area of the body as possible, followed by light fanning. The principle behind this is that a light breeze blowing across the body will evaporate the water, which will take along with it its heat of evaporation from the body thus cooling it and bringing down the temperature. Cold water should not be used because it will make the child uncomfortable and he may start shivering. In my day to day practice, I often see parents putting a strip of wet cloth on the forehead for bringing down the fever. It is of limited value.

TREATING FEVER AT HOME

What is fever?

- *Fever is a rise in the body temperature to 100 Fahrenheit or greater.*
- *Fever is the body's natural response to a viral or bacterial infection.*

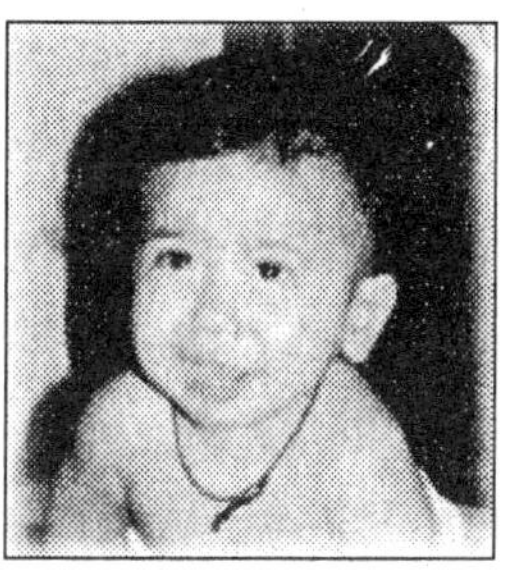

- *Fever is considered beneficial to help the body fight infection and usually is not dangerous.*
- *You may be able to realize that your child has fever by feeling his/her forehead, face or stomach, but it is not a very accurate method, particularly in low grade fever.*
- *Taking a temperature is the only sure way to know if your child has a fever. Normal body temperature may go up in the late afternoon or early morning.*

How to take temperature?

- *There are many devices to measure temperature like glass, digital or tympanic (ear) thermometers. Glass thermometer is the most cmmon variety. It is least expensive and very accurate.*

- *Devices such as temperature strips which are placed on your child's forehead*

are nt accurate. DO NOT USE THEM.

- Taking rectal temperatures should be avoided because it is difficult to ensure safety while measuring this way.
- Remember not to leave your child alone while taking his/her temperature.

Oral temperature

- Oral temperature should be taken only if your child is cooperative and five years of age or older. Young children may bite or break the thermometer.
- Tip of the thermometer should be kept under the tongue for 2-3 minutes.
- Tell your child to close the lips tightly without biting the thermometer.

Axillary temperature

- Take your baby or young child's temperature under the arm (axillary).
- Hold the tip of the thermometer in the centre of the armpit with one hand for 3-4 minutes.
- Axillary temperature is slightly lower than oral temperature. Table given below will help you to understand the axillary temperature readings. ADD 0.6 to the axillary reading.

Body Temperatures			
	Normal	Fever	High fever
Axillary	98.0°F	99.4°F	104.4°F
Oral	98.6°F	100.0°F	105.0°F

HOW TO TREAT FEVER AT HOME?

Without medicines

- If your child has a fever but is otherwise playful, eating and drinking, he may not need any medicine.

- Dress your child in lightweight clothes or preferably remove them to allow heat loss through the skin.

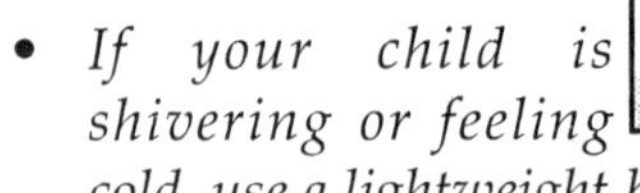

- If your child is shivering or feeling cold, use a lightweight blanket.
- Activity increases body temperature–try to keep your child quiet.
- Encourage your child to have extra fluids to prevent dehydration or extra loss of water (water, iced drinks, juices, or whatever he/she will drink).

With medicines

- Medicines to reduce fever are needed only to make your child more comfortable.
- You can safely use acetaminophen (paracetamol) every 4 hours which can be administered in a syrup or drops form. Remember to check the dose on the bottle.
- Your doctor may advise you to use nimesulide or ibuprofen. Frequency of administration and doses differ with different antifever medication. Always check with the doctor.
- Do not use aspirin for fever (it has been related to a serious illness, Reye's syndrome).
- Always give your child medication for fever if he/she has had febrile seizure (seizures when your child has a fever).
- Give your child a sponge bath with lukewarm water only (no cold water) if fever is higher than 104°F or if fever is not decreased 30-60 minutes after medication is given.
- Never leave your child alone in the tub.

- *Stop the sponge bath if your child starts to shiver.*
- *Never use rubbing alcohol for baths or sponging.*
- *Alcohol can cool your child too quickly and can be absorbed through the skin causing alcohol poisoning.*

When to call your doctor?

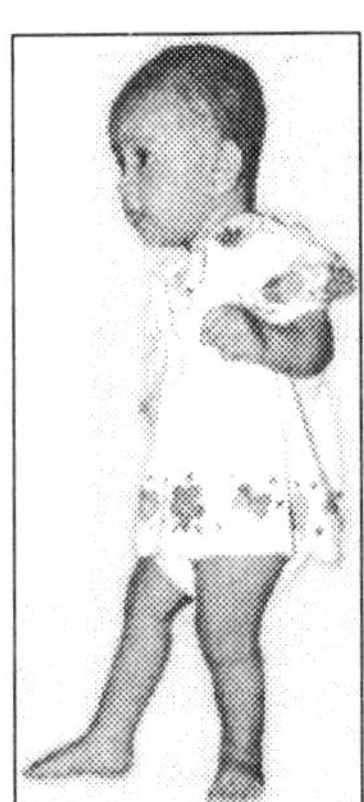

- *If your baby less than 6 months of age has a temperature 101°F or higher.*
- *If your child's fever is 104°F or higher.*
- *If your child has other signs of illness like vomiting, loss of playfulness or appetite.*

Caution!

This information should not be considered alternative to Doctor's advice.

2. Diarrhoea

In the majority of cases it is due to viral infection of the intestines. Benign and self-limiting, it again doesn't require anything else but electral or ORS solution to make up for the fluid losses in diarrhoea stools (i.e. to prevent the child from going into dehydration). Most of the diarrhoeas will correct themselves spontaneously in 2-3 days and in fact giving "over vigorous" therapy like antibiotics etc. may worsen the diarrhoea because the antibiotics kill the "good" bacteria in the intestines. These "good" bacteria prevent the "bad" bacteria from colonising the gut and so are beneficial in warding off infections. That's why there is an entity called "antibiotic induced diarrhoea". Of course if there is clinical or laboratory evidence to suggest that the diarrhoea is due to a bacterial infection, antibiotics are justified but to prescribe antibiotics for each and every case of diarrhoea and that too multiple drugs is not justified. Anti-motility drugs (drugs which reduce the motility of the intestines by reducing the muscle contractions) like Ridol, Imodium etc. are contraindicated in childhood diarrhoeas. Giving antibiotic injections and that too costly ones (in a bid to impress the parents) to a child for a simple case of diarrhoea is even more difficult to justify, except when the child is having a serious systemic infection with diarrhoea as one of its features (which is rare).

ORS therapy: It is a universally accepted treatment for diarrhoeas. It replaces the fluid and electrolyte losses that accompany the loose stools. There are many ORS powders available in the market, which have to be reconstituted by adding water. Ready made ORS in liquid form is also available as 200 ml bottles (often prescribed by the doctors costing about Rs 20/- for 200ml or Rs. 100/- for 1 litre) and is mentioned only to be condemned as the cost is prohibitive and it has no advantage over the freshly prepared ORS at home (which is practically free). To charge Rs 100/- for a litre of salt and sugar water is really swindling the patients. The instructions for reconstitution with water are written on the packet and should be strictly followed. Usually, one packet of ORS is dissolved in one 1 litre of boiled and cooled water. Babies don't like the taste of ORS much, as it is too salty (sodium is 90 Meq/L), particularly the WHO recommended ones. In such cases one can try ORS with a less salt content (i.e. 50 Meq/L). I personally prefer ORS with 50 Meq/L sodium in the usual cases of diarrhoea; and give ORS containing 90 Meq/L of sodium only if the stools are cholera like i.e. profuse and watery with a high frequency. Anyhow WHO recommends that 2 parts of its ORS should be offered with 1 part of ordinary water/ breast-feed as a supplement in between. This effectively reduces the sodium load to 60 Meq/L, the only difference being that in this particular approach, you are giving concentrated WHO ORS separately first and then offering plain water to the baby, so that they mix together in the stomach! Mothers should not make the ORS concentrated by adding less water than recommended to the powder. Dangerous incidents of salt "poisoning" have been documented by doing so. Sometimes a child will not take ORS, how much you try. In that case there is no alternative but to prepare it indigenously at home by adding 5 tsp of sugar and 1 tsp of table salt to 1 litre of boiled and cooled water along with some fresh lemon juice to make it tasty. In case the child rejects even this, one can go for rice water with salt to taste added to it. Coconut water, weak tea and barley water are also appropriate if the child doesn't accept any of the above liquids. ORS therapy should be abandoned if there is persistent vomiting, the child refuses to accept, there is no urine output for 8 hours or the child is becoming more dehydrated. All such children will usually require intravenous fluid therapy.

Many types of diarrhoea are blamed on an entity called "lactose intolerance". It means that the child will have diarrhoea if lactose (i.e. milk sugar) is offered to him. There are many lactose free tinned powders available in the market, which are given by doctors from day 2-3 of diarrhoea at the expense of breast milk, cow's milk or milk tins. There is no justification in such a step unless lactose intolerance has been documented by lab testing of the stools. So don't "abandon" milk (particularly breast milk) if the diarrhoea is not all right in 2-3 days. Another treatment forwarded by the doctors is dietary restrictions and to give ½ diluted milk during episodes of diarrhoea. There is no logic in this. The food that we eat is not causing diarrhoea, otherwise one should have diarrhoea daily whenever he/she takes full strength milk i.e. not ½ diluted. To say that during diarrhoea, the digestive capacity is reduced and therefore diluted milk is required is also not correct as the body's digestive capabilities remain the same during diarrhoea also. Similarly partial starvation/ fasting etc. are not good. In fact during diarrhoea, there should not be any restriction on the diet of the child and he should be allowed to eat whatever he feels like. Remember, good nutrition is important in any disease including diarrhoea and not starvation which will make the child even weaker and delay the recovery.

There is another entity called "toddler's diarrhoea." In this, the child passes loose stools frequently but surprisingly the child suffers from no adverse effects. Thus the child for all practical purposes is a healthy one, gaining weight adequately and not going into dehydration. His appetite is not curtailed and he is active and playful. Routine stool examination doesn't show pus cells or blood. Such benign diarrhoeas do not require any treatment and the child outgrows it with time. Unfortunately, this is the diarrhoea, which is most commonly treated the wrong way. The parents run from pillar to post, get all sorts of tests done and are prescribed all sorts of medicines, particularly shot-gun types, with no relief or only transient relief. If the parents are aware of this entity, and it is not rare, a lot of their anxiety will be relieved plus they won't go in quest of a cure where none is actually required.

***A new drug was launched by a multi-national company amidst great fanfare with the slogan "the drug reduces mortality." However due to a typing mistake the slogan went on print as "the drug reduces morality." The horrified publicity manager had to hastily call back all the literature published. ***

3. Vomiting

Most of the vomiting is due to irritation of the stomach (called gastritis), and so at the most, some antacids and antiemetics may be of benefit. Vomiting quite commonly presents itself along with diarrhoea; a condition called "gastro-enteritis". By and large, vomiting is self-limiting. **Vomiting doesn't always mean a stomach upset**. In fact any disease in the child ranging from ear infections, kidney infections etc. to brain fever can be the cause of vomiting. The chances of retaining fluids increase in vomiting if it is cold and palatable (ice-cream is a good choice). Also the chances of retaining are appreciably more if the child is offered the food that he wants. This is the same with adults. If they have the urge/appetite for a particular food, chances are less that they will vomit it out during periods of illness. It is better to give food in small quantities frequently, so that the incidence of vomiting will be reduced. So you should not force feed the child and not offer food/liquids that you consider appropriate but rather ask the child what he wants to take. If he says that he doesn't want anything, do not give, as it will almost certainly cause vomiting. It is better to start with plain water initially and if the child tolerates it, to proceed to glucose water, fruit juices, soups, liquid diet, semi-solid diet and so on.

4. Constipation

Constipation may be there when the child is suffering from an acute febrile illness. This is due to the dehydrating effect that the fever has on the body plus in illnesses, the gut motility may also be transiently reduced. This is self-limiting. Don't be bothered about it. Just give some extra fluids to your baby. Some parents have the misconception that unless the child has normal stools his fever or disease won't get better, which is erroneous. Chronic (long term) use of enemas or laxatives is strongly discouraged for transient constipation, as the child may become habituated to it and may find passing stools difficult without it in the long run. Often I have seen parents being prescribed suppositories (which are to be inserted anally into the child's rectum. It is a disagreeable way of treatment.

5. Stomach-aches

Another common problem in children is pain of the abdomen. While the commonest and an obvious cause is infection of the intestines (gastro-enteritis), sometimes no obvious cause can be detected and the diagnosis remains elusive. So if your doctor, after a thorough physical examination and some simple tests like stool and urine analysis, doesn't find anything wrong, don't be much bothered. Costly and sophisticated tests usually add little to the already available information. So desist from them unless a doctor strongly recommends them.

Many of the stomach-aches in childhood are "functional" rather than due to an underlying disease, which requires nothing else but psychological reassurance both to the parents and to the child. Also called as "irritable bowel syndrome (IBS)" this pain is usually peri-umbilical, dull aching type with vague localisation. There is no association with feeding or bowel habits. Contrary to popular belief, it can also be present when the child is sleeping though the incidence is much higher in an awake child. It is usually never present when the child is playing and enjoying himself and is mentally relaxed. **Remember, the pain for the child is real and not a made up, fictitious one**. So it should never be suggested that he doesn't have any pain or the pain exists only in his "head"; and not in his stomach. A calculated neglect of the pain (and not the child) along with reassurance helps in the child outgrowing the pain. The parents should understand that the child requires love, attention and security at all times and not while he is complaining of pain abdomen.

Compare this pain with malingering where the child makes up the abdominal pain whenever he is confronted with some unpleasant task, particularly going to school. This type of pain never occurs on holidays and subsides rapidly once the wish of the child is granted; e.g. he enjoys a day off from school. This doesn't mean that a day off from school is the treatment for this type of pain. This will only positively reinforce the behaviour and make it a vicious cycle. Since this type of pain is in the "head" and not in the stomach, parents should be strict and in no case should there be school avoidance. Rather the child should be told firmly that he has to go to school and that once he is in the class, the pain will become OK.

6. Coughs and colds

***Impatient patient to a doctor, "I know that whisky is no good in getting rid of the cold, but then, neither is the medical profession."* **

The commonest affliction of childhood, some children may have 10-12 attacks per year (since 1 attack may last for 1 week or so, parents may feel that the child is falling sick every 2-3 weeks). To the parents of such children, it appears that the child is never all right. Hardly has one attack subsided that the child again starts having cough and cold. The infections may vary from common cold with nose block to high fever, severe cough and congestion of the chest. Most of the respiratory infections are viral in nature, most common being common cold or flu. The best remedy for a blocked nose is frequent instillation of saline drops with intermittent cleaning of the mucus in the nose by buds or gentle suction. If some medicated nose drops is prescribed, it should not be used for more than 3-4 days as they can cause rebound congestion of the nose, because of which as soon as you stop the drops, the nose will again get blocked. If a common cold persists for more than 10 days, it indicates a sinus trouble (sinusitis) for which the doctor will prescribe some antibiotics.

*** Outside a chemist shop, a fellow was seen clutching a pole for dear life, like a statue not moving, frozen. The chemist asked the assistant "What's the matter with the guy. Wasn't he here earlier?"*

"He was. He had the most terrible cough and none of the prescriptions seemed to help."

Chemist: "He seems to be fine now, not coughing at all."

*Assistant: "Sure, he is fine. I gave him a bottle of strongest laxative as the cough syrup... now he dare not cough."***

Cough syrups should be used judiciously to suppress an irritating and hacking cough that disturbs the child much. Whatever syrup is given to the child should be well shaken, as omitting this step leads to diluted medicine being given first and concentrated doses when the bottle is finishing. The role of steam inhalation is questionable in treating respiratory infections. Of course the air that the child is breathing should not be dry. The best way to liquefy the tenacious mucus inside the lungs and expectorate it out (remember child will swallow it and you won't see him bringing it out) is to give plenty of fluids to the child. Tea, coffee, warm milk etc. may be quite beneficial. The purpose is to hydrate the child well so that the thick mucus present in the air passages, which is causing its irritation and hence coughing, becomes liquefied and thinned out so that the child can bring it out easily. The expectoration of such mucus plugs causes a substantial relief of the coughing bout. Many children vomit at the end of a coughing bout. This vomiting is not due to stomach upset, but is a reflex vomiting secondary to gagging due to excessive coughing. In such cases the problem to be addressed is not the vomiting but the cough, and therefore anti-vomiting medicines are of limited value in such cases. Diarrhoea is also often associated with respiratory infections. Actually it is a part of the disease spectrum and not a separate illness. As such, it doesn't require any specific treatment and starts subsiding as the respiratory infection starts improving.

Taking multivitamins cannot prevent colds, nor can swathing the child from head to toe in multiple wrappings of warm clothing prevent them. Colds are due to viruses, which are ubiquitously present in the air. How can one prevent a child from inhaling that air? The answer is simple: one cannot. So humans (both adults and children) had had and will have in future many episodes of colds and coughs. Vitamin C is quite popular as a preventive agent, but there is no scientific evidence to suggest that it is really effective. Similarly there are no shots (vaccines) against cold. The only way of reducing the frequency of colds in a child is to keep him away from a person who is suffering from such an infection, because colds spread from person to person via air borne viruses. Again it is practically difficult to carry out this suggestion. How can one isolate a child from his parents and his playmates, who may be suffering from colds?

The use of steroids, a popular therapy for treating fevers, cold etc. is not justified and in fact may be harmful. Steroids can bring down fever and symptomatically improve the patient, sometimes dramatically, which makes parents very happy. This is the reason why steroids are a frequent component of multi-drug prescriptions. The truth is that fever etc. are manifestations of an infection that the steroids may suppress. This is all the more not desirable, because now nobody knows whether the infection has worsened. In fact by the regression of symptoms like fever, one is lulled into a false sense of security that the patient is improving, whereas actually the infection may have worsened. It doesn't require much common sense to understand that fever, cough etc. are manifestations of some disease and if you cure the disease, the symptoms will automatically be cured. Unfortunately, because these symptoms are so obvious and because they are the cause of discomfort to the child, the parents want them to be relieved fast and once some improvement of the symptoms occurs, parents think that the child is on the road to recovery. Surely he is on the road to recovery provided the symptoms are not being suppressed by artificial means like steroids, but rather are getting better in the natural course of the disease. So remember the wise old adage: when you want to remove a problem permanently, strike at its roots (though sometimes it may be time consuming).

7. Sore throat: (Tonsillitis & Pharyngitis)

Both of them co-exist closely. The chief manifestations are sore throat, pain in swallowing and fever. The glands around the neck may become enlarged and painful. Again, viral aetiology is most common, so no antibiotics are warranted. Warm saline gargling may provide symptomatic relief. Usually in a matter of 3-4 days, the patient will be relieved even without medicines. In some cases, a bacterium called "streptococcus" can cause sore throat (pharyngitis). Rarely, these bacteria after an interval of few weeks (particularly in the age group of 5-15 years) may cause problems to the heart, joints etc. called "rheumatic fever/rheumatic heart disease". The only way of knowing that the throat problem is due to streptococcus and not due to viruses, is by means of throat culture (report takes 2-3 days to be ready). Streptococcal sore throat requires antibiotic treatment.

*** (Removal of tonsils): Surgeons and dacoits are similar. Both have a mask on their face and both carry knives for their jobs. ***

A common dilemma of parents is "Enlarged Tonsils". Remember that tonsils may be physiologically enlarged to an extent that they might seem to meet in the midline of the throat on gagging. However if the child is having no problems and the area around the tonsils is normal i.e. not red and inflamed, then no treatment is required. Tonsils have been blamed for respiratory problems, particularly recurrent respiratory infections. Parents believe that removal of tonsils is a permanent cure for frequently occurring cough, cold, nose block etc. Nothing is farther from the truth. Tonsils and adenoids are lymphoid tissues, which have been provided by nature to protect against infections. Any infection that threatens to enter through the nose or mouth meets as a first line of defence, the tonsils and adenoids. As is obvious, they protect against infections rather than being the culprits causing recurrent infections.

8. Nasal allergy: (hay fever/hives)

***In a seminar on allergy it was stated very nicely: "Anything under the sun as well as the sun can cause allergy." ***

The patient is bothered by persistent running nose (clear, watery discharge which if examined under the microscope shows eosinophils), sneezing, itching of the nose/throat and stuffiness of the nose. If this problem is seasonal and keeps on recurring during fixed months of a year, it is called "seasonal hay fever" and is usually due to allergy to pollens. If the problem is around the year, it is called "perennial hay fever." Common allergens are dust, mites, feathers, pets, moulds (fungal spores) etc. Some preventive measures recommended are that the floor should be wet mopped daily; curtains, bedcovers, carpets, furniture coverings, linen etc. should be laundered at least once a week and then exposed to bright sunshine; woollen articles and stuffed toys should be removed from the bedroom. The environment should not be too humid as it favours the growth of fungal moulds. The room and the air inside should be kept as clean as possible, particularly of air suspended particles like dust. Furniture coverings, bed sheets etc. may harbour mites and thus should be periodically laundered. All these measures will reduce the incidence of allergic attacks though not eliminate them completely, as it is very difficult to remove all allergens from the environment. Persistent nose problems like watering, sneezing etc. are often attributed to a deviation of the midline nasal septum. A slight deviation to one side is normal and is not responsible for these nasal problems. Surgical correction of this "deviation" is advocated as a permanent cure for persistent nose problems, but the results post operatively are mostly disappointing, if this is done without a careful and critical evaluation. In fact you should go for it only if it is certain that it is indeed the culprit. Since nasal allergy is a chronic, life long problem, the helpless patient accepts any sort of treatment including surgery (which in most cases is not required as it is of no benefit).

Treatment of nasal allergy: During the acute phase oral antihistamines/ decongestants work well (nowadays there are non-sedating single daily dose antihistamines available). Your doctor may also prescribe decongestant nasal drops. Once the attack is controlled, for prevention, prophylactic nasal drops (sodium chromoglycate drops or steroid nasal sprays) can be used.

9. Asthma

The incidence of asthma is increasing dramatically, due to the increasing air pollution. It is a chronic disorder where the airways are hyper-reactive to a variety of stimuli. This hyper-reactivity is reversible but recurrent. Recurrent attacks are a hallmark of asthma. The airways constrict in response to the offending stimulus (e.g. pollens, viral infection etc.), which narrows their lumen. As a result, breathing becomes laboured particularly during the phase of expiration (breathing out). Thus the child suffers from an increased work of breathing i.e. he has to strain his muscles of breathing in order to breathe out through the narrowed airway tubes (called bronchi). Sometimes as air is expelled out through these narrowed passages, an audible sound is heard called "wheezing", which most of the parents whose child suffers from asthma have heard sometime or the other. Wheezing need not always be audible. Often, only the stethoscope picks it up. Remember that wheezing though a characteristic feature of asthma may not always be present. In fact an asthmatic may present simply with chronic cough without wheeze or breathing difficulties. Also remember that all wheezing is not asthma (there are many other diseases that can cause wheezing). A helpful point in diagnosing asthma is a positive family history of asthma or allergies. In children, the stimulus that often precipitates an asthmatic attack is the common cold. Parents often give the history that the child had a running nose for 1-2 days and now has started having a tight cough i.e. an attack of asthma. Other allergens can also cause asthma, like in hay fever (refer above). Asthma can be without cough, so don't think why the doctor is diagnosing asthma when my child has no cough. The treatment of asthma is bronchodilators (drugs which dilate the constricted air passages) and steroids. Bronchodilators should preferably be delivered directly to the air passages rather than orally. Oral bronchodilators are less efficacious with more side effects like tremors etc. There are various ways of delivering bronchodilators to the lungs directly, e.g. by nebulization, use of inhalers, rotacaps, spacers, baby masks etc. The method most suited for your child will be decided by your doctor. For instance, inhalers are useful only for adults and older children. For smaller children, an assist device like spacer or rotahaler may be required. Steroids, the second mainstay of treatment, can be given by inhalation, but during an acute attack of asthma; they are given orally for 5-7 days. The use of deriphylline or an injection of adrenaline, therapies that were popular in the past, is nowadays seldom used and that too as a second line measure.

If there are frequent recurring attacks, some type of preventive therapy (such prevention only decreases the frequency of attacks, it doesn't stop them all together) is advocated. Usually inhaled steroids taken twice a day or inhalation of sodium chromoglycate is efficacious as a preventive therapy. Nowadays, a new generation of drugs called "leukotriene receptor modifiers" are available that are also of benefit in reducing the incidence of asthma i.e. they have a preventive role. Each case has to be individualised, as to what suits him the best. Your doctor may have to try out permutations and combinations of various drugs before striking the optimum balance. As the child grows older, in about 50% of cases, the attacks of asthma become less frequent and may even subside completely.

An asthmatic child should be allowed to lead as normal a life as possible. He should be allowed to play all types of games he loves. If exercise precipitates an attack of asthma (called exercise-induced asthma), it is readily preventable by taking some puffs of bronchodilators before the exercise. So activities of the child should not be curtailed. There is no need to cut down on any food until is proved that the child is allergic to that particular food (food allergies seldom cause asthma). The family members of the asthmatic child, particularly if the attacks are severe and frequent, require a lot of emotional support. It is always best to take the support of your social system i.e. friends, relatives etc. Also talk over these things with your doctor who will give a sympathetic hearing to your emotional problems and try to alleviate them as much as possible. On the whole, the outlook is not that bad and once you accept the situation, you start feeling better.

Triggers of Asthma

Allergens

Allergens are an important triggering factor of asthma. Some examples of outdoor and indoor allergens are:

1. Pollen
2. Mold
3. Animal dander
4. House dust/dust mites
5. Cockroach
6. Certain foods

Viral infections

Viral infections of the respiratory tract often act as a major aggravating trigger. Viral infections produce an added irritation in the airways, nose, throat, lungs, and sinuses. This irritation often precedes attacks of asthma. The exact biological mechanism for this is not known.

Sinusitis

An inflammation of the nasal sinuses, known as sinusitis, often begins as an upper respiratory infection. Childhood symptoms include wheezing, postnasal drip, night-time cough, and enlarged lymph nodes. Adolescents and adults may have headaches and sinus pressure of pain. Asthma may be aggravated by drainage of mucus into the nose, throat and bronchial tubes.

Irritants

Irritant can play a large role in triggering asthma. Some examples are:

1. Strong odors and sprays, such as perfumes, household cleaners, cooking fumes (especially from frying), paints and varnishes.
2. Other chemicals such as coal, chalk dust, talcum powder.
3. Air pollutants
4. Tobacco smoke
5. Changing weather conditions, including changes in temperature, barometric pressure, humidity, and strong winds, all are likely to affect and irritate airways.

Tobacco smoke and wood smoke

Tobacco smoke, whether directly or passively inhaled, has harmful effects on the airways and is especially irritating for patients with asthma. An increased incidence of asthma has been reported in children whose mothers smoke. No one should smoke in the home of an asthmatic patient.

Smoke from wood burning and heating stoves can be extremely irritating to asthmatic by releasing chemicals such as sulphur dioxide. Proper ventilation must be maintained if these devices are used.

Exercise

Exercise can also trigger an asthma attack. It is estimated that 85% of allergic asthmatics have symptoms of wheezing following exercise. Inhaled cool and dry air seems to be a strong asthma trigger. Long distance running, a longterm strenuous activity, is most likely to induce asthma and swimming the least likely.

Gastroesophageal reflux

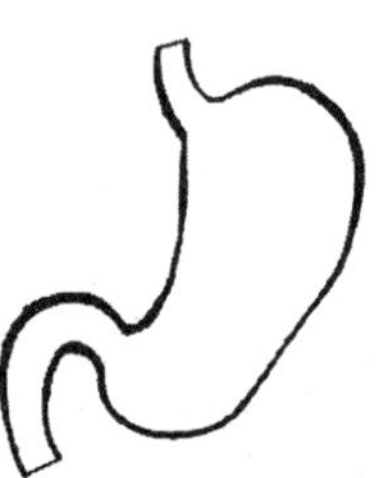

Gastroesophageal reflux, a condition characterized by persistent reflux of stomach acids, is common in individuals with asthma. Symptoms may include heartburn, belching, or spitting up (especially in infants). Nighttime asthma is common.

Industrial or occupational exposure to chemical irritants while on the job

Many cases of asthma in India are worsened or caused by exposure to occupational vapours, dust, gases or fumes. Typically, occupational asthma improves when the individual is away from the workplace for several days, e.g. weekends and vacation.

Sensitivity to medications, such as aspirin and sulphites

Five to 20% of adult asthmatic patients will experience an asthma attack as a result of sensitivities or allergies to medications. Medications that are known to induce asthma attack include:

1. Aspirin.
2. Other nonsteroidal anti-inflammatory medications in patients with aspirin sensitivity, such as ibuprofen, indomethacin, naproxen, etc.
3. Sulphites used as food and beverage preservatives.

Before taking any medication, (including over the counter medications) asthmatics should consult their physician.

Emotional anxiety

Emotional anxiety and nervous stress cause fatigue and may add to asthma symptoms and aggravate an attack. These psychological factors alone cannot provoke asthma and are considered more of an effect than a cause.

Your doctor can provide you with more information on the causes and treatment of asthma.

Taking a New Look at Asthma

Unfortunately... asthma prevalence, particularly in children, is increasing worldwide. It is underdiagnosed and undertreated.

Fortunately...

- *New methods are available for recognising, diagnosing, treating, and controlling asthma.*

- *Personal, social, and economic burdens of asthma can be minimized.*
- *Patient education increases the likelihood of lifelong success.*
- *You can make a difference.*
- *Asthma causes recurring episodes of coughing, wheezing, chest tightness, and difficult breathing. Asthma attacks can be life threatening. They can be prevented.*
- *Asthma is a chronic inflammatory disorder of the airways. Chronically inflamed airways are hyper-responsive; they become obstructed and airflow is limited (by bronchoconstriction, mucus plugs, and increased inflammation) when airways are exposed to various stimuli, or triggers.*
- *Common asthma triggers (that is, factors that make asthma worse) include viral infections; allergens such as domestic dust mites (in bedding, carpets, and fabric-upholstered furnishings), animals with fur, cockroach, pollens, and molds; tobacco smoke; air pollution; exercise; strong emotional expressions; chemical irritants; and drugs (aspirin and beta blockers).*
- *Asthma attacks (or exacerbations) are episodic, but airway inflammation is chronically present. Asthma is a chronic disorder requiring longterm management. For many patients, this means taking preventive medication everyday.*
- *Asthma can change over time. Asthma can be mild, moderate or severe; asthma attacks can be life-threatening. The severity of asthma varies among individuals, and it can change in one individual over time. Treatment decisions are made based on the severity of asthma.*
- *Asthma can be treated and controlled so that almost all patients can:*
- *Prevent troublesome symptoms night and day.*
- *Prevent serious attacks.*
- *Require little or no quick-relief medication*
- *Have productive, physically active lives.*
- *Have (near) normal lung function.*
- *Asthma is not a cause for shame. Olympic athletes, famous leaders, other celebrities, anal ordinary people live successful lives with asthma.*
- *Asthma may be preventable. For infants with a family history of asthma or atopy, it is highly likely that avoiding exposure to passive smoking and to domestic dust mite, cat, and cockroach allergens will help prevent the initial development of asthma. For adults, avoiding exposure to chemical sensitizers in the workplace is helpful.*

Identify and Avoid Triggers

- *When patients avoid exposure to asthma triggers (allergens and irritants that make their asthma worse), asthma symptoms and attacks can be prevented and medications reduced. Common triggers are listed below.*

Common Asthma Triggers and Avoidance Strategies

TRIGGER	TO AVOID
Domestic dust mite allergens (so small they are not visible to the naked eye)	Wash bed linens and blankets once a week in hot water and dry in a hot dryer or the sun. Encase pillows and mattresses in air-tight covers. Remove carpets, especially in sleeping rooms. Use vinyl, leather, or plain wooden furniture instead of fabric-upholstered furniture. If possible, use vacuum cleaner with filters.
Tobacco smoke (whether the patient smokes or breathes in the smoke from others)	Stay away from tobacco smoke. Patients and parents should not smoke.
Allergens from animals with fur	Remove animals from the home, or at least from the sleeping area.
Cockroach allergen	Clean the home thoroughly and often. Use pesticide spray–but make sure the patient is not at home when spraying occurs.
Outdoor pollens and mold	Close windows and doors and remain indoors when pollen and mold counts are highest.
Indoor mold	Reduce dampness in the home; clean all damp areas frequently.
Physical activity	**Do not avoid** physical activity. Symptoms can be prevented by taking a short- or long-acting inhaled beta2-agonist or sodium cromoglycate before strenuous exercise.
Drugs	Do not take aspirin or beta blockers if these medicines cause asthma symptoms.

10. Urticaria (skin allergy)

Red blotches, round or oval and raised from the skin surface appear on the body accompanied by itching. If it is associated with swelling of the lips and tongue, pallor, breathing difficulty or light-headedness, it may signify a serious disorder called "anaphylaxis." Under such circumstances the child should be taken to the doctor immediately. Otherwise urticaria is a benign condition and the best treatment is anti-histaminic drugs. The only problem with urticaria is that like asthma it is difficult to trace the allergen and hence it may be chronic and recurrent.

Skin Tips in Eczema

Small children and babies can wear cotton gloves to prevent them from causing more damage to the skin by scratching. Avoid scratching or rubbing the itchy areas.

Avoid frequent hot bath or showers.

Cotton underclothes and socks should be worn. Woollen clothes should be avoided.

Applying bath oils before bathing and a moisturiser after bathing will prevent skin from drying out. Avoid common soaps and increase the use of glycerine soaps, mild face washes and moisturisers.

Source: *American Association of Family Physicians*

11. Headaches in childhood

Parents tend to blame eyestrain or hearing problems as the main cause for headaches, which is seldom correct. The commonest causes for headaches in childhood are migraine, tension headaches, organic headaches and psychogenic headaches. Migrainous attacks cause a severe throbbing headache often followed by vomiting. The child wants to retire to a dark room. There is often a positive family history of migraine. Tension headaches are due to a continual stress during the daytime, which results in a headache in the evenings, mainly due to muscle soreness. Psychogenic headaches are a means of seeking attention or a means to escape from an unpleasant activity, say going to school. Organic headaches are due to a disease of the brain and should be taken seriously. Whatever the cause, headache should not be taken lightly. It is best to consult a doctor, primarily to rule out an organic cause such as a tumour of the brain or infection of the brain as the cause for headache.

12. Dental caries

*** A dentist was amazed when a lady came rushing into his chamber and said, "Doctor, I am in a great hurry. So do the extraction without giving anaesthesia." The doctor complimented her on her bravery and asked her to show the tooth to be extracted whence she called out to her husband following behind, "Come quickly and show the tooth. The doctor will do it without anaesthesia." ***

Food, high in sugar content and remaining in the mouth for a prolonged period is the commonest factor responsible for dental caries. Babies who sleep with the bottle containing sweetened milk in their mouth are especially prone to get it, called as "nursing bottle" caries. The tooth becomes sensitive to the temperature of the food and hence cold or hot foodstuff may hurt. Later on, there may be a constant pain and even a dental abscess (collection of pus). In the early stages of tooth decay, the decayed part is cleaned and tooth filling done. Later on, extraction of the teeth may become necessary. Even milk teeth should be cared for meticulously. Just because they are going to fall off at the age of 6 years onwards and replaced by new permanent teeth doesn't mean that they should be ignored. Milk teeth allow the child to speak and eat properly, have a good self-image and preserve the space for the permanent teeth.

To prevent dental problems, teeth should be cleaned regularly. The gums of even a small baby can be cleaned by wiping it with a moist cotton cloth. As the child grows older and cuts out the milk teeth, these can be cleaned by rubbing them with a soft cloth or a soft baby toothbrush. Toothpaste may be used even though the child tends to swallow it (it causes no harm). Cleaning should be done twice a day preferably, particularly before bedtime and after that the child should have no more food items. The second important step is to limit the intake of high sugar food particularly those, which are concentrated, viscous and have a sticky texture. The third and final step is to strengthen the tooth and this is done by fluoridation of the toothpaste. Caries of the milk teeth does not directly cause caries of the permanent teeth. Antiseptic mouthwashes, though a good way of protection against dental caries, are of little value in a small child, as he tends to swallow it, particularly before the age of 6 years.

13. Anaemias in childhood

It is a frequently encountered problem. The child looks pale and gets tired quickly. The best way to diagnose anaemia is by testing "haemoglobin" of the blood. Anaemia, in the majority of cases, is due to a nutritional deficiency of iron, folic acid or Vitamin-B_{12}. However any case of anaemia should be thoroughly investigated and one should strive to find a cause for anaemias diligently. If the doctor orders a battery of tests, it is worth the effort, time and money to get them done, because often anaemias can be a perplexing problem and the cause difficult to ascertain. Giving iron and other tonics indiscriminately for anaemias without knowing the type of anaemia is not correct. In fact iron is contraindicated in certain types of anaemias called "haemolytic" anaemias, the prototype of which is "Thalessemia" in which blood gets "destroyed" prematurely. Children suffering from this devastating disease are dependent on regular blood transfusions, as there is no definitive therapy for it yet. So prevention is best, which takes mainly two forms. One is to avoid consanguineous marriages (i.e. marriages among close relatives) and secondly is to go for genetic counselling. This can be done during the early weeks of pregnancy and if the baby in-utero is found to be having Thalessemia, it is advisable to go for therapeutic abortion.

14. Jaundice

Most commonly it is due to an infection of the liver called "Hepatitis". The liver is usually infected by the hepatitis viruses A, B, C and E, out of which A is the most common. The mode of spread of Hepatitis-A is feco-oral. This means that it can occur by contaminated water, fingers, flies, contaminated food etc. Hepatitis B and C are also common and the mode of spread is by intimate sexual contact, i.v. drug abusers, and blood transfusions and from a pregnant mother to her baby. The eyes may become yellow and the urine becomes dark yellow along with a decrease in the appetite of the child, apathy, right sided pain abdomen and nausea/vomiting. As opposed to Hepatitis-A; hepatitis B and C can become chronic and lead to liver failure and sometimes cancer of the liver. Hepatitis-E is rare and similar to A.

Treatment of Jaundice and Hepatitis: It is a common misconception that some sort of liver tonic e.g. Liv-52, Stimuliv etc. is a necessary medicine to treat jaundice. The truth is that these liver tonics are of questionable benefit. Liver is a very versatile organ capable of regeneration of the dead liver cells by its own and doesn't require liver tonics to keep itself fit and fine. Similarly, there is a misconception that fried, fatty food is contraindicated in liver disorders and should not be given to the child. This stems from the fact that in some children fatty food can cause more nausea. So often parents feed the child only high carbohydrate diet (e.g. Glucon-D) and even if the child asks for fried food, it is avoided, sometimes for weeks. This is not appropriate, because if the child cannot tolerate it, **he will not ask for it**. Even the sight of fatty food will repulse him. So if the child asks for it, it means that he will be able to tolerate it and so there is no harm in giving it. Finally many parents, even educated ones, go to "jaundice specialists"(quacks), who dip the hands of the child in water. The water, as if by magic turns yellow and the quack smugly tells the parents that the jaundice of the body has been "removed" into the water. In fact it is nothing else but a fraud.

Liver is the centre of control for diseases: It appears that parents and some doctors, too, have the erroneous notion that a liver problem is responsible for all sorts of indigestion, failure to gain weight, poor appetite, thinness, chronic and recurrent pain in abdomen etc. Whenever a child has these problems, the doctor often tells the parents that it is due to a liver problem which generates a lot of anxiety in the minds of the parents, while it is rarely true. The liver is normally palpable in a child up to 3 years and doesn't signify a liver pathology. Liver problems usually manifest as jaundice, deep yellow urine and nausea/vomiting with a marked decrease in appetite. Therefore to blame the liver for all troubles is injustice being meted out to a versatile and "innocent" organ of the body.

15. Cervical lymph nodes (neck glands)

Parents are quite worried over small pea-sized swellings, which they feel in the neck, behind the ear, at the back of the scalp etc. These swellings are due to lymph nodes (as parents correctly point out). Some of them are anxious that it may not be a tumour or T.B. glands. If the glands are freely mobile, less than 1 cm in diameter and not painful, it is reassuring and the only policy to be followed is a "wait and watch" policy. Parents should report if there is any increase in the size of the glands. Most of these glands persist due to some old illness of the scalp or of the mouth. There are no associated systemic complaints with these glands and are brought to notice only because one day, the parents happen to feel them.

16. Head injury

Head injuries are very frequent in children. They may topple down from the bed, trip and fall while running; fall down from a height etc. Fortunately most of the head injuries in children are trivial. However following a head injury, parents should always consult a doctor. If there is a change in the level of consciousness, persistent vomiting, irritability or drowsiness, convulsions; immediate medical help should be sought. External injuries like bruises or a swelling of the skull at the site of injury are of less concern than the possibility of a brain injury. Parents are anxious about the external visible swelling following the bump. Actually it is nothing else but a collection of blood below the scalp and nothing has to be done for it, certainly not aspiration or incision, as it subsides on its own in a few weeks.

17. Ear aches

This is also a very frequent complaint amongst childhood. It usually follows a respiratory infection like cough, cold etc. It is also more common in bottle-fed babies, particularly when they are nursed lying down. It is due to a collection of fluid behind the eardrum, which causes pain. Relief is achieved by spontaneous perforation of the eardrum with exudation of the pus. The treatment is antibiotics and analgesics. Parents are worried that the perforated eardrum may not heal and may lead to hearing problems later on. Fortunately in the vast majority of cases, these fears are unfounded as the eardrum heals completely with no residual hearing loss.

CSOM: It means chronic otitis media. Some children have chronically draining ears which do not respond to the common antibiotics. Any ear discharge that is persistently present even after 3 months is termed CSOM. It usually follows a perforation of the ear drum and a chronic infection of the middle ear. This infection causes pus to come out of the perforated eardrum outside the ear. The treatment of it requires a different kind of antibiotics, which are usually given for a period of 2-3 weeks till the ear is dry. After that the child may have to be put on a single daily dose preventive antibiotic for 3 months so that the ear infection does not recur. This is done so that the ear drum can heal and all focus of infection from the middle ear is removed. If it still does not work, then the option is surgical closure of the ear drum. In CSOM, some doctors also prefer instillation of local ear drops in the ear for a period of 7 - 14 days, a thing which is not ordinarily done in an ordinary acute ear infection (called ASOM).

18. Limb pains

A very common complaint of children is pain in the limbs. It may be a part of a viral illness in which case the child will also have fever, apathy etc. Some children complain of pain in the calf muscles, bones and joints, particularly at night time. This pain is present in both the limbs and is called "growing pains." It is common amongst school going children. It is a benign condition, which outgrows with age as the child reaches adolescence. In case of severe pain, local massage, hot fomentation and analgesics may be required.

19. Heart problems in childhood

***A surgeon while operating on a patient suddenly shouted, "Nurse, quick, get me my anatomy book (an anatomy book is one, which explains the body's layout). ***

They are mainly of two types, congenital (from birth) and acquired ("rheumatic heart disease" described earlier is the commonest in this category). All types of congenital heart problems are by and large, thanks to the modern advances and wonderful cardiac surgeons in India, treatable. For rheumatic heart disease, future prevention is very important which usually consists of giving a monthly injection of long acting penicillin, at least till the child is 18 years old and maybe much longer also. So the parents must without fail take these injections regularly, because if the child has a second attack of rheumatic fever, it may cause more damage to the heart. There may be some turbulent sounds coming from the heart heard by the stethoscope called "heart murmurs". If your doctor detects some murmur in the heart of the child and tells you that it is innocent or benign, there is nothing to worry about. Children frequently have these types of murmurs, even when the heart is completely normal. These are produced due to turbulence of the blood flow across normal heart valves. Many of these murmurs will disappear with time, but even if they persist there is no cause for alarm.

20. Convulsions/coma

***A patient came out of his unconsciousness after many days, thanks to the excellent treatment. One fine day he was declared fit and discharged from the hospital. He was readmitted half an hour later again with unconsciousness. His wife said that going through the hospital bills made this happen. ***

The term to a layman usually implies some spasmodic twitching of the muscles of the body like those of the face, limbs etc. But there are many types of seizures without any muscle twitching. An example is "absence seizures" (common above the age of 5 years) in which the child temporarily loses contact with reality and just has a staring, dazed look. Typically it lasts for a few seconds, after which the child comes out of his "absence" and resumes his normal functioning. The child has loss of memory for the seizure episode; i.e. he is not aware that some time is lost or that he had gone into a trance like state. So seizures needn't always be associated with twitching.

A type of convulsion associated with fever and occurring in the age group of 6 months to 5 years in an otherwise normal child is termed "**Febrile Convulsion**". These fits are benign, always associated with rising fever, subside spontaneously within 10-15 minutes and post-fit, the child is normal. Children will outgrow these fits (they subside, as the child becomes older than 5 years), and they have no ill effects on the development of the child. No investigations are required for such fits and also no long-term treatment with anticonvulsant is required. When the child is having fits, the doctor may give some injection (usually that of a drug called diazepam) to stop the fits. For preventing febrile convulsions, as soon as the child starts having fever, you can give Syrup Paracetamol and Syrup Diazepam to your child (for exact dose and schedule, consult your doctor) and then take the child to your doctor.

Convulsions that are recurrent are termed "Epilepsy". There may be a positive family history of epilepsy (paternal or maternal side). For diagnosing epilepsy and its exact nature, your doctor may order a test called EEG. Fortunately, there are excellent drugs, called anti-convulsants, available to control epilepsy so that the child doesn't suffer from recurrent fits. These drugs are usually to be taken for a period of 3 years. The type of drug and the dose required is decided on an individual basis and your doctor will guide you in it. If the child has been fit free during these 3 years or had only an occasional fit, then chances are good that he may not become an adult epileptic. Some precautions are to be observed for any person suffering from fits. Common sense dictates that the child should not be left unattended (i.e. without supervision) in places, where if he has a fit, there is a danger of physical injury to the child. Obviously, therefore the child should not be allowed to go to high places (e.g. rooftops) alone, should not be allowed near fire or water unattended, should not drive motorcycle alone etc. But he can attend school, play any game he likes, pursue his hobbies etc. The child should not be made to feel inferior to his peers. He should lead as normal a life as possible. Parents should not become over protective but rather have a positive approach towards the disease and inculcate the same in the child. Some of the greatest personalities (whose statures we can't even dream of achieving) like Caesar, Napoleon, and Einstein etc. suffered from epilepsy, which just goes to prove that greatness and excellence has no relation with epilepsy. So, why your child should feel handicapped in any way, if he is suffering from epilepsy?

Some convulsions are secondary to an insult to the brain e.g. meningitis, low blood sugar, calcium etc. Fortunately, by and large, these types of convulsions are transient and lasts a few days only. Once the underlying insult to the brain is treated, the convulsions also regress. Of course for these few days, the child may be put on an anticonvulsant, but usually secondary convulsions don't require long-term therapy. An exception is convulsions secondary to brain trauma, which may require a prolonged anticonvulsant therapy.

21. Worm infestations

Practically all children suffer from it sometime or the other. Worms have been blamed for all type of problems like teeth grinding, loss of appetite, poor weight gain, diarrhoea, chronic or recurrent pain in abdomen, listlessness or irritability in the child etc. Worms usually don't cause all these problems unless the worm load is very heavy. Rather than blaming worms, one should diligently search for other causes. For example if the child is having chronic diarrhoea or pain in abdomen, it is quite possible that it is not due to worms but to some other intestinal problem/ infection. Worms, particularly small thread like worms can cause peri-anal itching, particularly during night-time. Some worms like hookworms suck small amount of blood from the intestines and over a prolonged period of time can cause anaemia in the child. The larvae of some worms migrate through the lungs and at that time they can cause cough and wheezing. Worm infestation is treated nowadays with a single dose therapy, with gratifying results. People believe that worm medicine should not be given in cold weather, should be given only before going to bed etc. These beliefs are not true. Worm medicine can be given at any time. In a country like India, it is advisable to periodically de-worm your child twice a year at 6 month interval. Parents often query that even after giving the worm medicine no worms come out (i.e. was the medicine ineffective?). The medicine is very effective. Worms are seen in the stools only if they have become big. But eggs of the worms and larva cannot be seen by the naked eye, which are also killed by the medicine and comes out in the stools.

22. Diaper rash

The rash can be allergic or due to direct irritation of the skin by the chemicals like acid, ammonia etc. liberated from the urine and stools of the child. This rash may also be due to fungal infection (candida). Depending on the type of rash, specific ointments are prescribed. Some general measures are important. The diapers should be changed frequently. The area of the rash should be kept clean and frequently washed with warm water and soap. If possible, it is preferable to keep the area open to air (i.e. without diapers). Exposure to the air and keeping the area dry hastens the healing of the rash. While cleaning, the raw area should not be rubbed with towel, which might cause more rawness; but instead should be patted dry. If possible, use cotton rather than towel for cleaning.

23. Hernias

***A patient came running out of the operation theatre and made a beeline for the director's office. After having a glass of water and regaining back some of his composure, the reason he cited for "bolting" away from the operation table was: "The nurse told, 'don't worry, it is a simple operation.'" On seeing the puzzled look on the director's face, he said, "You see, the nurse was not telling that to me but to the doctor."* **

An intermittent bulge that appears and disappears is typical of hernias. It is due to coming out (herniation) of some content (e.g. intestine) of the abdomen, most commonly into the scrotum. The treatment is surgical. Parents are sometimes scared of surgery and search for a medical cure. There is no medicine or device that can cure the hernia. Wearing trusses and belts in order to keep the abdominal contents in check may do more harm than good. The operation for hernia is a simple one. One should get it done.

24. Undescended testis

Parents sometimes discover that one or both sides of the scrotum seem empty and they cannot feel any testis in that. In many of these cases the testis has retracted into the abdomen (called "Retractile Testis"). These testes, off and on, automatically descend back into the scrotum and retract back into the abdomen. Testes that have been seen or felt in the scrotum at any time are retractile, and don't require any treatment because it is normal. On the other hand, testes that are truly undescended and lie in the abdomen should be brought into the scrotum by operation. This should be done before the child is 3-4 years old, as the testis may atrophy and lose its function. Sometimes children are born with one testis only. This is of no concern, if the other testis is normal. A single normal testis can carry on the function of reproduction and the person won't be sterile.

Urinary tract infection (UTI): It is quite common in a child. Below the age of 1 year, the incidence is similar in boys and girls. After this it becomes more common in girls. It may present with discomfort and pain in passing urine, passing urine frequently, sudden bed wetting or lack of control over the passing of urine. It may also present with high fever with chills, i.e. shaking with fever. To diagnose UTI, a urine analysis and a urine culture is done. If the urine culture is positive i.e. it grows bacteria, it is a definite evidence that the child has got UTI. The treatment is to give antibiotics, which is usually given for a period of 10 days. One week after the completion of the antibiotic course, a repeat urine check is done to see that no bacteria is grown i.e., the child is free from UTI. If he/she is free from UTI, repeat checks are carried at 3 months interval for a minimum period of 1 year. This is because recurrent i.e. repeated episodes of UTI should be detected and treated early as repeated attacks may lead to damage of the kidneys. But by and large if not neglected and promptly and adequately treated, it is a benign disease with an excellent outcome.

Many children pass white coloured (milky) urine, which if not associated with other complaints like pain, increased frequency of passing urine etc. is usually normal and is due to the presence of phosphates and urates being excreted out in the urine. Similarly, parents complain that the urine which has been passed, say on the floor, leaves a whitish deposit. This is again normal and is due to the reason mentioned above. If ants come near the urine passed and seem to like it, one should check for presence of sugar in the urine, which may sometimes signify a serious disease like diabetes.

Similarly, the colour of urine varies from colourless like water to amber coloured to pale yellow to deep yellow. It usually depends upon the amount of water intake. If water intake is good, the urine will be on the side of pale yellow while if there is decreased water intake, urine tends to become deep yellow (as is seen in fevers, where there is a lot of water loss from the skin due to sweating). However, if in doubt consult a doctor, particularly in case of deep yellow urine, as it may be due to liver disease.

Prevention of UTI: the child should be made to drink plenty of water so as to ensure that he/she passes adequate amounts of urine. It is recommended that the anal opening after the passage of stools should be washed from front to behind rather than in the opposite fashion (as is normally done). This is done to prevent the bacteria of the stools from coming in front and thus infecting the urinary passage (most of the UTI are due to the bacteria of the intestines, which gain entrance via the urinary opening and then ascend upwards to infect the urinary bladder and the kidneys). Thus UTI is mostly an ascending infection as compared to most other infections which are blood borne.

25. Enuresis (Bedwetting)

The child is unable to control urination and

thus voids in the bed, pants etc. Usually bedwetting occurs during night when the child is asleep. A neonate is a natural enuretic and only by the age of 2-3 years is the child able to have some control over his voiding of urine. As the child masters it, he wakes up at night whenever he has the urge to pass urine. Such a child, by and large, is day and night-time dry and only occasionally, he may pass urine in his pants e.g. when he is busy playing or is in a deep sleep. Such rare occasions are normal.

Medical intervention is required only if the child is bedwetting after the age of 5 years. So if your child is bed-wetting say at the age of 4 years, it may just be that he requires some more time to be able to control it. Don't worry about it, as most likely the child will outgrow it with time. Above 5 years, for a bedwetting child, the doctor may prescribe some simple tests like urine examination and culture to rule out any disease of the urinary tract and if none is found (as usually is the case), the child is said to be suffering from "Psychogenic Bed-wetting".

This is the commonest type of bed-wetting and is usually due to conflict and stress during toilet training. For example, if a child of 3 years is unable to control voiding and wets his pants regularly, the parents may scold and humiliate him, undermining his confidence. This adverse psychological effect on the child leads to his being a bedwetter. It is important for the parents to realise that the child is not wetting deliberately. He wants to co-operate and would give anything to overcome the problem. But he has little control over the unconscious feelings that produce the wetting in his sleep. What he needs is more confidence in his ability to control the wetting and this can only be gradually built up with patience and help from the parents. All negative remarks and attitude of the parents should completely stop. Instead the general attitude should be one of encouragement. They can explain to the child that quite a few children have this problem but that practically all of them overcome it with time. They can express their confidence in their child, that he, too, will also surely overcome it. The child should be praised and encouraged if he doesn't bedwet one night or if the frequency of bedwetting is reduced. A chart can be maintained on a "to be reviewed weekly" basis and improvement found during one week over the preceding week should be lauded. The child can also be rewarded by giving him some coveted article like toy etc. on showing improvement. Intermittent failures should be ignored. Making the child drink less fluid after evening may be of some help. Waking the child up every night from deep sleep and making him urinate is of dubious benefit. Drug therapy for this condition is not satisfactory. The medicine may be able to control the bedwetting, but obviously the medication cannot be given for an indefinite period and so when it is stopped, the child again starts bedwetting. Some conditioning alarms are available that ring a bell when the bed is wet and are effective in some cases. **Usually within 6 months of seeking medical opinion, the child is cured irrespective of the type of therapy.**

What was discussed so far was about a child who never was able to control bedwetting (called "Primary Enuresis"). What about those children who had achieved control satisfactorily and now again have started bedwetting (called "Regressive or Secondary BedWetting")? In these cases, the usual cause is some change in the lifestyle and routine of the child or some emotional trauma to the child. Examples are like shifting to a new house, birth of another baby in the family, some tragedy in the family, the child starts his schooling etc. A secondary bedwetter is easier to treat and the problem is usually transient.

26. Eye problems

***An ophthalmologist operated upon both eyes of a patient whose vision was very poor due to cataract. Post operatively, he carefully removed the bandage from the eyes and dramatically asked the patient, "Can you see clearly now?" The patient said, "Show me your bill and then only I will be in a position to tell you whether I can see or not." ***

Four common types of eye problems are discussed below.

i. **Squint:** A condition in which the child appears cross eyed should not be taken lightly, particularly if the child is older than 6 months. If corrected early the results are excellent but if delay occurs, the child may continue to focus and see objects preferentially with one eye in order to avoid the discomfort of double vision. With time the non-used eye may become functionally useless ("blind") with a poor outcome and slim chances of restoring vision in that eye. So parents should always take squint seriously.

ii. **Myopia:** Also called as "short-sightedness", the child can see nearby objects but finds it difficult to focus on far objects, which appear blurred. The first inkling often comes during school going when the child may not be able to see the blackboard clearly, particularly if he is seated some rows behind. The child because of shyness and shame may not complain. So all parents should make it a point to periodically check whether the child's vision is good. Asking the child to read something written on the T.V. (for e.g. "Cartoon Network") at a distance that the parents can just read it clearly can be done at home also. If in any doubt, get the eyes tested. The child may feel ashamed to put on spectacles, as very few children in school wear them and so he is the "odd one" out. His classmates may pass comments that his eye sight is not good, he looks funny in the specs etc., all of which may lead to a sense of inferiority complex in the child at a tender age. Parents should be aware of this and anticipate it. The child should be given reassurance i.e. with specs you look good and grown up, that many adults including the highly successful one and celebrities also wear specs to look elegant.

Patient: "Doctor, I think I need glasses."
Teller: "You certainly do. This is a bank."

iii. **Foreign body in the eye:** The eye should be washed copiously in running tap water, which may remove small foreign particles. If the foreign body is visible and on the white (sclera) of the eye, parents may try to remove it by swiping it away with a moistened cotton applicator. If the foreign body is on the cornea (i.e. the black/brown central part of the eye), do not touch it and seek medical help. If some

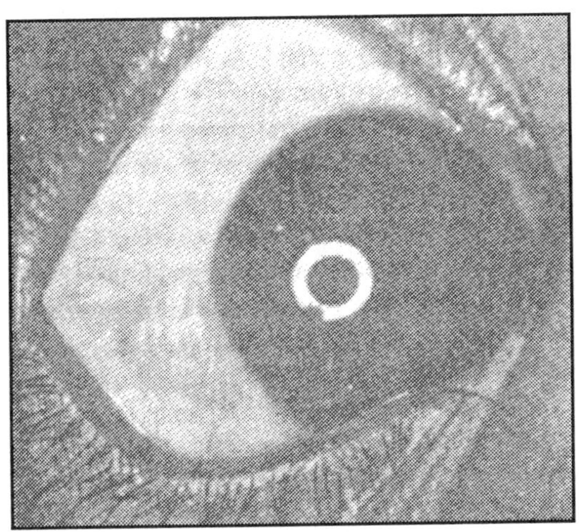

Night blindness: Formation of white ring in the eye as a result of Vitamin-A deficiency.

chemical like acid or alkali or hot oil etc. falls into the eye, the parents should wash the eyes copiously with tap water and seek urgent medical help.

iv. **Night blindness:** If the child sees less at night but well in the day time, it may be due to deficiency of Vitamin-A. The child should be shown to a doctor.

27. Malingering and hysterical conversion reaction

There is a slight difference between the two. In malingering, the child makes up some complaints like stomach ache, headache etc. to escape from a stressful and unpleasant situation e.g. going to school.

In hysteria, the patient may have abnormal behaviour, may be breathing fast and/or may act out a disease she/he has witnessed before e.g. Paralysis (as if the limbs are not moving), fits etc. This is done because the person is either psychologically disturbed or to achieve secondary gains like gaining love, sympathy and attention of the near and dear ones. The person usually feels neglected emotionally and so can have a hysterical conversion reaction.

Parent should be aware of these not so uncommon entities, so that they are not taken by surprise if the doctor tells them so.

CHAPTER 8

ACCIDENTS IN CHILDHOOD

KEY POINTS

- Nothing is more tragic than a healthy child dying of a freak accident. On hindsight, the parents realise that the tragedy could have been averted, if only they had been more careful. An immense feeling of guilt haunts them throughout their lives. For such parents, it is important to know that medical science doesn't put any blame on them. Such mishaps are destined by fate and one should not question the wisdom or the unfathomable ways of the ALMIGHTY. Such mishaps can happen to anyone. Retrospectively it is always easy to be wiser, but can anyone foresee or predict such a tragedy? The answer is an emphatic no.
- Children, particularly below 3 years have little sense of danger or self-preservation and thus are wholly dependent on adult supervision for their safety.
- Guidelines for prevention of accidents are discussed in this chapter. The purpose is "a wake up call" for the parents. I believe the best guideline is common sense of parents, who should have a nose for trouble and a sense of anticipation for a potential mishap.
- The parents cannot act as a 24-hour sentry to their child. Excessive concerns about safety will make them paranoid. The child's freedom and natural instincts will also be stifled. If you surround the child with all types of don'ts, the child is just like a caged animal. In spite of all precautions, you can only reduce the risk but cannot prevent accidents completely. Destiny always has a role to play. So don't have excessive concerns about safety bordering on irrationality or obsession. Just take normal precautions, without stifling the child.

Nothing is more tragic and heart rending than a healthy child dying due to some sort of accident or mishap e.g. the child may consume some adult medicines (poisoning), drown, choke on some object etc. When such a tragedy occurs, on hindsight, parents realise that the tragedy was preventable if only they had been more careful. Many "ifs" and "buts" torture their mind. That the child died due to their "negligence" is the nagging feeling of self-guilt that continues to haunt them throughout their lives. Children, particularly below 3 years, have little sense of danger or self-preservation and thus are wholly dependent on adult supervision for their safety. But sadly, preventable accidents continue to happen.

***A Sanskrit shloka translated into English is as follows: "O doctor, I salute you as the brother of the lord of death (Yamraj) but you are worse because Yamraj takes only life away, while you take away both money and life. ***

I remember a small infant who slipped from her mother's hug, hit his head on the floor (the fall was no more than 3 feet), and subsequently died in spite of our best efforts. This, of course, is a freak accident, for which one cannot blame the mother, but then the most important question is, will the mother reconcile to the fact that it was just an accident and not due to her mistake? She will always keep on blaming herself that if only she had held the child more tightly, this mishap would not have happened.

For all such parents who had the immense misfortune of their child having met such an untimely and tragic accidental death, it is important to know that medical science doesn't put blame at their doorsteps. Such mishaps are something destined by fate and one should not question the wisdom or the unfathomable ways of the ALMIGHTY. Remember that such mishaps can happen to anyone. Retrospectively, it is always easy to be wiser and to realise the mistake, but can anyone foresee or predict it? The answer is an emphatic no. By being careful, you just reduce the chances of a mishap occurring, you cannot eliminate it completely. So parents should strive to cut down the risk percentage for mishaps by taking adequate, precautionary measures.

Another case that comes to my mind is that of a 24-day-old baby, who was prescribed Triaminic drops by their family doctor for common cold and nose block. The mother in the early hours of the morning, when the baby was crying too much, gave him more than the normal dose. The baby was brought to our hospital in a very serious state. It was touch and go for him for 2 days. Fortunately he survived, but the mother developed a phobia for medicines. So after a month or so when she brought the child to me with the complaint of fever, I told her to give the baby 10 drops of paracetamol s.o.s. The next day the mother again visited my chamber saying that paracetamol is not working in bringing the fever down and whole night the child had high fever. On close questioning it was found out that the mother had given only 2 drops, because of her earlier very unpleasant experience! No wonder, fever was not coming down!

This chapter discusses guidelines for prevention of accidents. They are by no means exhaustive. The purpose is "a wake up call" for the parents. I firmly believe that

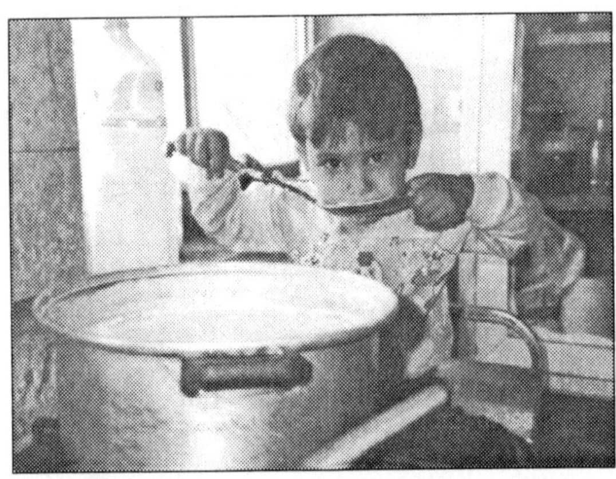

A recipe for an accident? : A 2-year old child sitting on a shelf in the kitchen, drinking milk from a pot on the gas.

the best guideline is common sense of the parents, who should have a nose for trouble and a sense of anticipation. Like for example, if they see a 2 year child moving towards the table, at the edge of which is a cup of hot tea, immediate danger signals should flash through their mind that the child may accidentally pull the tablecloth and thus pour the hot cup of tea on itself. I hope parents will go through these guidelines and judge for themselves, firstly how much they know and, secondly how much they follow practically in their day to day life in ensuring the safety of their child. If they reach to the conclusion that they are careless, wake up!

Obviously parents cannot act as a 24-hour bodyguard to their child. Excessive concerns about safety and sticking to "accident prevention" guidelines in a copybook style and religiously following them will make the parents paranoid. The child's freedom and natural instincts will be stifled and if you surround the child with all types of don'ts, the child is no better than a caged animal. In spite of all the precautions, accidents cannot be prevented completely. You can only reduce the chances of a mishap happening, but cannot eliminate it completely. Fate or destiny always has a role to play. So don't go to excessive lengths regarding accident prevention bordering on irrationality or obsession. Just take simple, sensible precautions, without stifling the child.

PREVENTION OF CHOKING/SUFFOCATION

1. Do not give the child any food that is big in size, particularly round things that the child can put into his mouth as a whole, as there is a danger that the child may choke upon it. This precaution is necessary till the child is old enough to chew or spit out such things (usually 4 years of age). Classical examples are nuts, buttons, beads, popcorn etc. Chop things that are large into small pieces so that the child may not choke upon it.
2. Do not allow a child with food in his mouth to run and play, jostle or bounce him.
3. Be careful with toys. They may have small detachable parts that the child may mouth and choke upon. Better buy the child toys that do not have detachable parts.
4. Be careful in disposing of button batteries. The child may mouth it. Even if it goes into the stomach instead of the windpipe, because of its alkaline nature, it has to be removed.
5. Don't allow the child to put sharp objects particularly sharp pencils in the mouth. Though the child most likely

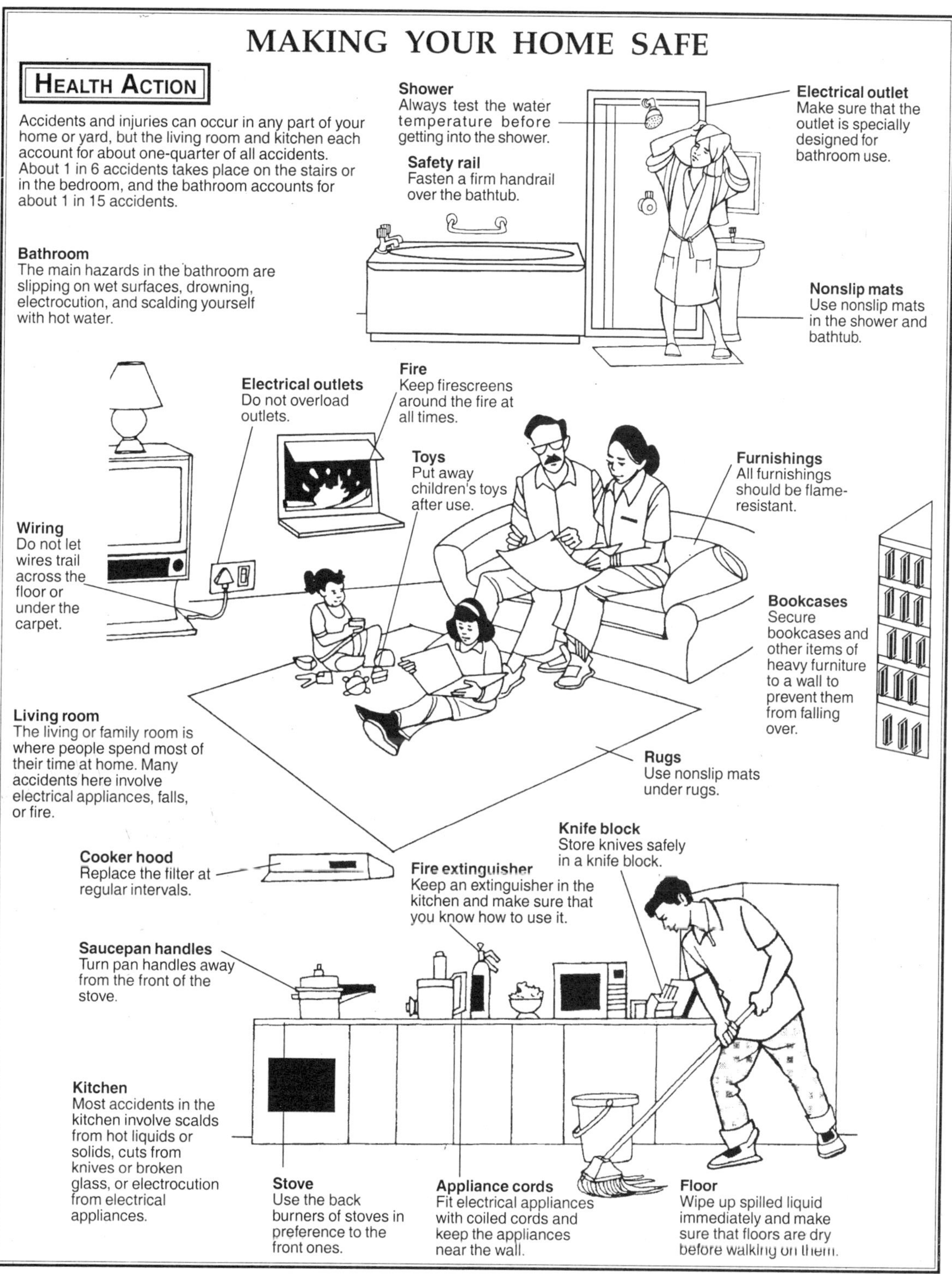
MAKING YOUR HOME SAFE
HEALTH ACTION
Accidents and injuries can occur in any part of your home or yard, but the living room and kitchen each account for about one-quarter of all accidents. About 1 in 6 accidents takes place on the stairs or in the bedroom, and the bathroom accounts for about 1 in 15 accidents.
Bathroom
The main hazards in the bathroom are slipping on wet surfaces, drowning, electrocution, and scalding yourself with hot water.
Shower
Always test the water temperature before getting into the shower.
Safety rail
Fasten a firm handrail over the bathtub.
Electrical outlet
Make sure that the outlet is specially designed for bathroom use.
Nonslip mats
Use nonslip mats in the shower and bathtub.
Electrical outlets
Do not overload outlets.
Fire
Keep firescreens around the fire at all times.
Toys
Put away children's toys after use.
Furnishings
All furnishings should be flame-resistant.
Wiring
Do not let wires trail across the floor or under the carpet.
Bookcases
Secure bookcases and other items of heavy furniture to a wall to prevent them from falling over.
Living room
The living or family room is where people spend most of their time at home. Many accidents here involve electrical appliances, falls, or fire.
Rugs
Use nonslip mats under rugs.
Knife block
Store knives safely in a knife block.
Cooker hood
Replace the filter at regular intervals.
Fire extinguisher
Keep an extinguisher in the kitchen and make sure that you know how to use it.
Saucepan handles
Turn pan handles away from the front of the stove.
Kitchen
Most accidents in the kitchen involve scalds from hot liquids or solids, cuts from knives or broken glass, or electrocution from electrical appliances.
Stove
Use the back burners of stoves in preference to the front ones.
Appliance cords
Fit electrical appliances with coiled cords and keep the appliances near the wall.
Floor
Wipe up spilled liquid immediately and make sure that floors are dry before walking on them.

Dangers to Avoid: Sharp objects in low drawers; polyethylene bags; electrical sockets; protruding pot handles; playing on the roads; hanging tablecloths or mats.

won't choke on it, there is a risk that the sharp point may puncture the area near the tonsils, which can lead to one-sided paralysis of the child.

6. Be on the watch if the child is playing with a plastic bag. He may cover his head and face with it (by pulling down the plastic bag over his face), leading to suffocation.
7. Long strings, threads etc. (particularly when the child is learning to tie some knots), can be dangerous. Accidentally the child may entwine the piece of cord around his neck.

PREVENTION OF BURNS INCLUDING ELECTRICAL

Majority of the burns in a child are scald burns (i.e. those caused by hot liquids). Common offenders are food, beverages and hot geyser water in the bathroom.

1. Never drink anything hot while holding a baby. The baby may accidentally jerk or make some unexpected movement, spilling the contents over him and you.
2. Keep matches, lighters etc. out of reach of the children.
3. Have a fire extinguisher at home.
4. Don't use tablecloths or mats that a child can pull off the table and so cause any hot liquids kept on the table to spill over him.
5. Turn pot handles away so that they don't protrude from the edge of the cooking gas.

Dangers to Avoid: Bottles on low shelves; unsupervised garden pool; climbing on unstable chairs; inadequately fixed stair carpet; teddy bear's eyes; unguarded fires.

6. When you are ironing cloths, never leave it unattended. If the phone rings or you have to do something in the midst of ironing, make sure the iron is out of reach of the child.
7. Always cover the electrical outlets. A child loves to plug and unplug things in the electrical outlets. Tape tightly any joint or naked wire. Replace worn out cables.

PREVENTION OF DROWNING

1. Never leave a child under 3 years unattended, even, in a bathtub. They can drown in that small an amount of water also.
2. Never leave a child unattended near a swimming pool. Children are not "water safe" before the age of 3 years. So start swimming lessons only after that age.
3. Household water storage systems like tanks, drums etc. should be out of reach of your child. Else, the child may lean over them and accidentally topple inside.
4. If your child is diving in swimming pool, make sure that the area where he dives has adequate water levels. People have been killed (by head injury) while diving in too shallow waters and banging their heads against the floor of the swimming pool.

PREVENTION OF HEAD TRAUMA

1. Always keep the side rails up in a crib.
2. The staircases and the rooftops should have side railing.
3. Teach the child to cross the road safely at the age of 5-6 years. Before that, never leave the child without you holding him in areas of traffic.
4. Do not teach a child to ride a bicycle before the age of 7-8 years. Ideally the child should have a helmet on when riding a bicycle.
5. Baby walkers, though convenient, are responsible for many accidents as the walker can trip. The child may topple over and bang his head. So use them with your close attention on it.

Reaching out for the bottle: Note the feet of the child, the open drawer (to get support of one hand), the other hand reaching out for the bottle, which is still some cms. away. A perfect recipe for an avoidable accident.

6. While riding on a scooter or car, always use some restrain for the child like seat belts. On a scooter the child can be strapped to the mother with some sort of belt or harness.

PREVENTION OF POISONING

***One person tried to commit suicide and took sufficient amount of a medicine, which exceeded the lethal dose. Yet miraculously, he survived. His wife remarked, "O God, why the tablet was not of the mentioned strength." ***

1. Keep all medicines out of reach of the children. Open tablets, capsules etc. should be disposed. Tightly screw the cap of all medicine bottles.
2. Discard all old, used medicines.
3. Never use medicines from an unlabelled or unreadable container.
4. Store medicines in their original containers and never in food or beverage containers.
5. Drugs and medicines are not the only source of poisoning. Chemicals, insecticides, petrol, kerosene, all sorts of house cleaners etc. are things which the child can ingest. Keep them in a safe place out of reach of the children.

Parents should take pains in taking precautions to prevent a mishap. A casual attitude and a carefree approach that nothing can happen to my child is to be condemned. Remember that no one can predict when and where a tragedy will strike. So, parents should keep their eyes and ears open, use their common sense and spend some time and energy in making the child's surroundings "accident free."

FIRST-AID

Key Points

1. Children suffer from cuts and bruises, bleeding, ingestion of toxic products etc., as a part of their carefree and exploratory lifestyle. Because of this, parents should strive to know the basics of first aid and dealing with common emergencies.
2. The basics involve a lot of DO'S but also include a lot of DON'TS i.e. measures the parents should not undertake unless they have received training in that. Such emergencies which should not be dealt by the parents and require professional and expert care should be taken to a doctor immediately or at least his opinion sought telephonically.

Discussed in this chapter are the common injuries suffered by a child and their first aid management.

Eye

***An eye specialist had his door to the nursing home designed in the shape of a human eye with pupil, iris etc. A doctor commented, "Thank God, he is not a gynaecologist." ***

Foreign body in the eye: The eyes should be washed copiously with running tap water, which will usually remove the small foreign particles. If the foreign body is on the conjunctiva (the portion of the eye that is white) and is visible, parents may try to remove it by a moist cotton tipped applicator, by gently sweeping the foreign particle along with it out of the eye. Any foreign body, which is on the cornea i.e. the pigmented central portion of the eye, should not be touched. Similarly penetrating eye injuries should not be handled in any way by the parents, but expert consultation sought as soon as possible.

Chemical Burns: Sometimes chemicals like acids, alkalis, hot oil etc. may spurt in the eye. Parents should wash copiously the eye with running tap water for at least 15-30 minutes and in the mean time seek professional help. No solution or eye drops should be used without expert advice.

Nose

Epistaxis: It means bleeding from the nose and is a common and recurrent complaint, particularly during childhood. The common causes are nose infections i.e. viral upper respiratory tract infection and nose picking. Whatever the cause, the situation is quite alarming to the parents, many of whom panic, particularly if it is their first experience. Actually it is by and large a benign condition and easily controllable, even at home.

First of all the child should be made to sit leaning forward. The commonest mistake is to make the child lie down. By doing so, blood doesn't come out from the nose and so the parents are quite happy that the bleeding has stopped, but actually it is just a false sense of security, because the blood is trickling backwards in the throat now, which the child goes on swallowing. After sometime, the child may vomit out this blood, which will enhance the anxiety of the parents. So it is better to be aware of the bleeding, rather than being blissfully ignorant about it by making the child lie down.

After the child is in the sitting position, apply pressure with the thumb over the bleeding nostril so as to compress it against the midline nasal septum for 5 minutes (a similar method of compression is used when one wants to blow his nose in which case he puts his thumb against one nostril and then blows out the other nostril).

If this is not able to control the bleeding, then a cloth soaked in ice water and applied to the nostril externally (not to be put inside the nostril) with the same technique of compression of the nostril as described above will usually stop the bleeding i.e. in this, the cloth is put between the thumb and the nostril. Cold constricts the blood vessels and so helps in stopping the bleeding.

If still bleeding doesn't stop, take the child to the doctor with compression still applied.

To prevent recurrent nosebleeds, the child should be instructed not to do nose picking. The room air should not be dry. Humidification of the air that the child breathes decreases the incidence of nosebleeds. Another useful advice is to apply a lubricant like Vaseline inside the nose by cotton tipped applicator twice daily for a month, to keep the nasal mucosa lubricated.

Nosebleeds are by and large not serious and though the quantity of blood lost may seem to be large, actually it is not so. Nosebleed is certainly not a reason to panic and can be controlled quite easily. The child never usually loses a quantity of blood that can make his condition serious and endanger his life.

Foreign Body in the Nose: Parents should exercise restraint. Though there is a lot of anxiety and an urge to somehow remove the foreign body by any means quickly, the parents should remain calm and not take matters in their hands. They may worsen the situation by pushing the foreign body backwards and therefore make it all the more difficult to retrieve afterwards. A foreign body in the nose is not an emergency and there is plenty of time to take the child to a doctor.

Nasal Trauma: The nose is a vulnerable part of the face and liable to be hit by ball, fall, fist etc. The child may have a swelling and bluish discoloration of the nose where he has been injured. Local application of ice can be done to reduce the swelling and if the nose is bleeding, then measures mentioned above should be undertaken. Under no circumstances should an effort made to manipulate or try to set back in place the disfigured or crooked nose secondary to trauma.

Ear

Trauma: An interesting study shows that parents are responsible for nearly 50% of ear trauma, usually in the form of injury to the eardrum. Parents commonly put cotton tipped applicators inside the ear for cleaning the ear, which leads to injury. The ears of a child don't require periodic cleansing. Instillation of oil/glycerine in the ear is a much better alternative. The softened wax is expelled out spontaneously.

Foreign Body: A foreign body in the ear is not an emergency and therefore the parents should refrain from doing any manipulations. It is always better to take the child to an ENT specialist. The only exception is when a live insect enters the ear and causes a lot of buzzing, in which case it may be killed by putting oil or alcohol in the ear.

Mouth

Burns: This can be caused by the child accidentally swallowing hot liquids or can also be caused by the accidental ingestion of chemicals like detergents, bleaching powder, potassium permanganate granules, drain cleaners, phenyl, and toilet cleaners etc., all of which are either acidic or alkaline in nature. Soap ingestion is benign.

The parents should not try to make the child vomit. Whenever the child swallows anything toxic, the immediate urge of the parents is to induce vomiting, either by putting a finger deep inside the mouth or by making the child drink water with a lot of salt in it. These methods are dangerous in the case of ingestion of acids or alkalis. As first aid, parents should give the child plain water or milk to drink, the quantity of which should not exceed 15ml/kg (because it may then itself cause vomiting by bulk effect on the stomach); so as to dilute the caustic and take him urgently to a doctor. Parents should never give weak acids like vinegar etc. in case of an alkali ingestion and weak alkali like baking soda in case of an acid ingestion. Though the idea theoretically appears attractive (that the acid and alkali will neutralise each other); practically it is dangerous as a lot of heat is produced during neutralisation and temperatures may even reach up to 100° C inside the stomach. This can itself cause a serious burn and may perforate the stomach or the food pipe.

Trauma: The most common form of trauma is dental. Sometimes the tooth may be avulsed from its socket. Under such circumstances, the best thing to do is to clean it with water and try to gently put it back in the socket, before taking the child to the dentist. If this is not possible then the teeth after cleaning should be transported to the dentist immersed in water or milk. This way the viability of the tooth is maintained and the chances of its uptake i.e. the tooth being successfully replaced back in the socket are good. After a gap of 2 hours, the tooth may no longer be viable. (The same principle applies when an organ like a finger or a hand is severed due to trauma. In these cases, the severed organ should be put in a clean plastic container, surrounded on all sides by lots of ice and transported to the nearest hospital.)

Poisonings

The ideal thing is prevention. Potentially toxic things like adult medicines etc. should be kept well out of reach of the child. But surprisingly, this very obvious and common sense fact is overlooked in a vast number of cases, as is evident by the number of children brought to the emergency department of the hospital with some sort of poisoning.

After the consumption of anything toxic, if you can reach a doctor within 10-15 minutes, then it is best to go to him as soon as possible. In case medical facilities are not available at hand, the only first aid that parents can give is to induce vomiting. Remember inducing vomiting after 2 hours of ingestion is seldom of any use and should not be attempted if such a delay has occurred.

Also do not induce vomiting under the following circumstances:

1. If the patient is unconscious or convulsing.

2. In case of ingestion of acids, alkalis or hydrocarbons like kerosene, petrol etc.

How to induce vomiting?

Caution: The parents should do it only in case medical facilities are not at hand and a doctor cannot be contacted even telephonically. If you can contact a doctor on phone, then tell him the nature of the poisoning, how long before has the poison been consumed etc. and then follow his advice. Only in the absence of any medical guidance, should vomiting be induced by the parents, keeping all precautions mentioned above in mind.

The medicine of choice for induction of vomiting is Syrup of Ipecac, but its availability is very limited in India; while in western countries all parents are advised to keep this syrup at their homes. Syrup of ipecac is given in the following doses:

< 1 year	:	10 ml
1 - 10 years	:	15 ml
> 10 years	:	30 ml

Since it is rarely available in India, the best way to make the child vomit is to make the child drink soap water in India (15 - 30 ml of liquid hand soap or powder for washing clothes in a small amount of water). Do not induce vomiting by giving hypertonic salt solutions as cases of salt poisoning due to it have been reported.

N.B. : The child may inhale cosmetic powder with serious consequences. The talcum powder is in the form of a very fine powder and if inhaled, it can spread as a thin sheet all over the lungs thus seriously hampering oxygenation of the blood. Parents should be careful while handling talcum powders and not let a child play with it.

Articles Ingested with no or Low Toxicity (No treatment required)

Ballpoint ink	Hair dyes	Bar soap, bathing soap
Hair oils	Battery (dry cell)	Mascara
Candles	Toothpaste	Chalk
Cigarettes	Clay (modelling)	Water colours
Crayons	Adhesives (glue)	Teething rings
Detergents (anionic)	Slaked lime	Eye makeup
Dry indoor paint	Hand lotion and cream	Latex emulsion paint
Lipstick	House lizards in food	Newspaper
Fertilisers (non-nitrate)	Pencils (lead and colouring)	Shampoo
Shaving lotions and cream	Shoe polish	Thermometers

Things of Low Toxicity (removal/ treatment necessary if large amounts consumed)

After shave lotions	Body conditioners	Colognes
Deodorants	Fabric softeners	Hair dyes and sprays
Indelible markers	Perfumes	Suntan lotions
Nail polish	Nail polish remover	Skin lighteners
Bleaching lotions	Hair vitalizer	Toothpaste (fluoride)

Skin

Skin can be contaminated with poisons, both corrosive and non-corrosives. The treatment is washing the affected area copiously with a lot of water. A special mention is to be made about skin contamination with organophosphorus compounds e.g. compounds like insecticides, tick-20. They can be significantly absorbed through the skin and hence the skin should be washed thoroughly with soap and water for at least 30 minutes. The person who is washing should take care that he himself doesn't get contaminated with the poison.

Burns

A common injury; there are 5 common types of burn injuries:

1. By hot liquids or gases (like steam): also called scald burns.
2. By hot solids: like burn by touching a hot iron.
3. Electrical burns: where a current passes through the body and cause burns at the site of entry and exit of current. Burns due to lightning can also be included under this category.
4. Chemical or caustic burns: By the falling of corrosive material on the skin.
5. Flame burns: where the clothing catches fire by a flame or the person suffers burns due to direct contact with a source of flame like gas stoves etc.

FIRST AID DURING BURNS

It is estimated that approximately 50% of patients dying due to burns do not die as a direct result of the burn injury but rather due to indirect effect, out of which the most common is inhalation injury to the lungs. The smoke and carbon dioxide/carbon monoxide emission from the fire suffocates the person, who dies as a result of lack of oxygen.

Given below are some practical tips when faced with a fire or a burn:

1. If the clothing catches fire, do not run, rather fall down on the ground and roll. The person giving first aid should immediately wrap such a person with a blanket so as to choke off the air supply to the flames, which thus gets extinguished.
2. If there is a fire indoors with lot of smoke, crawl beneath the smoke. The reason is simple. Smoke being lighter tends to rise up. Remember that nearly 50% of deaths are due to smoke inhalation rather than due to the direct effects of fire.
3. Smouldering clothes / clothes covered with hot liquids should be gently removed.
4. In hot tar burns, the tar should be removed by application of mineral oil or any hydrocarbon solvent, which dissolves the tar. An alternative method is to apply ice over the tar. It makes the tar hard and non-sticky, after which it can be easily peeled off the skin.
5. Jewellery, particularly rings, bracelets or any circular object encircling the body should be removed immediately, because post-burn, there is a lot of swelling. Therefore these objects may act as constricting bands and interfere with blood supply to that part of the body.

6. Cold compresses (and not ice) should be applied to the area of burn or alternatively the burnt area should be washed under free flowing tap water. Do not apply any ointments over the burns, but rather wrap the patient in a clean, dry sheet and take him to the hospital.
7. Any vesicle (i.e. the clear fluid filled swelling post burn) should never be pricked.
8. Electrical burns mainly due to an inquisitive child poking something in the electrical sockets are by and large not dangerous, contrary to popular belief. On the other hand, high tension wires (those running between electric poles) are dangerous. In case a person comes in contact with such a wire, the best way to dismantle his contacting body area is by a dry stick. Never try to catch hold of the child or the adult and yank him away. You will also get electrocuted with the same disastrous consequences as the original unfortunate victim.

HEAT PROSTRATION

In India, where summers are extremely hot with the mercury climbing to 46-48° C; emergencies due to heat prostration are very common, particularly if one is doing manual work outdoors and undergoes a lot of exertion in the open blazing sun. There are two types of ill-effects due to extreme heat:

1. **Heat Exhaustion:** Patient continues to sweat in this condition (as compared to the entity called "heat stroke" described below). The patient loses a lot of water and salt from his body due to the continuous ongoing perspiration. As a result the patient feels weak, dizzy, and may have blackening before the eyes and fall down on the ground in a state of disorientation. Gradual acclimatisation to the strong heat and a liberal intake of salt and water can prevent this. Water intake by itself, though helpful, may not be adequate and should be supplemented by salt. It is not a serious condition. Immediate first aid measures include taking the patient to shade, loosening his clothing, blowing cool breeze over him by fanning and most importantly, offering him plenty of water and salt supplementation.
2. **Heat Stroke**: In this, the patient's body temperature rises very rapidly and is usually over 40° C i.e. 106° F. The tendency to sweating is impaired and thus you have a unique combination of a person with a high fever and yet dry! (not sweating). The patient will be in a state of deranged sensorium and delirious. The first aid measure consists of removing the patient in a cool place and then showering the patient with a stream of cold water along with fanning. Urgent arrangements should be made to take the patient to the nearest hospital, as the sickness may prove dangerous. On the way to the hospital also, the above first aid measures should be carried out.

BITES (Snakes, Scorpions)

1. **Snake bites :** Most of the snakes are non-poisonous. Therefore a feeling of

panic should be replaced with a calm and cool approach. Even if the snake is poisonous, medical care today can save 95-99% of poisonous snake bite victims provided they reach the hospital without much delay.

As immediate first aid, the following points are important:

- *Nearly half of the deaths due to snakebites occur due to the intense fear of impending doom. An utter sense of helplessness and resignation preys on the patient's mind. Therefore a very important aspect of first aid is "solid" reassurance to the patient to allay his intense anxiety. Some form of sedative to allay the anxiety is also useful and can be given to the patient.*
- *Contrary to popular belief, the patient should not be kept awake and walking; instead he should be made to lie down, the bitten part should be at a lower level than the rest of his body and immobilised. The patient should be encouraged to relax and go to sleep.*
- *Incising opens the bitten part to ensure a free flow of blood in the hope that the snake venom will be washed out "with the free flowing blood" has been found to be of little value. Similarly sucking the bitten part in the belief that you will suck out the snake venom and then spit it out is no longer recommended. So don't do them.*
- *Applying ice over the bitten part or giving electrical shock to the bitten part is also harmful and should not be done.*
- *The only thing, which should be done, is to tie a tourniquet (a tourniquet is a circular band applied around the arms or the legs and in emergencies can be made of any material including a piece of cloth). It should not be tied tightly. An acceptable way to judge the "tightness" of the tourniquet is that you should be able to pass a finger beneath it quite easily (the tourniquet should be loosened every 10 minutes and retied). Numerous cases have been seen where the patient has lost his whole limb due to the choking of the blood supply by the tourniquet. This happens because the bitten limb tends to swell very rapidly. Thus a tourniquet which initially was loose enough now becomes a very tight constricting band. Hence the need to open and retie the tourniquet every 10 minutes.*
- *Shift patient urgently to the nearest hospital where further treatment can be given.*

2. **Scorpion Bites :** The same general measures as discussed above for snakebites apply with the exception that local application of ice is recommended as it helps in relieving the pain a lot.
3. **Bites due to wasps, hornets, bees**: They are by and large harmless, except in occasional cases who are hypersensitive to the sting in which case they may start having swelling of the lips, will complain of light-headedness and breathing difficulties. Such patients should be urgently rushed to the hospital. Apart from these cases, the best first aid is to apply meat tenderiser locally and if it is not available, to apply papain powder locally, which causes rapid relief of pain.
4. **Bites (animals and humans):** The bitten part due to animals (common offenders being dogs, monkeys) or human beings should be thoroughly and copiously washed with a running

stream of tap water for at least 15-30 minutes. You can then apply a mild antiseptic over it like spirit or betadine. Do not try to cover the bitten part, but after this first aid, take the patient to a doctor immediately, the major concern being the risk of developing tetanus or rabies. The doctor will decide as to what further steps should be taken.

***Surgeons hate the physicians very much for their talking about various, endless theories and ifs and buts regarding a disease. Surgeons don't talk but cut. One day they together committed some criminal negligence and the patient died. When asked by the judge what their last wish was before hanging, the physician replied, "I want to give a lecture on my favourite subject for 1 hour." The surgeon said, "Hurry and hang me fast before this fellow opens his mouth." ***

CHOKING

This may be a life-threatening emergency and every second is precious. In choking, a thing (food bolus or any foreign body like marble etc.) that the child has put into his mouth sometimes may go into the windpipe. As a result there is a partial or complete obstruction of the windpipe and the child is deprived of Oxygen. The usual history is that the child will have an excessive bout of coughing in an attempt to expel the foreign body out, failing which the colour of the lips and tongue of the child may turn blue. In most cases, the child is able to eject the foreign body out and usually no intervention is required. But if the child is having breathing problems and the colour turns blue or ashen; it is a very serious emergency. There are certain don'ts that the parents should never attempt.

- *Never attempt a blind finger sweep of the throat of the child in an attempt to remove the foreign body. Your finger may push the object even downwards and may convert a partial obstruction of the windpipe into a complete one.*
- *The following manoeuvre (described in detail below) should be undertaken only if the child is showing no breathing and is aphasic (i.e. cannot bring any sound from his throat or in other words cannot vocalise at all). Under no circumstance should it be tried if the child is having some respiratory efforts. If you try it in a child who is having some breathing of his own you may dislodge the foreign body and convert a partial obstruction into a complete one, with fatal results.*

THE MANOEUVRE

It is different in children under 1 year and those above 1-year.

- ***Child less than one year**: Give 4 blows on the back of the child followed by 4 blows to the front of the child's chest. The blows are given with the heel of the hand. The child is positioned face downwards on the rescuer's arm, so that the face is lower than the rest of the body. After giving these blows, the child's mouth should be opened and the back of the throat examined for any foreign body. If visualised it can be removed by forceps or even by a "scoop" of the finger (remember here you are able to visualise the object and therefore it is not blind finger sweeping, which as mentioned above is contra indicated). In case the object is not visualised, then the rescuer should give artificial respiration to the child (described below) and then repeat the same sequence of events.*

Back blows (top) and chest thrusts (bottom) to relieve foreign-body airway obstruction in the infant.

- ***Child more than one year:*** *In this case, instead of chest thrusts, abdominal thrusts are used. The child is made to lie down on his back with the head end lower than the rest of the body. The heel of one hand is kept on the abdomen between the navel and the end of the breastbone. The heel of the other hand is placed on top of the first hand and a thrust is given in an upward and inward direction. 6 rapid thrusts are recommended after which the mouth is visualised as stated above. If the object is not seen, artificial respiration is given and the sequence is repeated. Abdominal thrusts can also be given in a standing position with the rescuer standing behind the victim.*

Abdominal thrusts with victim standing or sitting (conscious).

ARTIFICIAL RESPIRATION

The best way to give artificial respiration is mouth to mouth. The patient is made to lie down on a flat surface. Firstly the rescuer should position himself at the head end of the patient and do what is called "jaw thrust". In this, the rescuer puts both his thumbs below the angle of the jaws, and then lifts both the jaws forward by

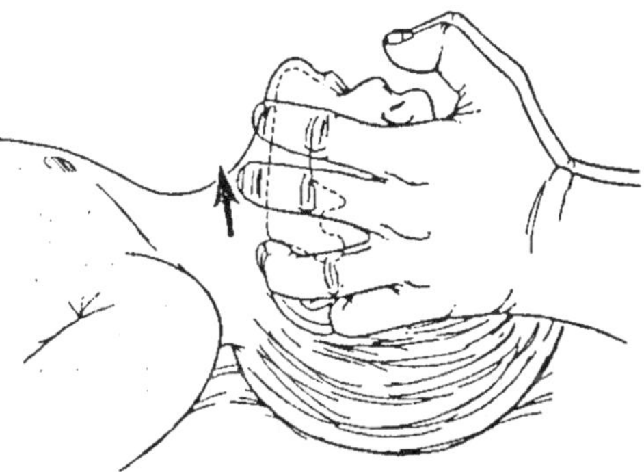

Combined jaw thrust-spine stabilization manoeuvre for the paediatric trauma victim.

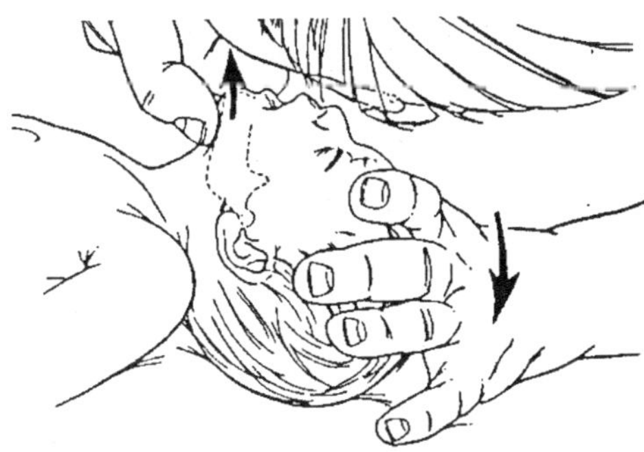

Opening the airway with the head tilt-chin lift manoeuvre. One hand is used to tilt the head, extending the neck. The index finger of the rescuer's other hand lifts the mandible outward by lifting on the chin. Head tilt should not be performed if cervical spine injury is suspected.

applying steady pressure in an upward direction. (Chin lift and head tilt is another way of making the airway patent). Once this is done, the rescuer comes to the side of the patient and with one hand pinches the nose of the patient tightly shut. With the thumb of the other hand on the chin of the patient, he opens the mouth of the patient slightly. After this he puts his own mouth over the patient's mouth so as to completely make an air tight seal. Then he blows air into the patient's mouth. His eyes should be looking at the patient's chest and as he blows in air, the patient's chest should rise as it does in normal breathing. If it doesn't rise, either the pressure that the rescuer is using in blowing the air is less or the seal between the lips is not air tight; as a result of which air is escaping from there rather than going into the patient's lungs. Once the chest rises, the rescuer should terminate his blowing in of the air and open the nose of the patient by taking his hand off it. The patient will passively exhale as can be judged by the downward movement of the risen chest wall. Once this is accomplished, the rescuer should again seal the nose of the patient and blow in the air. There is no need to take the mouth off the patient's mouth, because then the rescuer will have to make an air tight seal between the lips again.

The rate of artificial respiration should be 30 breaths/min for a child and 20 breaths/minute for an adult. Artificial respiration (i.e. mouth to mouth) is also of prime importance in a nearly drowned patient or in one who has suffocated due to inhalation of some noxious fumes, smoke etc.

These things require practical training and parents keen on learning artificial respiration and other life saving measures should enrol themselves in courses on these.

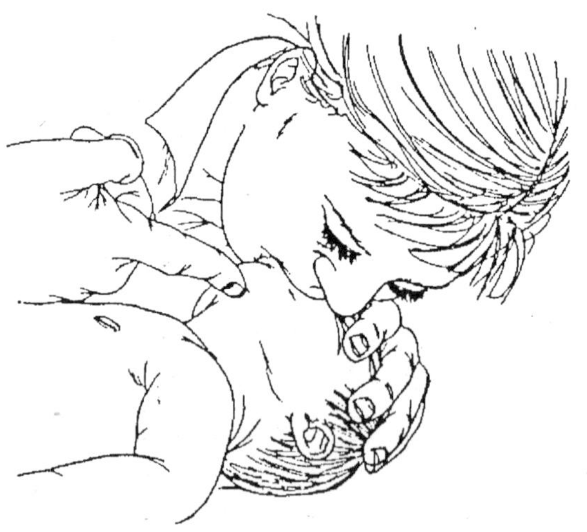

Rescue breathing in an infant. The rescuer's mouth covers the infant's nose and mouth, creating a seal. One hand performs head tilt while the other hand lifts the infant's jaw. Avoid head tilt if the infant has sustained head or neck trauma.

Rescue breathing in a child. The rescuer's mouth covers the mouth of the child, creating a mouth-to-mouth seal. One hand maintains the head tilt; the thumb and forefinger of the same hand are used to pinch the child's nose.

FIRST AID IN CUTS AND BRUISES

Children suffer, off and on, from minor scratches, abrasions, bruises etc. These usually are minor. If the wound is having dirt, parents should clean it with soap and water and then apply some antiseptic like dettol, betadine, spirit etc. followed by sterile dressing. In dirty wounds, risk of contracting tetanus is there and therefore the child should be taken to a doctor; who will give a shot of tetanus toxoid, unless the child has been fully immunised against it.

Sometimes wounds may be big, lacerated or gaping in nature and bleed a lot, causing anxiety in the parent's minds. Actually it is quite simple to control bleeding. The golden principle is use of pressure. Put clean cotton, handkerchief or any piece of clean cloth over the bleeding source and tightly compress it with your hands. Sometimes the cloth you have put may get soaked right through and blood may start oozing from it also. There is no need to panic. Over the soaked cloth, put another clean cloth and again apply firm and steady pressure over it. Never remove the soaked cloth and replace it with another cloth. Instead go on layering one piece of cloth over the other. Keep the pressure maintained for at least 8-10 minutes before you ease it to see whether the bleeding has stopped; i.e. the soakage of the cloth by blood has decreased to a great extent. Even if the bleeding has stopped, don't remove the cloth covering over the wound. Instead take the patient to the nearest medical centre.

FRACTURES

The only first aid required is to minimise motion of the fractured parts to lessen the excruciating pain. Splinting the fractured part does this. A splint can be anything, which is stiff. Usually the most common material used is a piece of broad wood. The splint should ideally be also supporting the joints before and the joint after the fracture, in addition to the fractured site. For example in a suspected fracture of the forearm, the splint should extend beyond the wrist (i.e. the joint before) and the elbow (i.e. the joint after the fractured part). Don't try to manipulate the bones or "straighten" them or "fix" them. Instead put the splint parallel to the fractured part and then wrap both the fractured part and the splint together with clothes. For practical purposes, even three handkerchiefs, one each tied around the two ends and one in the middle will suffice. During transport to the hospital take care that the fractured part is kept as motionless as possible and not jostled too much.

In any case of a trauma patient, while handling the patient, take great care that you don't 1) extend or flex his neck 2) the spine i.e. the backbone should not undergo any motion (flexion, extension or rotation). In other words, the patient should be lifted by at least 4 persons in the same state that he was lying on the ground, particularly avoiding any motion of the neck or backbone relative to the rest of the body. Otherwise it can lead to an injury or severing of the spinal cord and result in paralysis.

CHAPTER 9

CRYING PATTERN IN A CHILD

KEY POINTS

- **Crying:** This is one of the most common, perplexing and irritating dilemmas faced by the parents as the child is unable to communicate why he is crying.
- **Sensitivity:** There are some babies who are extra sensitive during the first few weeks and require a lot of cuddling. The parents should keep their presence of mind and cool, particularly during the night and not get angry with their baby, for it only worsens matters.
- **Infantile Colic:** This condition begins at the age of 2-4 weeks and subsides by 3-4 months. The baby typically starts crying in the evenings. The cry may last for hours and is resistant to the usual soothing methods. It is a very testing time for the parents, as the baby cries for hours together in a stereotyped fashion day after day. Worse, there is no guaranteed method to get rid of it. The parents have to wait till the child becomes 4 months +, when the condition subsides regardless of the management strategy. The parents require more counselling than the baby, for whom this is a harmless condition.
- **Tackling crying:** The best thing to do is to admit your feelings of irritation and laugh it out with your spouse. Laughter and a sense of humour is the best antidote for stress and irritability. Parents should also realise that the baby is not doing it deliberately. If she is crying, there is always a genuine and valid reason behind it. She is too small to do it purposely so as to be mad at you, to throw tantrums or use crying as a means to "irritate" you.

Crying is a baby's way of telling you he needs something - that something is not quite right. In the first few weeks and months, crying is your baby's main way of communicating with you. There are a lot of myths surrounding crying: that he is crying because he is 'naughty' or because he wants to be picked up and that you will 'spoil' your baby if you do so. Another myth is that a certain amount of crying is good for young babies because it 'exercises their lungs' and makes them "mentally tougher" if not attended to immediately. Parents believe that if they respond immediately to crying of a baby, the baby may become "spoiled." Remember a baby below the age of 4 months cannot be spoiled and so should be attended to with all love and attention whenever he/she cries. Research has proved that mothers, who responded quickly to their babies' cries in the early months, were the ones whose babies cried significantly less in the second half of their first year. They found that from about 4 months onwards, babies whose crying had been ignored earlier tended to cry more. Prompt response to the baby's distress during the first six to eight months is important because it helps build a trusting relationship between mother and baby.

Crying is one of the most perplexing and irritating dilemmas faced by parents. A child till the age of approximately 2 years cannot verbalise and explain the reasons for his crying. So, the parents are at a loss as to why the baby is crying. Even the doctors find it difficult to pinpoint the cause of crying. If the baby goes on crying and is not soothed by the efforts of the parents, it really becomes a tense situation for them. First of all, they don't know why the baby is screaming his head off and secondly the baby is not getting any relief. Obviously, the first thought that comes to the mind is that the child is having pain somewhere, which is quite often true. But there are a number of other reasons also as to why the baby cries. Some of the common causes are mentioned below.

COMMON CAUSES FOR CRYING

1. Normal Crying Pattern of a Newborn

New-borns cry at night for the initial 4-6 weeks and sleep during the day. This is just the opposite of what adults do (called "circadian rhythm.") It is very disturbing to the parents because they can't get proper sleep during the night time. However they should realise that it is not the baby's fault but just a continuation of the intra-uterine pattern. During fetal life, the mother's activities during the daytime have a rocking effect on the fetus and thus lull him to sleep. During night the opposite happens. This pattern persists after the baby is born and only by 4-6 weeks is the baby able to change and fit its sleep rhythm to the adult pattern.

2. Crying During Passing Urine/Stool

She may cry and strain temporarily while passing urine or stool (parents may misinterpret this as the baby having some problem in her urination or stooling, while **actually it is normal**). If the stool is very hard or the baby is having dysentery (loose stools with mucus and/or blood), then the baby may cry due to pain while passing stools. Similarly, if the baby has urinary infection, he may have pain while passing urine and may cry. But in the majority of cases, in a small baby, it is normal if the baby strains, groans or cries while passing stool/urine.

3. Hunger

This is the most common reason, and can be easily dealt with by feeding. Particularly, during the first few months, the most common cause of crying is hunger, which of course most of the parents learn to recognise over a period of time. Also, the natural impulse of a mother, whenever her baby is crying, is to offer milk to it. If the baby is crying due to hunger, it will suck vigorously and be satisfied.

There are two exceptions to this. Firstly, even if the baby is hungry, her mood should be good! The baby may have been left unattended and hungry for a length of time that exhausts her patience. Examples are when the parents have to prepare milk in a bottle that is not washed. During this time, the baby may go on crying with hunger. When finally you offer milk to her, though she is hungry, she is also angry! So she may balk at it initially. However if you gently persist and say soothing words to the baby, take her in your lap and caress her, it is usually enough to calm her! Then she will start sucking nicely.

Another cause may be that though the baby is hungry, yet for some reason it is unable to have a smooth, uninterrupted sucking of milk. Examples are when the nose of the baby is blocked (the baby will have to leave the nipple intermittently to breathe through the mouth) or the baby is having cough (she has to leave the milk whenever she wants to cough). The hole of the nipple may be too big (too much milk may flow, giving her a sensation of choking. She may even have a bout of coughing if some milk goes into her windpipe) or too small (she has to strain and suck a lot to get the milk). The hole of the nipple may become clogged with some milk/sugar particle (so that the baby in spite of sucking does not get milk). A change in milk formula and hence the taste of the milk may also affect her. Whatever the reasons, a baby who is unable to have a smooth supply of milk will become angry and irritable and thus cry. The parents must keep all this in mind before reaching to the conclusion that the crying of the baby is due to a cause other than hunger.

4. Pain

The baby may cry if the gas in her stomach has been incompletely eructed out due to less burping/no burping after her milk intake. So, parents should burp their baby properly. Pick him up, hold him over your shoulder and pat his back. The parents should also check whether any external factor is causing the baby discomfort (e.g. there may be something pricking the baby or the bedding may not be comfortable). Bites of ants and mosquitoes may make the baby cry. The baby can't scratch herself to relieve itching and so parents have to scratch and massage the affected part. Another common reason is pain of the ears, particularly if the baby is suffering from cold and cough.

*** A couple went to the hospital to have a baby. The doctor told them that he had invented a new machine that would automatically transfer a portion of the mother's labour pain* *to the father. Both the husband and wife were in favour of it. So the doctor set the knob at 10% for starters, explaining that even 10% was probably more pain than the father had ever experienced before. As labour progressed, the doctor adjusted the machine to 20% pain transfer.*

The husband was still feeling fine. At this, they decided to try for 50%. The husband continued to feel quite well. Since it was obviously helping out his wife considerably, he encouraged the doctor to transfer ALL the pain to him.

The wife delivered a healthy baby with virtually no pain. She and her husband were ecstatic.

When they got home that afternoon, they found the milkman dead on the porch! **

5. Heat and Cold

If the temperature of the surrounding air is uncomfortable i.e. too hot or too cold, the baby may cry because he may feel cold and miserable or hot and uncomfortable (parents may have wrapped him in excessive clothing that the state of weather doesn't warrant). Parents should check it out and take steps to make the environment comfortable.

6. Is He Wet ?

A baby may cry if her diapers are wet and soggy. Check the nappy. Many babies dislike having a wet or soiled nappy, as it makes them feel uncomfortable

7. Loneliness

Maybe he needs your phsysical presence to be reassured and comforted. Babies have a natural and instinctive urge to be held close and be given lots of contact comfort.

8. Boredom

Some babies really do want to be in the centre of things all day. So try and prop up your baby in such a way that he can see and hear you, all the time if possible

9. Getting Undressed

Some babies dislike being undressed–they are frightened by the feel of their skin being exposed to air, and hence may cry. While dressing, you could try keeping the baby calm by laying a towel, nappy or shawl across the chest or stomach. This can be very soothing.

10. Over-stimulation

Some babies, if they are too much stimulated, may react by becoming irritable and tense. Instead of it being easier for them to fall asleep, it may be harder. (A similar situation occurs with adults when their mind is in a state of excessive stimulation). Though the baby is fatigued, it has to "wind down" its tensions. Parents may be at a loss and fail to understand why their baby, in spite of being tired and not having slept in the afternoon, is not falling asleep. If the parents force the baby to sleep, she may resist and cry frantically. Then gradually, as she becomes exhausted, the crying stops and the baby goes to sleep. For such a situation, it is best for the parents to "wind down" their babies by rocking her, caressing her, talking to her in a soft melodious voice etc. before sleep.

11. Extra-sensitive Babies

There are some babies who are extra sensitive. If they are in a strange environment away from home (e.g. when you visit someone), they may be acutely uncomfortable and be agitated. These babies are tense and restless, fretful and fussy during the first few weeks and require a lot of cuddling and fondling. Some parents may have experienced that the baby starts crying the moment they put the baby on the bed (thinking that it has slept, while actually the baby is yet not in a state of deep sleep). While, if they carry and rock her or sing some soft melodies, the baby is soothed and goes on sleeping. For such babies, it is best for the parents to be patient and put her in bed only when she is in a deep sleep in their laps. During her sleep also, the baby may easily get startled, get up and start whimpering on a slight noise or by a change in her position etc. Usually she will go back to sleep if the parents murmur soothing words, pat and caress her. It is important for the parents to keep their presence of mind and cool in the middle of the night and not get angry with their baby, for it will only worsen matters. Such babies do best on:

- *Some sort of a pacifier (e.g. a rubber nipple in their mouths in between feeds)*
- *A quiet regime: i.e. quiet and dark rooms, few visitors, low soothing voices, soft melodies etc. During daytime, such babies should not be stimulated much e.g. too much noise, too much T.V., too many visitors etc., otherwise they may become too excited and take a long time to wind down & relax sufficiently to fall asleep during night-time.*

12. Infantile Colic

There remains a subgroup of babies (and their number is quite large), who cry because of "Infantile Colic." Colic means intermittent pain. These babies suffer from intermittent spasmodic pain of the intestines. The condition commonly begins at the age of 2-4 weeks and subsides by the age of 3-4 months. The baby typically cries in the late afternoons or evenings, the cry is more or less continuous, may last for hours and is resistant to the usual soothing methods. The baby's abdomen may become distended, it may pull its legs up on the abdomen, the face may become flushed and the baby may even perspire. Many babies will pass flatus and/or stool and this may provide relief to the baby. This picture is not limited to a single day but may occur more than 3 times/week and continues till baby is 3-4 months old, when it stops regardless of the management strategy.

It is indeed a very testing time for the parents. Parents become distressed even if their baby cries for 5-10 minutes. Imagine the agony of the parents whose baby cries for hours and that too in a stereotyped fashion day after day. Worse there is no guaranteed method to stop it. These parents just have to wait and wait with a lot of patience and heartburn for their baby to become bigger. The parents wonder how long the baby can keep this up and not become exhausted. They wonder how long they can stand it without becoming "crazy."

***Doctors in a mental asylum had a meeting and decided that one of their patients was potentially fine. To test it, they went to see* *a movie with the patient. In the movie theatre, there were signs of wet paint on the seats. The patient puts a newspaper first and then sits down upon it. The doctors are excited because they think that he is in touch with reality now.*

Why did you put the newspaper?" they ask him.

*He answers, "Simple, so I will be higher and get a better view of the movie."***

When a baby has infantile colic, the mother's first instinct is that something may be wrong with the baby's feeding. If the baby is on breast milk, the mother may attribute the crying due to some thing wrong with her milk.

Given below are some guidelines for managing such colicky babies:

i. The parents are not to be blamed and their way of upbringing is not the cause for the baby's crying. Thus they should not harbour feelings of guilt

ii. Colic has nothing to do with the type of feeding. Changing formulas or switching from breast milk to bottle feeds is not recommended. However if the baby is on cow's milk, you may try to give the baby formula milk.

iii. The parents should take heart from the fact that it is a fairly common condition that will subside with time, their baby is otherwise healthy and that the baby has no ill-effects due to this. In fact such babies prosper a lot. So it is just a matter of time and patience.

iv. Various methods have been suggested to soothe the baby. The parents should try them and, by trial and error, find out for themselves what suits their baby the best. Rocking the baby gently in the cradle or in their laps, offering a pacifier, turning on soft music or singing a lullaby to the baby, creating a calm atmosphere around the baby with a soothing blue night light are some of the routine methods to be tried first. If the baby is still not soothed, then taking the baby out for a ride in the car sometimes work wonders. Colicky babies are usually more comfortable lying on their stomachs. Thus they may get relief by being laid with their stomach on the parent's knees and their backs being gently massaged and rubbed. A hot water bottle may be tried (ensure the water is not too hot) that can be placed under the stomach of the baby with the baby lying stomach down on it.

v. The doctor may prescribe a sedative to the baby if the crying is too long and not being relieved. In very trying conditions, enemas or suppositories may be given to the baby whence the expulsion of gas or stool may afford relief to the baby.

vi. Picking the baby up and loving and cuddling it will not spoil the baby. The parents should do it at the first sign of distress in the baby.

vii. Finally, the parents should accept the condition in a calm and resigned way, think about it as transient that will go away with time; and half the battle is won.

Counselling of Parents

It often happens and almost all parents must have faced it sometime or the other that the baby's crying shows no signs of stopping. It tests the nerves and the patience of the parents. In spite of your best efforts to calm her, the baby may thrash her arms, kick her legs, scream more and just refuse to be comforted. You run out of ideas and feel completely helpless. These reactions are painful to you. You feel sorry for the baby, at least in the beginning. With time, you feel increasingly inadequate, as you are unable to control her. With some more time, when the baby rejects your efforts you cannot help but get mad at the baby. Inwardly you are irritated while outwardly you may try to console her. But there is a limit to everything including your patience and it may so happen (and it does happen often) that you blow your top and get angry with the baby, at the world and at yourself. But this doesn't help and you realise after sometime that you had lost self-control and unnecessarily got angry with your baby. This makes you feel ashamed and guilty, which in turn may make you tenser.

What the parents should realise is that every parent gets angry at such trying times and there is no need to feel ashamed or guilty about it, as it is a normal humanly feeling. The best thing to do is to admit your feelings and laugh it out with your spouse. Laughter and a sense of humour is the best antidote for stress and tension. Besides you should realise that your baby is not doing it deliberately and that she is too small to be mad at you or to throw tantrums. If she is crying, there is always a genuine and valid reason behind it.

In the case of "infantile colic", when the baby cries for hours on together and repeats the same routine day after day, it may bring the parents to the end of their tethers, so much so that they may feel that it is beyond their endurance power. When you feel so much exhausted, it is time that you take some rest. At least once or twice in a week, the parents should spend "quality time" together e.g. going to movies, visiting some close friend etc. Ask the help of some friend, neighbour, relative or a baby sitter to look after the baby in your absence. The parents often hesitate doing this thinking that they are inflicting their baby on someone else and so shirking from their responsibility. But you should realise that a few hours off from your baby is very important for you to keep your sense of balance, and that it is equally important for your baby and your spouse that you do not start cracking under the mental strain and irritability. If you can't arrange for someone to "baby sit", then the best option is for the parents to take time off in rotation. After all, the baby doesn't require two worried parents at a time to listen to her. Everything that helps you from getting too preoccupied and obsessed with the baby's crying, and thus helps you in maintaining "sanity" helps you, your spouse and your baby in the long run.

BOTTOM LINE: As you get to know your baby better, you will find that you understand what his cries means more readily. In the beginning it's mostly trial and error, but if you respond to your baby's need quickly in these early months and do the best you can to comfort him, you will find that he discovers other, less distressing ways to communicate with you as he gets older.

CHAPTER 10

SLEEP PATTERN IN CHILDREN

KEY POINTS

- **Sleep rhythm:** A newborn baby doesn't have a fixed pattern of sleep. The baby may sleep too much in the daytime while during the night it may keep awake. A regular sleep rhythm is established by 3-4 months of age.
- **Falling asleep with the parents**: The child has to be weaned (after a particular age) from the habit of his falling asleep with the parents. Tuck his favourite toy in the bed along with him and tell him to make it go to sleep along with him. The child will gradually associate sleep with the toy and his association of sleeping with the parents lying down besides him will weaken as a result.
- **Bedtime struggles**: The children are in a state of "evergreen love" with life and don't want to withdraw from the events of the day. Thus they are reluctant to fall asleep. The most important cause for bedtime struggles is the absence of clear cut and consistent limits set by the parents regarding acceptable bedtime behaviour. The best remedy for bedtime struggles is that the parents deal with it firmly and set a definite time for "lights out." After being put to bed, the child may try to engage parental attention in various ways like "I want water, I want to go to toilet" etc. Don't bow to these requests. Handle them in a firm but neutral fashion. For e.g. you can tell him firmly that he just had water or just had peed. When children realise that nothing will help, no matter what they do, they usually give in to their fatigue and fall asleep.
- **Night waking**: The child frequently arouses from sleep and does not go back to sleep easily, causing distress to the parents. If the parents are firm and can continually ignore waking, whining and fussiness of their child in the middle of the night (this may result in increased crying initially), the problem is solved within a week.
- **Parasomnias:** These are divided into nightmares, night terrors, night walking and night talking. Parasomnias are benign and not of much concern unless too frequent.

Sleeping problems are the most common complaint of mothers and fathers in the first few years. And more often than not, being a parent means having to get used to NOT sleeping fitfully almost every night. Let's face it. You need your baby to sleep at night not just for her sake – you need sleep too to remain sane and function effectively. For this, it is important to know that there's a great variability in babies' sleep patterns and needs.

Just as every pregnancy and every birth is different, so too, is every baby. Some babies need 20 hours of sleep a day, others only 10. Some will sleep for 3 to 4 hours at a stretch. Others never more than 15 to 20 minutes at a stretch (i.e. a short nap). Such sleep patterns are in-built and there's little you can do to change it. But what you can do is to influence your baby's attitude to sleep. Establishing some kind of ritual with regard to sleep time is a fundamental requirement for many babies. And though there are no magical solutions to sleeping problems, here are some ideas you might like to try.

YOUR BABY MIGHT LIKE

- *Being fed to sleep, then moved gently into bed.*
- *Being rocked (Research shows that the effective rate is about once a second).*
- *Being patted on the back or head when put to bed.*
- *Being sung to.*
- *Walking around with he nursed in your arms or in a sling.*
- *Being pushed backwards and forwards in a pram or stroller.*

Such rituals may take up to an hour for the first week or so, but gradually your baby will get the message: "It's time for sleep". After a month or so, most babies will quite miraculously fall asleep after two to three minutes of whichever ritual they are accustomed to i.e. they become conditioned to that ritual.

It is also very important to help the baby understand the difference between night and day. Some of the useful steps that the parents can try (when it is night) are:

- *Make sure the baby's room is dark so that she doesn't think its day time.*
- *Leave lights off when feeding.*
- *Change nappies quickly, burp the baby and put her back to bed quickly without play and talk as during the day.*
- *Make sure she is comfortable and securely wrapped. Put your baby to sleep in the same cot in the same room each night.*

Good Night Sleep.

NORMAL SLEEP HABITS

***One mother was trying to impress upon her daughter the virtues of getting up earlier. "Look", she said, "it is the early bird that catches the worm". The daughter asked, "Mama, what about the early worm which got caught?" ***

Sleep is a pleasant thing that nature has blessed us with. It is a means of rejuvenation. Sleep is the best antidote for fatigue and those who have a good, sound sleep feel mentally and physically relaxed the next morning. Even a one day old baby (who doesn't even know the meaning of sleep), dozes off after satisfying her hunger.

The parents are often worried about how much the baby should sleep. There is no definitive answer to this question, simply because every baby has her own pattern and duration of sleep. However, a newborn sleeps approximately 18 hours/ day, which is reduced to 12 hours/day by the age of 2 years and then to 8-10 hours/ day by the age of 6 years. Remember babies, unlike adults don't have worries and tensions, and thus cannot suffer from insomnia (sleeplessness) at least till the age of 2 years. Thus they cannot miss out on their full quota of sleep. So parents should not worry about it.

A newborn baby doesn't have any fixed pattern of sleep and so parents may complain that the baby sleeps too much in the daytime while during the night it keeps awake. New-borns cry often at night for the initial 4-6 weeks and sleep during the day. This is just the opposite of what adults do. It is very disturbing to the parents because they can't get proper sleep during the night. The parents want that in some way, the baby should sleep more in the night and thus disturb their sleep less, a feeling that is quite natural. One possible solution is that the parents try to keep their baby awake in the daytime which is difficult as the baby will continue to sleep. Parents should realise that it is not the baby's fault but just a continuation of the intra-uterine pattern. During fetal life, the mother's activities during the daytime have a rocking effect on the fetus and thus lull him to sleep. During night the opposite happens. This pattern persists after the baby is born and only by 4-6 weeks is the baby able to change and fit its sleep rhythm to the adult pattern.

As babies get older they cut down on their sleep. By the end of first year, the child may be having 2 naps, one in the afternoon and one in the night. As the child grows older, he may even forego the afternoon nap and sleep only during night.

Parents should inculcate in their child the habit that he should go to bed after dinner and not engage in any activities post dinner like play, watching T.V. etc. In Indian custom, the child mostly sleeps with the parents till he is 5-6 years old or even more. It becomes a habit with him that unless the parents (at least one of them) is not in bed with him, he cannot go to sleep. In western countries, the culture is to make the baby sleep in a separate room by the age of 6 months or earlier, which is difficult for us to accept as we think it as being "harsh" to the baby.

MAKING CHILD SLEEP ALONE WITHOUT PARENTS

Some or most of the parents may have a desire to have some free time for themselves after dinner, after the daily baby care ritual. The pre-requisite for it is that the child should be asleep! But the child doesn't sleep without the company of his parents. So, the child has to be encouraged and trained to sleep alone, without the parents.

If you tuck up an active child in the bed forcefully and tell him firmly that he should sleep alone, you may find that the child may not sleep and instead engage in some solitary play or self-talk in the bed. Intermittently he may ask for water, request you to come to bed with him, tell you that he is feeling afraid being alone etc. If you relent to his pleas, you have to go to bed with him in an effort to make him sleep, thus defeating the whole purpose. Therefore you have to be firm in your determination to let the child fall asleep by himself. Initially you may find that the child is sleeping quite late and just wants to be awake and enjoy "life", in spite of the fact that he is tired and there is "sleep" in his eyes. But gradually your perseverance and patience will pay off, particularly as the child starts getting bored being awake. He realises gradually that keeping awake and "fighting" fatigue is not that appealing an idea. There are three important things to be kept in mind, as follows:

1. Anything that stimulates a child's mind and lets his imagination work overtime should be restricted to a minimum possible after the evening e.g. an exciting game. This will help him to "wind down" his mental energy rather than stimulating it further and so making it difficult for him to sleep.

2. If the child comes in the drawing room to sit along with you from his bed and waits for you also to come in bed, it is best to eliminate all sources of entertainment and stimulation from him at that time. The parents should forego temporarily watching T.V. All this is done to make the child feel "bored" so that he will not think that being awake means fun. You will have to accompany him back to bed, but you should make it clear that you will stay with him for sometime only and then go out. In the time that you are in bed, you cam narrate to him his favourite tale. The routine might end with a positive statement like "go to sleep now, sweet dreams. See you in the morning." And after kissing and hugging your child a final "good night", you can come out of the room.

Television Tiredness.

Bedtime. A story from father is better than a late romp just before going to sleep.

3. In your endeavour to make him sleep alone without your having to lie down with him for an hour or more, it is best to give him a favourite animal like teddy bear, doll etc. and tuck the teddy bear up also like a baby. The child may

be told to make the toy go to sleep along with him. In this way, the child will gradually associate sleep with the toy and his association of sleep with your lying down besides him will weaken as a result.

4. Some children wish that you should lie with them for some time (say 10-15 minutes) at bedtime. Others may want that they should be told a story before going to sleep. These are genuine requests and the parents should agree to them.

SLEEP PROBLEMS IN CHILDHOOD

They can be divided into three broad categories:

1. **Bedtime struggles**: The child finding it difficult to fall asleep.
2. **Night waking:** The sleep of the child is interrupted during the night.
3. **Parasomnias**: Nightmares, night walking, night talking and night terrors.

1. Bedtime struggles

It appears that children are in a state of continuous and everlasting love with life and thus are reluctant to withdraw from the events of the day. Hence in spite of their feeling sleepy, they are reluctant to sleep, not wanting to terminate their social activities and wanting to explore and learn more what life is all about. As the child grows older, a struggle for autonomy and independence with his parents regarding who actually is in control of his life may lead to bedtime struggles.

The most important cause for bedtime struggles is an absence of clear cut and consistent limits set by the parents regarding acceptable bedtime behaviour. There may be lack of a fixed bedtime i.e. the child goes to bed sometimes at 8 p.m. and sometimes at 10 p.m. depending upon when the parents go to bed. If the child sometimes sleeps in the afternoon and sometimes not, his night routine will also be disturbed leading to bedtime struggles. So either the child should have an afternoon nap consistently or forgo it completely. A regular routine allows a circadian (day and night) sleep rhythm to develop. The best remedy for bedtime struggles is that the parents firmly deal with it and set a definite time for "lights out." If the child resists going to bed, just ignore it and put him to bed at the same time every day. However if you find that the child routinely is keeping awake even 1 hour after being put to bed, it means that the child is not sleepy at that time and so you have to postpone putting him to bed by say half an hour the next time. Gradually, by trial and error, you will know the appropriate time for putting the child to bed. Having established a regular sleep routine, the parents should put him to bed at that particular bedtime hour every night. Suppose the child goes to bed at 9 p.m. Now if parents put him to sleep at 8 p.m. one day (because they are tired), bedtime struggle may ensue, as the child won't sleep before the accustomed time.

After being put to bed, the child may try to engage parental attention in various ways like I want water, I want to go to toilet etc. All this is in spite the fact that the child recently had been to toilet or had drunk water. Parents should be firm in not responding to these demands of the child, who uses them to gain parental attention and postpone his sleep.

Don't bow to these requests (these are just excuses), but rather handle them in a firm but neutral fashion, without getting irritated at the child. For e.g. you can tell him firmly that he just had water or just had peed. If he still insists, firmly tell him that you won't do it as you feel that it is not necessary. When children realise that nothing will help, no matter what they do, they usually give in to their fatigue and fall asleep.

Other measures to help in making the child sleep are to have a pleasing and relaxing bedtime routine. This may involve bathing the child before bedtime, changing his clothes to a comfortable nightwear, telling him his favourite story etc. Then again, a favourite toy or doll kept beside him, which he likes and enjoys, is a big help in "winding" him down so that he can fall asleep.

2. Night waking

In this, the child frequently arouses from sleep and does not go back to sleep easily, causing discomfort to the parents. It should be kept in mind that almost all children wake up in the night. During the stage of partial arousal, they may moan, but if the parents reassure them verbally and pat them, they will go back to sleep. This is normal. But if night waking is prolonged so that the parents also have to be awake and make all sorts of efforts to put him back to sleep, then it is a problem. There are various reasons why the child does so, and once the parents understand them, the remedy lies in eliminating them.

1. The child routinely doesn't go to sleep without some sort of active parental intervention like rocking him, carrying him etc. So when he gets up at night, he again requires an active parental intervention for sleep re-induction. Therefore the parents should gradually cut down on their active interventions to lull the child to sleep so that the child is conditioned to sleep without these interventions.
2. Some of the parents are over sensitive, and as soon as the child starts moving or whining in bed, they pay much attention to it. At the slightest noise from the child, the parents will sit up in bed, pick the child up, fondle him and make a lot of fuss about it. This is counterproductive as it perpetuates and encourages night waking. The treatment strategy is to delay the parental response to the baby's whining for several minutes so as to give an adequate opportunity to him to fall back asleep. Picking the child up is not to be done. Instead the parents should rely on verbal reassurance and gently patting him.
3. Another reason may be that the parents are giving the child middle of the night feeds, e.g. a bottle of milk. Feeding at night is a learned habit after the age of 6 months. Normally, a child after 6 months of age doesn't require night-time feeds, unless parents have made this a learned habit, in which case the child will frequently awake at night. The solution is to initially make the night feedings "brief," substitute it with water and then gradually to cut it down completely.

Finally and most importantly, if the parents are firm and can continually ignore waking, whining and fussiness of their child in the middle of the nights (this may result in increased crying initially, which the parents have to ignore completely), the problem is solved within a week.

3. Parasomnias (nightmares, somnambulism etc.)

***There is some consolation in the fact that even if your dreams have not come true, neither have your nightmares. ***

Parasomnias are specific events happening only during sleep. These are of 4 types:

i. **Nightmare**: It is a bad, frightening dream. An occasional nightmare occurs now and then in most individuals throughout life and is normal. But if the nightmares are recurrent, cause frequent nightime awakenings and also distress during the daytime (by recollecting them), it is troublesome. A child awakening immediately after a nightmare will be alert and remember the contents of the dream. If he doesn't wake up, then next day he can recall the dream, if not completely, at least partially.

To reduce nightmares, the child should not be allowed to watch or listen to horrifying, violent or frightening things, especially prior to bedtime. Neither should the child be made to believe and imagine about ghosts, devils, spirits etc. Parents, particularly if their child is not behaving properly and irritating them, sometimes try to frighten the child into submission by the idea of ghost e.g. they may say, "if you don't behave, the ghost will come and take you." A night-light or keeping the door slightly ajar also may help to alleviate the childhood fears.

Whenever the child has a nightmare, the parents should reassure him that it is only in his dreams and that nothing of this sort happens or is going to happen in real life. The best way is to talk out the contents of the dream and convince the child that the dream is over and that he is safe in bed. By and large nightmares do not have an adverse effect on the psyche of a child, unless they are frequent, in which case a psychological assessment may be needed.

ii. **Night terrors:** The child becomes frightened and agitated in the middle of his sleep. He may scream, cry, thrash around; his eyes may be open and dilated and give the appearance of a "glassy stare" ahead. But although seemingly awake, the child actually is in a state of deep sleep and difficult to arouse, so much so that he even refuses to acknowledge parental presence in the bed. Upon awakening, the child has no memory of the event (compare it with nightmares). Although frightening to the parents, night terrors are benign and self-limited.

The parents should not worry about it. The only thing required of them is to simply observe the child while he is having such an episode and not to intervene by trying to wake him up, because it only prolongs the event. When night terrors are too frequent and disturbing to the parents (it never harms or disturbs the child, as he doesn't have any memory of it!), then several nights of anticipatory awakening before the usual time of the event will eliminate future episodes. Supposing the child is having recurrent episodes at 3 a.m. Then the parents should awaken him at 2.45 a.m. for several nights (i.e. before the event actually takes place). This is recommended only when the night terrors are a source of chronic stress to the parents.

iii. **Sleep walking:** Also called somnambulism, it is a phenomenon in which the child gets out of bed and then moves about in a confused and clumsy state. As is the case with night terrors, the child seemingly appears awake, but actually he is in a state of deep sleep and difficult or impossible to arouse to full awareness.

The treatment lies in the understanding that the condition is self-limiting and not dangerous to others. The parents should not make efforts to "shake" the child to wakefulness as it may lead to agitation. Rather, the environment should be made safe so that the child doesn't self-injure himself; the child merely observed and gently led back to bed. As in the case with night terrors, if the episodes are frequent and disturbing, then several nights of anticipatory awakening before the usual time of sleep walking is of help.

iv. **Sleep talking:** In this benign condition, the child utters something while asleep. The parents are often aroused and alarmed by their child's verbalisations. It may persist throughout life, but the condition is benign. No treatment is warranted for it.

CHAPTER 11

SCHOOLING OF CHILDREN

KEY POINTS

- **Type of School:** Child can be sent to school at the age of 3 years+ with the caveat that the school should be an informal play type of school where the child learns while playing. Formal schooling should start only at the age of 5-6 years.
- **Initiation of schooling:** Whatever you tell him about schooling at the prepatory stage should be true and actually happen when the child goes to school. Due to an acute anxiety of going to school for the first time, initially the child cries, clings and makes excuses. This is the critical point where the parents should put a stone on their heart. In the initial few days, someone not likely to waver in the face of the child's distress should accompany the child to school. The most important thing is that there should not be any school absenteeism because of crying or excuses.
- **Modern day schooling:** The child is overburdened with books, homework, exams and what not. On reaching home, he is back to the books and homework in a never-ending drab and monotonous schedule. The parents also have to sit with the child and make him complete his homework. Children are taught all type of things that have absolutely no bearing on their future career/ profession.
- **Corporal punishment:** Teachers give corporal punishment to cower the child into submission. By doing so, they create a fear "psychosis" in the child, and render his personality into one of a submissive or alternatively a rebellious child.
- **Tuition:** It fosters a culture of dependency, making a child dependent on others for success. The teacher who cannot do the job required of him/her at school, lured by the monetary factor, is more than willing to come home and teach the child.
- **Poor school performance:** The treatment lies in the cause and has to be individualised. Firstly seek medical opinion if the child's performance is poor at school. If a medical cause is ruled out, the help of the teachers should be sought. If the child is still unable to cope, it is better to make him repeat or study in a lower grade.
- **Parental attitude:** Most of the children are of normal intelligence and by and large do reasonably well. It is the parental pressures and expectations that put a big strain on them. We are making neurotics out of our children by burdening them with our high expectations. Inculcate good and positive habits of studying etc. in your child, but do it at his pace and his capability to cope up with it.

WHEN TO START SCHOOLING FOR YOUR CHILD?

School readiness involves a physical, social and emotional capacity to cope up with an alien environment. The demands are many. The child should have bladder and bowel control, should be able to overcome stranger anxiety and be away from his mother at least for some time. He should have a fair expression of language, both receptive and expressive. Although there are individual variations, usually these abilities are not present before the age of 3 years. It is not essential that you should send your child to school at the age of 3 years. You can wait for 1-2 years more i.e. till the child becomes 4-5 years old. The school should be an informal play type of school where the child learns while playing, and not a formal school where they have the classical school type strict protocol and discipline.

Some of the reasons why a child should be sent to school at 3 years are given below:

1. The child starts getting bored at home at the age of 3 years+. This is the time when he yearns for company, particularly of children of the same age group, with whom he can play and have fun. A play school is ideal for it.
2. The child starts learning the concept of schooling. The child learns to interact with others, becomes disciplined and learns social and mutual co-operation. He learns that everyone has his own rights and independence, including himself.

Home alone: Yearning for companionship of counterparts.

3. He learns a lot of things in play school like A-Z etc. while enjoying himself and takes justifiable pride in it.

The magic of books.

4. The parents get some free time when the child is away to school!

I think that informal schooling should continue till the child is more than 5 years, after which only formal schooling (i.e. from Class 1) should begin. Formal schooling requires the ability to read, write and do arithmetic (popularly called as the three R's). These involve control over the fine muscles of the hand and fingers, a fine eye to hand co-ordination, comprehension and abstract reasoning. Since these faculties are not developed before 6 years of age, hence children below 6 years are not mentally and developmentally geared for formal schooling (i.e. learning the three R's).

A child should be put in a class, the standard of which he is able to cope up with, i.e. the syllabus should not be beyond the child's comprehension. It doesn't matter that the child goes to school one year late e.g. he is put into class 1 at the age of 7 years. One year doesn't make any difference in the overall life of a child. But inability to cope up with the lessons and always struggling to "stay afloat" definitely will have adverse psychological consequences for the child.

WHICH SCHOOL TO PREFER IN THE INITIAL STAGES?

The ideal school at the age of 3 years is one where there is a lot of fun and joy for the child, along with learning of the basic and elementary things like knowing A-Z, names of common things, animals, colours etc. This learning should be in the spirit of play and fun; and not disciplinary where the child is made to sit at one place in the classroom for 3-4 hours and then taught things formally. The teachers over there should have a genuine fondness and love for the children and should be able to interact with them at their level. They should also enjoy taking part in fun and games with the small children and not have the attitude of just going through the motions, without being involved with the children closely. A child should like the teacher as a friend rather than having a feeling of awe or terror for him. Parents should make efforts search for a school that meet these requirements. The reason is simple. The child should not be put under pressure at a small age. He should learn things in the spirit of playing. This way there is a positive development of the child.

A good school should stress on the all round development of the child rather than focussing only on academics. Schools take great pride that 90% of their students achieve 1st division, and this is also the main factor that the parents consider for decision making. It is praiseworthy that the average academic level of a school is very good, but schools should also see to it that each child develops to his full potential. All round development doesn't mean that the child should be taught all things sundry like music, sports, debates, paintings, acting in dramas etc. They are desirable, but much more important is that the child is ingrained with a basic sense of value, self-confidence and positive self-esteem.

***A student nominated the dumbest doctor as the best teacher, taking everyone by surprise. On being asked the reason, he said, "Every time he opens his mouth, I go to the library to check whether what he is teaching is correct. This way I have learnt a lot." ***

An important dictum of any school should be "democracy builds discipline." A good teacher knows that if he/she acts in a dictatorial fashion, he/she is enforcing himself/herself upon the children without letting them freedom of self-expression. So a good teacher strives to do collective project work, entailing the co-operation of all the students, listening and discussing with them various ways of approaching and solving a specific problem so that the children are stimulated and thus develop to their full potential. The teacher should also be able to pay individualised attention to each and every child, and therefore the size of the class should be less than 30 students ideally.

SHOULD EXAMS BE HELD FOR PROMOTION TO NEXT CLASS?

Personally I am not in favour of burdening the child and hence the parents with formal exams, at least till class 3 and preferably till class 5. Exams place a lot of stress on the child and the parents. The child, if he is unable to cope with the mental pressures of exams and doesn't do well, may land up feeling depressed and inferior. If the child fails, the parents undergo a lot of anguish, may feel guilty plus consider that their child is not intelligent, which may give them sleepless nights.

How to judge whether a child should be promoted or not? His full year's general performance should be taken into account and if satisfactory, the child should be promoted automatically to the next class till class 5. The teacher should monitor the progress of the child, have meetings with the parents, and point out to them the strengths and weaknesses of the child. They should tell the parents in which fields and subjects the child requires more attention and care, so as to iron out any shortcomings in the child.

Alas, this is not the state of affairs today. Modern day's schooling means that the child is over burdened with books, studies, homework, exams etc. As a result, schooling becomes a dreary task that has to be undergone as there is no other choice.

SHOULD A CHILD BE GIVEN HOMEWORK?

Much homework should not be given to the child. The child already is in school from 8 o'clock to 3 o'clock. He gets up at 6 o'clock to reach school by 8 o'clock. On top of it, when he reaches home by 4 P.M., the thought uppermost in his mind is that he has to complete his homework. In fact, the school timings of a child are roughly equal to office timings of a government employee. When such employees reach home, they are usually tired and stressed out. *Do they have to do any homework?*

The parents also have to sit with the child and make him complete his homework, only after which, they can feel relaxed. The parents may not always be good teachers. This is because 1) they get upset when the child is slow in picking up things or doesn't understand. This is because they are anxious that he should learn things properly and quickly. 2) The parent's way of teaching may be different from that of the school teacher. When they try to teach the child anything in a particular way, the child may say that this is not the way their teacher told them. And believe me a child always considers the teachers correct! So, the child who is already baffled at school will be more baffled when his parents present things to him in a different way at home.

The only solution to reduce the homework and in general the burden of studies is to reduce the syllabus of the child and not teach him things which will be of no importance to him in the future.

I still remember that in school they taught me all complex chemical formulas and reactions, equations and what not, which we were supposed to remember by heart. Why to talk of school? Even in medical college they taught me how to make mixtures in pharmacology, which has no relevance today, as all drugs are produced by companies and the doctor doesn't have to make and dispense mixtures. Now when I look back, I realise that 70% of what was taught to me has no relevance to my job and profession as a paediatrician. Yet the "wise" bureaucrats (present day education policy makers) sitting in their posh chambers have little practical knowledge and awareness that they are converting children into beasts of burden and creating neurotics out of them. As a result, children are made to slog and taught all type of things which have absolutely no bearing in future on their profession or means of livelihood.

SHOULD THERE BE CORPORAL PUNISHMENT?

To cane or beat a child for simple errors is not correct. Yet many teachers do so as they feel "spare the rod and spoil the child." Also physical punishment cowers the child into submission, so that a large part of the teacher's headache is over. By doing so, they create a fear psychosis in the child and render his overall personality into one of a submissive or alternatively a rebellious child, that can be carried forward into adulthood. Children if dealt with a firm hand and made to understand the difference between right and wrong, between desirable behaviour and behaviour that cannot be condoned, will surely do their best to stay on the right path. After all, there is a strong desire in the children to please their elders, particularly parents and teachers. No child will deliberately do something to annoy his teacher in school. Agreed, some children are by nature a bit aggressive, "naughty" and on the lookout for fun. Such children are few. The teacher can talk to their parents about them or even resort to other forms of punishment like making him stand, turning him out of the class etc. But, to inflict a physical blow or to pinch, twist his ears etc. to cause them physical pain is callous.

SHOULD THE CHILD UNDERGO TUITION?

Because of the vast syllabus and lots of homework, parents go for private tuition, usually employing the same teacher who teaches their child at school.

Tuition is a means of burdening the child at home also. He has already spent such a lot of time in school that he is mentally and physically exhausted. Yet on reaching home, instead of some mental rest and relaxation, he is back to the books in a never-ending drab and monotonous schedule.

Tuition fosters a culture of dependency. The child begins to depend on others for success. Some parents, as soon as they come back home from work, will "retire" with their child in a separate room and then start tutoring him. If there are two children, then the mother and father divide the onus of teaching them, one child "belonging" to one parent. If parents do not have the time and the energy, they hire a tutor. All this inculcates a culture of dependency in the child. The child never learns how to study by himself and daily waits for his parents or the tutor to teach him. This habit lives on and even when the child goes to a higher class, he never has the confidence, habit or the will to self-study. Instead someone has to regularly sit with him and make him study. This is detrimental to the development of a child.

Therefore parents from the very beginning should encourage the child to study and do homework on his own, their role being supervisory. Definitely one doesn't expect the child to do all the studies by himself, but then parents should only intervene when the child faces a problem and solicits their help e.g. he doesn't know subtracting 2 numbers. Then the parents should only guide and make him understand how to do it e.g. keep 11 matchsticks and take away 6 to illustrate 11 minus 6. An important aspect of teaching is to make the subject interesting, simple and lucid so that less emphasis is laid on mugging and greatest emphasis is laid on understanding. Once the child understands the basic concept, he gains self-confidence and can reasonably tackle similar problems on his own. Similarly for spellings, it is important for the child to learn the phonation of the word and then try to learn its spelling. Suppose the child has to spell "ball". By its pronunciation, it is evident that it starts with "B" and also has "L" in it. So the child instead of blindly cramming the spellings and trying to remember them by heart should learn to associate the spelling with the way words are pronounced.

PREPARING A CHILD FOR SCHOOLING

Two important issues to be addressed for preparing a child to start schooling are:

i. **Separation Anxiety:** The child has difficulty separating from the parents temporarily to spend some time alone in an alien place i.e. the school. This is a normal phenomenon occurring in many children. With time and firmness on the part of parents, this anxiety decreases as the child becomes acclimatised to the school environment.

Children are bound to be anxious and fearful when they are first sent to school, a completely unknown place as compared to the warmth and security of his home. (Why to talk about only children? Even adults are filled with anxiety if they have to leave the security of their home and embark on a journey to the unknown). On the first day, the child may not make a fuss right away, but after sometime may start missing his mother and then become worried and frightened. So ideally, the initial few days in school should be short, say 2 hours or so, so that the child gradually gets acclimatised to tolerate a short absence of his parents. Sometimes it so happens that the mother's anxiety is greater than the child's is. If the mother says good-bye three times over with a worried look on her face, the child may think that something is amiss or wrong. He gets the idea that something awful may happen if he stays in the school without his mother. Therefore parents should accompany him to school everyday with a cheerful and confident expression on their face.

Many children make a great fuss going to school in the initial few days to weeks. They cry a lot, become increasingly clingy and do not want to leave their parents. They may start crying right from the time that they leave the house, a cry which increases in intensity as the school approaches nearer; and peaks as the classroom comes into view. On the way to school, they may make excuses like "my stomach is paining etc." All this is a natural reaction to an acute anxiety of going to an unknown place. In a bid to escape from this, the child's starts crying, clinging and making excuses.

This is a critical juncture where parents have to be strict and put a stone on their heart. The cry and the pleading of the child is sometimes so heartrending that the parents melt and don't send their child to school that day, of course after eliciting a promise from the child that tomorrow he has to go to school like a nice child. The child in his anxiousness to be spared of school that day will make such promises, but do you think he will keep it up? Next day, again some or the other excuse will pop up. So the most important point for the successful induction of a child into school is that there should not be any absenteeism. The child has to be firmly dealt with and made to understand that he has to go to school. Once the child finds that there is no alternative and that his pleadings, crying and excuses are all in vain, these things die out and the child after a few days will start going to school without much fuss. In some children this time period may be quite prolonged, as long as 3 months +. But the parents should continue sending him to school if they want that their child to have a successful induction to schooling. They can discuss the matter with the teacher, who already knows and understands the plight of such parents because this is not the first time that she is encountering such a case. In fact, such cases are much commoner than you imagine.

On the other hand, if you bow down before the cries and pleadings of the child, you are reinforcing the behaviour instead of letting it "die out." The child knows that by crying and pleading he can escape school, and so will use it again and again. As goes the wise old adage "nip the thing in the bud", parents should strive for it, though sometimes they may feel remorse and pity for their child.

ii. **School readiness:** The child should be mentally and emotionally prepared to go to school. He should have some idea of what a school is like and what it is for.

The child has to be mentally prepared before initiation of schooling, so that he / she can acclimatize to the new atmosphere. Parents should build the concept of schooling in the child's mind by saying that "everyone goes to school and that they also went to school. Schooling is necessary because in school, you learn a lot of things and become big like Mummy and Daddy." For the child, parents are his idols, whom he tries to emulate. So, if he associates schooling with the idea of becoming like his parents, it is a positive reinforcement for him. You should also prepare him mentally for a stay away from the parents for a limited time. You should reassure him that as soon as the school time is over, you will be there to fetch him. This is important because many children, in the initial few days of schooling are scared of the prospect of their being left alone without the parents. After all they are leaving the security of the home to go to an unfamiliar place. Some may harbour the fear that the parents may leave them forever. Some may consider it as some sort of punishment for them, because they did something, which the parents didn't want them to do.

Whatever you tell him about schooling at this prepatory stage should be true and actually should happen when the child goes to school. Many parents, in order to make the child "more ready" for schooling, paint a rosy picture that school is a place where there is a lot of fun and games, where he will enjoy himself. But when the child actually goes to school, his "sky high" expectations are brought down to earth. When he finds that the picture is not all that rosy, that all is not play and fun, that no one is paying any special attention towards him, he may get disillusioned. He may think that his parents have lied to him, just to push him out of the house and make him go to school. Therefore, never present a false and exaggerated, rosy picture of the school to the child.

Some useful guidelines for parents are:

1. Parents must know that they are being good parents by forcing the child to go to school rather than being "bad" parents, as they are doing it for the good of the child.
2. The child should be reassured that his problems like stomach-ache etc. are due to "worry" and will become O.K. on going regularly to school.
3. In the initial few days, when the child is going to school, someone who is not likely to waver in the face of the child's distress e.g. the father or some other adult should accompany the child to the school. As the school comes nearer, the crying and other complaints of the child increases in the same proportion and intensity, which makes the parents, particularly the mother, waver and take the child back home half way from school. They think that let us give him some rest today, tomorrow he will be more agreeable. Alas tomorrow never comes, and the same behaviour is repeated by the child. It may assume such proportions that the parents become hapless and seriously consider postponing schooling for a period of 1 year. So someone, who will not waver in the face of the child's pleadings, should accompany the child to school daily till his anxiety level abates. Teachers should always be taken into confidence and their help sought.
4. In severe cases, graded anxiety reduction may be useful e.g. if the school duration is of 6 hours, for first few days, the child can be sent to school for 2 hours. Once he becomes acclimatised to it, it can be gradually

increased in increments over a period of time.

5. For children with recalcitrant symptoms, a child psychologist should be consulted.
6. The most important thing is that there should not be any school absenteeism. Longer the school absence, more difficult it is to rehabilitate the child and make him go to school. The second most important thing is that if the behaviour of the child is not positively reinforced (by not sending him to school); the behaviour automatically tends to die out over a period of time.

SCHOOL PHOBIA

Some of the common reasons are as follows:

1. **Teacher factors:** It is quite possible that a particular teacher is making the child fearful and the child dreads his/her very presence and hence develops a school phobia. Examples are when the teacher beats the child, humiliates him etc.
2. **School Bully**: These are "aggressive" students who get a perverse pleasure in bullying other children to submission and "rag" them whenever the opportunity arises. Your child may be afraid of such characters and hence devise excuses to stay away from school.
3. **Lesson Problems**: The child is unable to cope up with the ongoing lessons, even though other students are by and large able to. The child may thus undergo stress, leading to school phobia. Under such circumstances, it is better to firstly get the child medically examined, like his mental developmental status, intelligence quotient (I.Q.), any hearing or visual problems etc. If the child is normal, then it is possible that you have placed your child a grade higher than he can cope up with. Remember some children are able to cope up with class 1 at the age of 5 years; some may do so at the age of 6 years. Both categories are normal and an early school goer is in no way more intelligent than a child who goes to class 1 at the age of 6-7 years. So it is for the parents (in conjunction with the teachers) to decide whether the placement of the child is in the correct class and if not so, then there is nothing ashamed of in getting your child repeat the class. This is because he is unable to cope up with the standard of the present class and so how can you expect him to cope up with a higher class.
4. **Miscellaneous**: There may be other reasons like the child being afraid of reciting in school, afraid of asking the teacher to go to toilet etc. The adults may consider these reasons minor, but for the child they may be terrifying enough to develop a school phobia. So the parents should ask the child in a tactful way about all the things that he is scared of during the time he spends in school.

"School phobia" usually manifests itself in the form of some physical complaint, because the child cannot directly tell the parents that he will no go to school. Therefore, various "excuses" like stomach-ache, headache, and dizziness comes up in the morning before leaving for school and if the parents take them as genuine and not send the child to school; these complaints tend to subside during the daytime.

CURE OF SCHOOL PHOBIA

The important thing is that the child should not miss schools, because then it becomes all the more difficult to cure it. The parents should find out what exactly is making the child fearful of school. Talking with the child and the teachers may reveal the cause. Most likely it will be one of the factors mentioned above (at the age of 3-4 years, it is usually separation anxiety). If the parents feel that the cause is not separation anxiety but something else like a stern teacher, a bully etc., they should not hesitate, but rather go and discuss the matter openly with the principal or the class teacher. Once the parents have an idea of the child's fear, they can take steps to rectify it, alone; with the help of the teachers; or with the help of doctors.

Schooling: A child engaged in homework though it is her birthday. A typical example of formal schooling. Note the stress on the child's face.

POOR SCHOOL PERFORMANCE

There are many reasons like depression, anxiety (paradoxically anxiety in some children enhances their school performance, as they fear that if they don't do well in school, they will be ridiculed), physical causes such as chronic diseases leading to prolonged school absenteeism, visual and hearing problems etc. Then there are some specific psychological diseases like learning disabilities, hyperactivity, autism, mental retardation, chromosomal anomalies like Down's Syndrome etc. which may make the child a poor school performer.

Sometimes a child is overwhelmed by the huge amount of syllabus and the furious pace of teaching and struggles to keep pace with it. If he fails in his efforts, he will become depressed, feel helpless and thus a poor school performer.

The treatment lies in the cause and has to be individualised. It is always better to seek medical opinion, if the child's performance is really poor at school. After a medical cause like learning disabilities, mental retardation, hearing and visual problems etc has been ruled out, the help of the teachers should be sought. If the child is still unable to cope up, it is better to make him repeat or study in a lower grade.

PARENTAL PRESSURES ON THE CHILD

Parental expectations may make the child over conscientious. He keeps going over the lessons that he has already learnt or the exercises he has already finished for fear that something is missing, incomplete or incorrect on his part. This is due to a lack of security in the child, plus the fact that the child has set very high standards for himself (mostly parent induced) that everything should be 100% perfect and no mistakes should be made. This quest for perfection may put him under great stress. The parents should imbibe in the mind of child that he by and large knows all the lessons, is intelligent enough and even if he doesn't remember a few things or makes some mistakes, it is all right.

A corner of his own: Give him space to flourish.

Finally, the most important thing for the parents to realise is that most of the children are of normal intelligence. It is only the parental pressures and expectations that put a big strain on the child. As I mentioned before in this book, we are making neurotics out of our children by burdening them with our high expectations. By all means, think positively, inculcate good and positive habits of studying in your child, but do it at his pace and his capability to cope up with it; and not at the pace and the standards that you deem necessary.

CHAPTER 12

TOILET TRAINING

KEY POINTS

- All anecdotal reports of a child being toilet trained early (before one and a half-year) are due to a "conditioned reflex" whereby the child becomes conditioned to strain reflexly whenever he feels the potty seat under him. The child is not conscious of the bowel movement nor has it come under his control. He has to be retrained later on in life, which will be a true and learned training. Retraining is harder, so don't toilet train a child before he is ready for it.
- What is readiness for toilet training? It consists of the following 3 points:

1. **Anatomical readiness:** During the first year, the muscles controlling the bladder and bowel are not fully under the control of the nervous system. Obviously, the child should attain neurological control over his muscles for defecation and urination, before he can be toilet trained.
2. **Psychological readiness:** How do the parents judge that the child is ready psychologically? This is by clues provided by the child whenever he has the urge to eliminate; e.g. the child may pause in what he is doing or have a sudden fleeting change in his facial expression. Once the child is ready psychologically, the role of parents is to educate the child in toilet training, patiently, at his pace.
3. **Educational process:** Toilet training is an educational process, rather than being disciplinary. It is inherently obvious, but often overlooked, that the child is really the only person who can control the muscles and impulses of elimination. Therefore, equally obviously, the parent's only role should be in helping the child to exercise this control. The child should be first made to understand the goal i.e. acceptance of the toilet as the appropriate place for elimination. Then on receiving a clue for elimination from the child, they should take him to the toilet.

- **Enuresis (bedwetting):** The child is unable to control urine voiding, usually during night, even after the age of 5 years. It is usually a psychological problem due to coercive toilet training. There is conflict and tension between the child and the parents over the issue of toilet training. The child is forced to be toilet trained and if he is unable to control his impulses, the parents get angry and humiliate the child. This undermines the confidence of the child and leads to his being a bed wetter.
- **Cure:** Parents should tell the child that quite a few children have this problem, which is transient and he will overcome it with time. The child should be praised and encouraged if he doesn't bed wet (called positive reinforcement). Negative reinforcement, i.e. scolding or humiliating the child makes the cure difficult. Patience and tact on the part of parents helps.

TRUE V/S CONDITIONED TOILET TRAINING

An important part of a child's development is to achieve control over his passage of urine and stool. From birth till the age of one and a half-year, the child passes both urine and stool involuntarily in his diapers. Only after that is some sort of control achieved. Culturally, human beings, as opposed to animals, are supposed to pass urine and stool in the toilet. We associate it with a sense of cleanliness.

In their eagerness to make the child toilet trained; the parents want to start it early and most of them harbour the "grossly erroneous" concept that it is an art that has to be learned by the child and taught by them. So they go about it in a most sincere and serious manner believing that they should and can make the child toilet - trained; the earlier the better. They think that if they take their child to the potty, make him sit there, and say something like "sss, soo" etc. in a long drawn out voice, the child will ultimately associate it with the fact that the parents want him to pass urine and so will do so. Incidentally, there is no such "sound" invented for passage of stools; and even if there is one, I am not aware of it.

What I have come across often is that at the age of 7-9 months (when the child is able to sit without support), the parents will make him sit on the potty at a specified time, usually for 20-30 minutes. Firstly parents will notice the usual time in a day that the child passes stools, which is usually after having food; as a reflex called "gastro-colic" reflex is active at that time. Then daily, at approximately the same time, they will carry the child and make him sit on the potty.

More often than not, the child will pass stools in the potty, as it is his usual time to pass the stools. The parents consider this to be a sign of success. They think that their baby is becoming toilet trained at as young an age as 8-10 months, and so are understandably pleased with themselves that their efforts and perseverance are paying dividends. They take pride in letting others know that their child passes stools in the potty at such a young age. On hearing this, other parents also want to try it out, thus perpetuating this type of "toilet training".

Unfortunately, all such parents are labouring under a delusion, which I am afraid is borne more out of ignorance than anything else. As modern education doesn't teach us practical aspects of baby care, educated parents also harbour such "erroneous" ideas. All anecdotal reports of a child being toilet trained early reflect only one thing and that is "conditioned reflex." The child is conditioned after a few days to pass the stools by straining reflexly, whenever the child feels the potty seat under him. The child is really not conscious of the bowel movement nor has it come under his voluntary control. It just reflects a training that is based on conditioning the child rather than a true and real toilet training (remember Pavlov's experiments of conditioning reflexes with the dogs). Infact all such children have to be retrained later on in life, which *now* is a true and learned training. It is believed that retraining of such children is more difficult than those children who have not been toilet trained and conditioned earlier. So I don't recommend toilet training before the child is ready for it.

READINESS FOR TOILET TRAINING

It depends upon the following three important aspects:

1. **Anatomical readiness**: During the first year, the muscles of the lower half of the body including the muscles that control the sphincters of the bladder and bowel are yet not fully under the control of the nervous system. It is obvious that firstly, the child should gain neurological control over the muscles used for controlling defecation and urination, before he can be toilet trained. When this full neurological control comes differs from child to child. A similar analogy exists for walking also. As mentioned in another chapter ("Growth and Development"), the age at which a child starts walking differs from child to child. Some may achieve it at the age of 1 year while others may achieve it as late as 18-21 months. This is due to a difference in the timing of the full neurological control of the muscles of the legs, and until that happens, the child simply cannot walk. Therefore, attempts to make the child walk before he is anatomically ready for it, is futile and simply a waste of the time and energy of the parents. I have encountered many parents who make their child "walk" with the help of the walker, under the mistaken belief that that their child will walk earlier. I am afraid it doesn't quite happen that way, both for walking as well as for toilet training.
2. **Cognitive (psychological) readiness**: The child may be anatomically ready for toilet training i.e. he may have attained full neurological control of the musculature; but he must also be ready psychologically for it. This comes a few months after the anatomical readiness. Before that the child doesn't possess the ability to understand the elimination process and to solicit the necessary parental help in pursuit of this venture by means of clues.

How do the parents judge that their child is ready psychologically? This is by means of cues provided by the child whenever he has the urge to urinate or pass stools. This may be non-verbal e.g. the child may pause in what he is doing, there may be a sudden fleeting change in his facial expression or he may pull or tug at his diapers. It may also take be verbal in the form of grunting, or use of relatively clear language incorporating words relating to elimination process (as used by the parents).

3. **Educational process:** Toilet training is an educational process, rather than being disciplinary in nature. It is inherently obvious, but often overlooked, that the child is really the only person who can control the muscles and impulses of elimination. It should, therefore be equally obvious, but often it is not, that the parent's main thrust should be in helping the child to exercise this control rather than taking matters in their own hands and forcing the child to be toilet trained. The child should be first made to understand the

goal, and that is acceptance of the toilet as the appropriate place for elimination.

Once the child understands that stools and urine should be passed in the bathroom and that his parents want him to do so, he will try to do so. This is because of the child's innate desire to please his parents (which is a powerful motivation for the child in achieving most of the developmental milestones).

The parents can then take the child to the toilet and make him assume the appropriate posture for elimination. All this should be done in a calm and relaxed fashion. It may happen quite a few times, that before they can put the child on the toilet, the child may already have eliminated. This should not discourage or frustrate the parents; rather they should regard it as a part of training.

After all, if the parents also undergo training in any field (say computers), they also will make many a mistake before they can learn the art. If the tutor thinks of his pupil as "good for nothing" and scolds him and ridicules him, the pupil will have a sense of insecurity and indecision. He is bound to create more errors and end up making a mess of the whole thing. In fact he may land up hating the training and not want to do it any further. On the other hand, if the tutor is patient and understanding that such errors are apt to take place and praises the pupil for even small achievements, the pupil will be encouraged and stimulated to give his best, and will end up completing the training successfully.

It holds true for toilet training also, where parents are the tutors and their child is the disciple. Parental praise and approval for small successes and progress is a very powerful stimulant for the child to master the art. The parents should also not be in a hurry to "finish" the course of "toilet training" within a particular time frame. Parents should be patient and willing to tolerate lapses on the part of the child, without getting angry with him or ridiculing him, because this will undermine his confidence and make the task of training more difficult. It may sometimes happen that on picking up the clue from the child, you take him to the potty and make him sit there, but the child doesn't eliminate even after a reasonable time period. On asking, the child may reply that he doesn't have the urge. But as soon as you remove him from the potty seat, he may void in his pants. Or he may void before you can take him to the potty. You should be understanding under both situations, understand that the child is trying his best to learn and master the art. Under these circumstances, to blame the child and punish him or get angry with him is not rational. Be patient and understanding; he will definitely master the art; some may do it sooner, some may take some time.

But if the child is coerced to become toilet trained and the parents get angry and frustrated, the child will resent both the process of toilet training and the trainers' i.e. the parents. Subconsciously, some children will harbour this resentment and to "take it out", he will do just the opposite of what is desired of him. That is, he will try to displease his parents because that is his way of getting back at them. Whenever he makes the parents angry, he derives a sense of morbid satisfaction that his "doings" provoke the parents. A good deal of trouble in the families centering on toilet training is due to this "war" between the parents and their child. And this war is nothing else but a battle for control i.e. who really is the "boss?" The parents feel that the child should follow whatever is told to him. The child, on the other hand, is at a stage when he is striving for autonomy and self-control. He wants to do things in his own ways. One side or the other may win such wars, but the wars are never won without causing considerable damage and pain to both. *(Incidentally, the "biggest war" fought between the parents and the child is over the issue of feeding and not toilet training).* Parents should handle these important issues, delicately and with tact, letting the child believe that he is in control. The parental role should be to guide the child in achieving developmental progress. Battles only make things worse and complicated.

It is important to note that a total laissez fare attitude is also not the most useful attitude for the parents to adopt. They should make it clear to the child that toilet training is an important goal that the child should strive to attain and that they personally want the child to achieve it. And once the child is prepared psychologically for it, the role of the parents is largely to encourage the child in attaining this goal at his pace and not at their pace!

BEDWETTING (ENURESIS)

The child is unable to control urine voiding, usually during nightime. A neonate is a natural enuretic and only by the age of 2-3 years is the child able to have some degree of mastery over his voiding of urine. As the child masters it, he gets up at night whenever he has the urge to pass urine and tells his parents. Such a child, by and large, is day and night-time dry and only occasionally, he may pass urine in his pants e.g. when he is too busy playing or when he is in a deep sleep. Such rare occasions are normal and the child should not be made conscious of it or scolded or made to feel guilty.

For children who are not able to achieve this control, doctors prefer to wait till the age of 5 years before considering it as a problem. So if your child is bed-wetting say at the age of 3 ½ years, it may just be that he requires some more time to be able to control it. Don't worry about it much as most likely the child will outgrow it with time. Above 5 years, for a bedwetting child, the doctor may prescribe some simple tests like urine examination to rule out a problem with the urinary tract and if none is found (as is usually the case); the child is said to be suffering from "psychogenic" bed-wetting.

This is the commonest type of bed-wetting and is usually due to stress felt by the child during the time that he was being toilet trained. For example, if a child of 3 years is unable to control himself and wets his pants regularly, the parents may scold or beat him, humiliate him and convey to him "you are good for nothing "type of attitude. This type of toilet training where there is conflict and tension between the child and the parents (called "coercive toilet training") undermines the confidence of the child, plus he secretly resents the whole process. This adverse psychological effect on the child leads to his being a bed wetter. For such a problem, it is important for the parents to realise that the child is not wetting deliberately. He wants to co-operate and would give anything to overcome the problem. But he has little control over the unconscious feelings that produce the wetting in his sleep. What he needs is more confidence in his ability to control the wetting and this can only be gradually built up with patience and help from the parents. All negative remarks from the parents should completely stop. Don't humiliate or demean the child. Instead the general attitude should be one of encouragement. They should explain to the child that quite a few children have this problem but that practically all of them overcome it with time, as it is transient in nature. They can express confidence in their child that he, too, will also surely overcome it. The child should be praised and encouraged if he doesn't bedwet one night or if the frequency of bedwetting is reduced. A chart can be maintained on a "to be reviewed weekly" basis and improvement found in one week over the preceding week should be lauded. The child can also be rewarded by giving him some coveted article like toy etc. on showing improvement. Intermittent failures or worsening should be ignored. Making the child drink less fluid after evenings may be of some help. Waking the child up every night from deep sleep and making him urinate is of doubtful benefit. Drug therapy for this condition is not satisfactory. The medicines may be able to control bedwetting, but obviously they cannot be given for an indefinite period and so when they are stopped, the child may again start bed wetting. Some conditioning alarms are available those ring a bell when the bed is wet and are effective in some cases. Then there is another way of treatment called "bladder training." It is found that many enuretic children have a low bladder capacity. So during the daytime the child is encouraged to postpone urination (when he feels the urge) as long as possible. Parents can help by diverting the attention of the child during this voluntary "urine retention." *Usually it is seen that within 6 months of seeking medical opinion, the child is cured irrespective of the type of therapy.*

What has been discussed so far is about a child who never was able to achieve control (called "primary enuresis"). What about those children who had achieved control satisfactorily and now again have started bed-wetting (called "regressive or secondary bed-wetting")? In these cases, the usual cause is some change in the lifestyle or routine of the child or some emotional trauma to the child. Examples are shifting to a new house, birth of a baby in the family, some tragedy in the family, when the child starts his schooling etc. Secondary bed wetters are easier to treat and the problem is usually transient.

CHAPTER 13

CHILD PSYCHOLOGY AND ASSOCIATED PROBLEMS

KEY POINTS

- **Up to 1 year (infancy stage):** The key issue is formation of a strong emotional bond between the child and parents.
- **1-3 years (toddler stage):** Key issues are formation of a good "self-esteem", a desire to be autonomous, the child's frequent use of the word "NO" and his overwhelming desire to please parents with his actions.
- **3-6 years (pre-school stage):** The child lives in a world of fantasy and perceives himself as the "centre of universe." Sibling rivalry is common at this age.
- **More than 6 years (school going stage):** The child involves in organised peer group activities, hobbies and development of skills.
- **Discipline:** Verbal/non-verbal expression of disapproval is an effective disciplinary method for all age groups. "Time out" is an effective method for extinguishing harmful or disruptive behaviour.
- **Behavioural problems**: Many of the behavioural problems like thumb sucking, head banging, temper tantrums, nail biting, breath holding etc are attention seeking devices or a means for tensional outlet. Frustration, fatigue, hunger, loneliness, and inadequate parental attention exaggerate them. On the other hand, behaviours like "infantile" stuttering, lisping, pica (dirt eating) etc. are non-attention seeking and go away with time.
- **Sibling rivalry:** One of the best ways to help the older child get over the jealousy and hence rivalry of having a younger sibling is not to make him feel a rival at all. The child should be made to act as if he is a "third" parent to the younger one.
- **Parental attitude**: They should accept the child as it is; with all his goodness as well as shortcomings, without feeling dejected that the child is not one of their "dreams." They should not have "unrealistic" expectations from him.

How do you tell the difference between a psychiatrist and a patient at the mental hospital?

"The patients are the ones that eventually get better and go home!"

NORMAL PSYCHOLOGICAL DEVELOPMENT

It is divided for simplification into 4 age groups: infancy (up to 1 year); toddler (1-3 years); pre-school (3-6 years); and school going (more than 6 years). The psychological development in these groups is discussed below one by one.

Infancy (Up to 1 Year)

Contrary to common belief, a child below the age of 4 months cannot be "spoiled." Therefore parents are encouraged to respond to every cry and distress of the child with immediate attention and love, and can pamper him a lot. Setting limits for older infants (more than 4 months) is important as they can use crying, fussiness etc. as a means for manipulation.

The key issue in infancy is formation of a strong emotional bond between the child and parents. These attachment bonds form the basis for a meaningful and fruitful human relationship throughout the life span. How to judge that such a bond is being formed satisfactorily?

- **Social smile:** A powerful criterion (during 1st 6 months) is "social smile." The mother and child derive mutual pleasure in "talking" and interacting with each other. The child responds by feeling pleased and satisfied, which he overtly manifests as an innocent smile that he flashes off and on during such an emotional interaction. If the child does not smile back by the age of 3-4 months, there is something developmentally wrong with him or the child is being grossly neglected emotionally by the parents.
- **Separation anxiety:** Another important criterion (after 6 months) is "separation anxiety." A baby who is normally attached to his mother is at ease in the mother's lap. If some stranger approaches him, he becomes wary, his facial expression changes and he turns towards the mother for reassurance. If taken off the mother's lap by a stranger, the child may start crying. The child's distress on seeing a strange face and further distress on separation from his mother indicates that the attachment process is proceeding normally.

Toddler (1-3 years)

- **Self-esteem and "mirroring":** A toddler is in a state of continuous love affair with this world. He is enamoured by his activities and excited by what he finds in the world around him. An important developmental aspect is the formation of a good "self esteem." For this the key concept is "mirroring", namely the information the child gathers about himself by the facial expression and comments of those around him. If the parents feel delight in the toddler's emerging skills and independence, this is reflected back to him as positive information about self. Over many years, the facial expressions and comments of parents become internalised within the child as deep-seated convictions about his self-worth.

If the child's doings are met with a constant frown and displeasure from the parents, he will harbour feelings of negative self-worth. All children have feelings of both positive and negative self-worth. The overall balance depends on the parental and the societal approval and appreciation of his acts and skills versus the disapproval. Thus, a child gains insight about self from what the world around him reflects back.

- **Autonomy and independence:** Another core issue is the desire to be autonomous and independent, which manifests itself as the child's acquisition and frequent use of the word "NO." Children's use of 'no' either by verbal expression or in action through behavioural opposition signifies the powerful wish on their part to be in control of themselves. Because of this strong mindedness and the frequent use of 'no', this age is aptly termed the terrible "twos."
- **Parental-child conflict:** One of the biggest stumbling blocks in the parents reconciling to this is the poor judgement of the child at this age. "Rash and dangerous" impulses of the child (e.g. fiddling with the electrical outlets) elicit in the parents a sense of duty, which they have to fulfil by themselves saying "no" to the child. The first noticeable conflict between the child and the parents surfaces now, and while absolutely essential, is experienced as unpleasant by both. It portends disagreements in the future and places parents in the difficult position of "the heavy." Therefore the ideal way of child upbringing is to strike a balance: autonomous but harmless behaviour; though may appear seemingly foolish to parents, is supported, while dangerous and disruptive behaviour is consistently and calmly limited. Parents should not cave in and give in to every demand of the child in order to avoid a direct confrontation with the child and thus "smooth" the relationship, as this only leads to the child becoming a tyrant.

2-year old child: By and large independent. She uses her brains to pull the stool and climb on it so as to reach the tap for brushing her teeth.

- **Desire to please others:** Another very important point is the toddler's wish and a powerful one, too, to please his parents with his actions. This should be reconciled with the child's equally powerful wish for self-control. If the child's playful explorations are not encouraged and his wish for autonomy is not respected i.e. by too many parental "noes", he will try to prove that in other fields (commonly eating and toilet control); parents just cannot control him. If however, there has been an optimum balance and the child is not frustrated by too many "noes", then he has the powerful urge to please his parents. The child will then internalize the parental attitudes and take pride and joy in accomplishing what the parents' desire.

Pre-School Child (Age 3-6 years)

- **Fantasy world:** A world of fantasy surrounds the child. It may include the boastful wish to be big and powerful and to show it off. Pre-schoolers perceive themselves as the "centre of the universe." They believe that everyone around them should be aware of their thoughts and pay due attention to them. Sibling rivalry is common at this age with competitive struggle for parental affection.
- **Unrealistic fears:** The "fantasy" thoughts of the child may manifest themselves as fears about ghosts, monsters, darkness etc. The pre-school stage of mental development comes to an end when the child learns to moderate his fantasies of power and privilege by identifying with the rules for self-control as well as reality.

The School-Age Child (more than 6 years)

The child becomes involved in organized peer group activities, where there are certain rules and codes of conduct. The child starts devoting time for the development of skills and academics. He starts having personal hobbies as a means of recreation and past time. At the same time they begin to exclude other children from certain activities, because they are perceived as not "suitable" for that particular activity. It is at this stage that parental expectations weigh down heavily on the child, particularly the parent's desire for their child to excel in academics and other fields. Parents should avoid pressure on the child to perform according to their unrealistically high expectations, to avoid the emotional turmoil and depression in the child of failure to "live up" to his parent's expectations.

ISSUES IN PARENTHOOD

- **Feeling of guilt:** In many situations, parents may feel guilty regarding child-rearing. Common instances are when the mother is a working woman, the baby has some handicap, the child is an adopted one, there is preference for one child over other etc. Whatever the reason for guilt, it acts as a stumbling block in disciplining the child, as the parents expect too little from the child and too much from themselves. Or they are vacillating (because of guilt) when the child needs firmness. A child knows when he is getting away with too much naughtiness and is also aware of the limits imposed upon him by the parents. Guilty parents pretend not to notice when the child misbehaves, thus not setting the limits desired. Let the child realize that an occasional angry outburst from their side is normal if he tries to cross the limits imposed. Parents should not feel guilty about their anger and act "conciliatory and softly" towards the child afterwards, because it conveys the impression to the child that the parents have committed some wrong by punishing or scolding him.
- **To be firm and friendly**: Parents should remember that they can be both firm as well as friendly. If the parents are firm when the situation demands and set consistent limits, the child understands it. Also it is an important

part of the training of the child for the future. He learns to distinguish between the desirable and undesirable, and so is reasonable with people socially, as he grows older. Parents should act and behave like older friends of their child rather than imposing strict and rigid codes of conduct, as is done by some nannies, grandmas' etc. By acting as friends, the parents share in the fun and play of the child. They also overlook simple, harmless pranks of the child. While, if too strict a discipline is enforced, there will be too many limits set on the child. Most of his actions will be monitored and met with "nos." The child will chafe at it and want some freedom without anyone keeping an "eagle eye" on him and constantly finding fault with him or criticising him. Don't give too many warnings or say too many "no's" to the child. E.g. "Don't touch the lamp, it will fall down and break"; "Don't go out, you will get lost" etc. This doesn't mean that you should give your child carte blanche and let him do whatever he wishes. Warnings are necessary if there is a danger of some harm and also to set limits on the child's unwanted behaviour. But some parents go on saying "no" to practically all things; "don't do this, don't do that" etc. This undermines the self-confidence of the child, who feels that whatever he does is in some way wrong, because his parents are always finding fault with him and telling him not to do this, not to do that etc.

In rearing children, parents undertake an often tiring and frustrating task. The major difficulties in parenting are:

- **Physical and emotional exhaustion**: Caring for a child means a lot of effort and hard work. This is partly compensated by the child's positive reinforcements in the form of joys and smiles. Parental exhaustion decreases their emotional responsiveness towards the child and hence when the parents feel at the end of their tethers, it is always advisable to take some rest and "quality time" out. (Please refer to the chapter on "Parental Concerns and Anxieties."). Impatience, chafing and disapproval from the parental side are a part and parcel of child rearing.
- **Unfulfilled expectations from their child**: Parents may nurture unrealistic fantasies about their child that may be a latent manifestation of their own unmet desire for respect and admiration. Putting it in another way, parents may expect the child to excel and do well in those fields in which they were not successful. Parents have to adjust to the temperament and the limitations of the child and this involves accepting and reconciling to the loss of the "fantasy" child that was hoped for but did not materialize. Ultimately parents should accept the child as it is, with all his goodness as well as shortcomings, without feeling frustration and dejection that the child is not one of their "dreams."

DISCIPLINE

1. **Corporal punishment:** The term discipline while frequently used to mean some sort of punishment actually is derived from the word "disciple"

which means to teach. By complimenting good behaviour, and setting consistent and appropriate limits for unwanted traits, the child is made to distinguish between the desirable and the undesirable, the good and the bad. Punishment, when necessary, should be age appropriate and not psychologically destructive to the child. Corporal punishment is not only less effective than positive reinforcement, but also potentially harmful. It teaches a child that physical aggression is an acceptable way of dealing with anger. In the long run, it makes them insolent and rowdy.

1. **Strictness or permissiveness:** In discipline, either strictness or permissiveness is not the main issue. Good hearted parents who are not afraid to be firm when the situation demands get good results with either moderate strictness or moderate permissiveness. On the other hand **strictness** that comes from harsh feelings and is too rigid, not appropriate to the situation or **permissiveness** in which parents are vacillating and filled with indecision as to how to deal with the child can lead to poor results. The real issue is the attitude the parents have in rearing up and managing the child and what attitude is engendered in the child as a result.

- **Strictness:** Some parents may lean towards a moderate amount of strictness, it being a part of their nature. They should stick to their convictions that what they are doing is correct and thus not have indecisions in their minds. This type of strictness is not harmful as long as the parent-child emotional bond is a secure one. Strictness is harmful when the parents are rigid, harsh and chronically disapproving (chronic don't do this, don't do that, i.e. chronic "noes") plus the strictness doesn't take into consideration the child's age, individuality, and the situation. In other words, it is inflexible.
- **Permissiveness**: Parents who on the other hand are easy going by nature, who are not strict about the child's mannerisms as long as it doesn't transgress harmlessness, can also raise good children, as long as these parents are not afraid to be firm about matters that they consider important and crossing certain limits. There are some parents who are too permissive. They literally allow the child to get away with murder. They turn a blind eye and look the other way whenever the child commits some act that is not to be condoned. They do not demand much from their child and lets him rule the roost. These types of parents are usually indecisive and timid or more commonly harbour some sub conscious guilt vis-à-vis the upbringing of their child. The children of such parents are apt to be tyrants and demanding, raising a racket and throwing all types of tantrums whenever their wishes are not being fulfilled. This is because they have never been disciplined and no limits set upon them firmly. So they consider that whatever they do, think or want is correct and should be complied with.

2. **Family atmosphere:** Thus, the most important factor in discipline is not strictness or permissiveness, but

growing up in a loving family atmosphere where the child feels wanted, being loved and wanting to love in return. In discipline parents have to act as guides, as they are older and mature. Therefore the responsibility of parents is to see to it that their child is on the right track, and if not, to deal with it firmly.

3. **Punishment:** The best test of a punishment is the effect that it has on the child. If it has hurt him very much, the punishment was too harsh. On the other hand, if it makes the child repeat the same behaviour, uncaring towards the parental "no", it is missing fire. Once in a while, the parent's anger may get out of control and they may slap the child. It is acceptable, as long as it is not used as a "routine" technique by the parents in disciplining the child.

4. **Threats**: Avoid threats, particularly those about which you are not serious or are not in a position to carry out. Once the child realizes the hollowness of the threat, it destroys the parents' authority. Scary threats, as those of a policeman or a ghost are wrong. A threat should be used judiciously and should be real. Harmless behaviours like temper tantrums, sulking, fussiness, whining etc. are most effectively extinguished by consistently ignoring them and not by means of threats.

A child on a chair in a corner of a room with his face towards the wall.

VARIOUS METHODS OF DISCIPLINE

1. **Verbal or non-verbal expression of disapproval:** It is an effective means of punishment for all age groups. Verbal disapproval is more effective when combined with positive instructions on appropriate behaviour. Another important concept of discipline is that the focus should be on the misbehaviour which should be pointed out to the child as undesirable; and not on belittling or humiliating the child.

2. **Learning by experience:** Some types of behaviour are most effectively extinguished when the child learns by experiencing the negative consequences of his actions. By verbally telling him not to do a particular thing may not be effective and he may go on repeating the action. But when he experiences the negative consequence of his action, it is extinguished. For example, if you tell the child that he should always hold the hands of the parents when they are in the market, the child may not do so, and instead enjoy being independent and running here and there. Now, once if the parents hide themselves, so that the child after his bit of fun cannot locate them, he will get very anxious and start crying. After a brief interval

of his crying, when you appear and explain to him why he should hold hands, he will do it regularly afterwards, because he has learnt that if he doesn't, he may get lost and may not be able to locate his parents.

3. **Delaying privileges**: Delaying things that the child likes till other less pleasurable tasks are completed is also effective. For example, the child may love watching cartoons on the T.V. Parents can lay down the pre- condition that they will allow him to watch it, only if he first, say, completes his homework. Similarly, if the child mishandles his toys, they should be removed, if he spills juice on the ground, he should be made to clean it up etc., before giving him more juice etc.

4. **"Time out":** It is an effective method for extinguishing disruptive behaviour. It works in a child of even 8 months and consists in temporarily boycotting him, i.e. withdrawing him from social interaction temporarily. Parents should maintain a calm demeanour and avoid engaging in angry lectures or negotiations with the child. An isolated, but not frightening, spot should be chosen for the "time out" and if in spite of one warning, the child persists in some undesirable behaviour, he should be led firmly to that spot and let him remain there, devoid of any social interaction or other interesting thing. Consistency and perseverance are vital for the success of this technique. Initially the child may show resistance and may not remain in the isolated spot or start creating a racket if put there. It is at this point that the parents consider it a useless technique and give up. But as mentioned before, perseverance and patience pays dividends. Once the child knows that if he does something undesirable, he has to "retire" to the isolated spot, come what may, he will be less disposed to displease his parents and at the first warning will terminate the undesirable behaviour. The length of "time out" should be brief, approximately 1 minute for every year, to a maximum of 5 minutes. This technique loses its effectiveness once the child becomes 5 years +. When the "time out" period is over, the child should be welcomed back to the social setting without further mention or discussion of his misbehaviour. After time out, it is important to help the child learn the socially appropriate behaviour, and to compliment positive behaviour on his part.

5. **Giving child choices:** Don't give the child too many choices, i.e. "do you want to...?" If you ask the child whether he will have food, whether they should dress him up, what clothes he wants to wear etc., you are asking for trouble as the natural instinct of the child, particularly during ages 1-3 years is to say "no". Then you have to argue and persuade the child. Ultimately you spend a lot of your time, energy and patience in making the child do what was necessary in the first place anyhow. So it is better not to offer him a choice in the first place in the form of a question. Rather when it is lunchtime, just lead him to the table or start dressing or undressing him up when

required, all in a casual and nonchalant manner.

FACTORS EXAGGERATING BEHAVIOURAL PROBLEMS

- **Fatigue**: If the child is tired after too much stimulation and play, he seeks rest, just like an adult. Adults usually will pursue some hobby like reading a magazine, watching T.V. etc. or will go to bed for rest. A child unfortunately is too small to have hobbies as a means of recreation and tension outlet. Plus sleeping is the last thing that is in his mind. Therefore, he craves for parental attention and love when tired. So it is the duty of parents to hug and cuddle the child and make him feel relaxed, after which he can be gently lulled to sleep.
- **Hunger:** Some children become irritable and edgy when they are hungry. Thus some of the below mentioned behaviours may be exaggerated. A child, usually, will not start eating as soon as he comes home, particularly if he is also tired. However after some "quality time" relaxation with his parents, he can be offered food, which he will eat ravenously.
- **Lack of parental attention (boredom/ loneliness):** It happens many a time that the parents are too busy in their work or in some social gathering or absorbed in watching an interesting episode or movie on the T.V. The child may be trying to attract their attention at the same time, like he may want to show them something or simply seek their company. But due to lack of parental attention, he feels neglected and left out. So as an outlet for his tension and frustration, he may exhibit some of the behaviours listed below:
- **Frustration:** It may be that the child is frustrated and feels "low" due to reasons like the day in school was not good, he had a fight with his friends, the teacher scolded him because he didn't know certain thing which the teacher asked etc. Naturally, at this time, he turns towards his parents for love and sympathy. Parents should be shrewd and alert enough to pick this up and gently ask the child what is bothering him. They should lift up the spirits of the child and also provide some means of entertainment like his favourite toy, video games etc. as a vent for his frustrations. One good thing about children is that they don't keep any hurt or grouse in their heart for long, as adults do. So once they get love from their parents, they quickly become satisfied and return back to normal instead of prolonged sulking.

COMMON PSYCHOLOGICAL PROBLEMS OF THE CHILD

***A psychiatrist once asked a patient, "When people get disgusted, they say 'go to hell.' What do people in hell say when they get disgusted?" The patient replied, "They say go to India and meet you." ***

1. Lisping

Children in the initial months of speech development often do not pronounce words clearly. Lisping or substitution defect (e.g. 'th' for 's') is a common, normal developmental phenomenon, which is considered abnormal only if it persists beyond the age of 5 years.

2. Stuttering

Many children stutter to some extent. The pronunciation is not clear plus there may be a pause and repetition of the syllables without further words of the sentence forthcoming for a while. The young child is not conscious of this non-fluency or repetitions. A child's vocabulary is limited and his expression power in combining words to form sentences, particularly long ones, is limited. As a result, the words seem to come out in an outpour, albeit brokenly. This is because, in his mind, the child has something to narrate but while putting these thoughts into words, he is not that fast and smooth. He has to "search in his mind" for the words to express himself. This is a normal phenomenon and parents should not be concerned if the speech of their child is not fluent and smooth initially. If parents have noticed, stuttering increases when the child is excited about something and eager to tell them some narration, which he considers funny and interesting. He bubbles along, repeating in an effortless manner. This is a normal phenomenon till the age of 3-4 years. This phase usually remains for 6-12 months after which it passes off, provided parents don't pay any attention to it and don't show concern or anxiety about it. Parents should not be bothered about it, as it is a transient condition, occurring in many children and which they outgrow with time. Parents feel that there is something wrong with the tongue whenever the child has any speech difficulties. But tongue-tie has got nothing to do with. However, persistence of stuttering beyond 4 years of age is not normal and is then referred to as "stammering." It can persist in adulthood also. An adult suffering from stammering is very aware and conscious of his speech and any situation, which makes him tense, nervous or more self-conscious, aggravates the condition.

This is usually due to mishandling of the earlier situation (i.e. stuttering).

Things to do (for stuttering)

i. Give him the attention he deserves when he is speaking to you. Do listen with patience and understanding because he is telling you something that he considers important.

ii. Let him finish what he is saying, no matter how much difficulty he is having.

iii. Eliminate as much as possible the causes of tension and frustrations in his daily routine. Maintain a calm and relaxed atmosphere at home. This can be done by slowing down your own pace and by handling routine things in an easy and unhurried manner.

iv. Try to speak more slowly, clearly and calmly to him. If you speak in short, simple sentences and at a slower tempo, he will find it that much easier to achieve fluency. If you are relaxed and unhurried, he is apt to feel more relaxed when he is speaking to you.

v. Sometimes a playmate or another adult may bring to the child's notice his way of speaking. Should this happen and the child ask his parents for guidance, the parents should reassure him by saying that everyone gets entangled while speaking once in a while if they are excited or talking very fast, and that there is nothing wrong with him.

Things to avoid

i. Don't make him self-conscious or give it the label of "stuttering" or any other label. Once the child's speech is "labelled", it means to him that something is wrong with him.

ii. Never discuss in his presence the "trouble" he is having with his speech.

iii. Try to avoid becoming anxious about his speech. Most children go through this phase. Anxiety can be transmitted to the child and remember a child's perception and understanding that something is amiss is very acute.

iv. When he speaks to you, your facial expression should be deadpan and not a give away clue that you are in some way bothered about his way of speaking.

v. Do not ask the child "to speak more slowly", "take a deep breath etc." In fact do not make any suggestions.

vi. Do not reward him for periods of fluency, neither force him to repeat something that he has got "entangled" with.

vii. Do not ridicule him, because this will lead to a lowering of his self-esteem and confidence, which will only worsen the problem.

3. "Mirror" writing

Many children, during the initial few months of learning to write, often confuse words while writing and so may write "b" for "d", "P" for "p" etc. This decreases with time and is no cause for concern. However if the problem is persistent, and the child seemingly cannot understand that he is making a mistake, it may be one of the indicators of a non-benign problem called as "Dyslexia" for which medical help should be sought.

4. Mathematical problems

Another common problem that children have is in reciting 1-100 in the initial few months. They will come to the nines and then get confused as to what follows it. To give an example, child may speak fluently up to 29 or 39 and then forget that 30 and 40 comes after that. If some adult tells them, they will again start fluently 31, 32.... This is also transient.

5. Bedwetting

This is a very common problem and is called as "enuresis." The child usually wets the bed at night-time. This phenomenon is normal up to the age of 5 years and only after that the parents should seek medical intervention. For more details on this, parents are referred to the chapter on "Toilet Training."

6. Tics

***A man was collecting brains of different medical specialists for study. The brain of psychiatrists was the most expensive. On being asked the reason, he replied, "You have to collect the brains of a lot of psychiatrists to make it weigh 1 pound." ***

They are repetitive, purposeless, automatic movements and are a means of outlet for tensions. Examples include throat clearing, nose sniffing, grimacing, eye blinking etc. Though these behaviours may be irritating to the parents, it is best not to call attention to them directly. They disappear more quickly if ignored rather than if the child is made conscious of them. Though these movements are harmless, yet they may be socially embarrassing and in some cases signify an underlying psychological problem, particularly if associated with mouthing obscenities and aggressive behaviour. Thus if they are recalcitrant and severe, the help of a child psychologist should be sought.

7. Dirt eating (Pica)

This is another harmless behaviour that many children undergo as a part of their growing up, usually between 1-3 years of age. It is postulated that it may be due to iron deficiency in the child. So it is better to get the child checked for them. A trial of iron therapy can also be given. Though the child usually outgrows this behaviour, it should not be ignored. The best approach is to give the child more attention and to keep an eye on him so that he can be checked whenever he mouths the "dirt." The second way is to provide him with more satisfactory and interesting activities. The side effect of dirt eating is the possibility of worm infestation and chronic lead poisoning.

8. Rocking, head banging and head rolling

These are all tensional outlets, which are by and large benign and pass off, as the child grows older. The child is sometimes not getting the emotional satisfaction that he craves for and so is under mental stress. This is released in various ways.

"Body rocking": It occurs at about 6 months of age. In sitting or crawling position, the child rocks forward and backward. Vigorous rockers have been known to move their cribs across the room. Frequently present when the child is tired or near bedtime, this behaviour continues for 15-30 minutes. It usually ceases by the age of 3 years.

"Head rolling": A lying down child rolls his head from side to side, the resultant friction often causing a bald patch at the back of the scalp. It starts at the age of 7-9 months and subsides by the age of 2 years.

"Head banging": It typically begins at the age of 8-9 months and ceases by the age of 4 years. Children may bang their head in various positions. Thus the front or the back of the head may hit a solid object repetitively. Episodes of head banging may last as long as 3-4 hours. Out of all these, the only one, which can cause any harm to the child is head banging, particularly if he bangs it against a hard surface. But the child never gets any serious injuries, only maybe some bruises and bluish discoloration. It is advisable to keep the cot padded if the child indulges in such behaviours. Also parents should pay more attention to the child's emotional needs.

9. Nail biting

It is different from the other tensional outlets mentioned above in that it doesn't outgrow itself but persists into adolescence and even adulthood. Under situations of tension or nervousness, some adults also start biting and chewing upon their nails.

In this way, their nervous energy is released, which makes them feel calmer and relaxed. Apart from the fact that it doesn't appear socially appealing, it causes little harm. Parents can keep the nails of the child cut short, so that they have nothing to chew upon.

10. Thumb-sucking

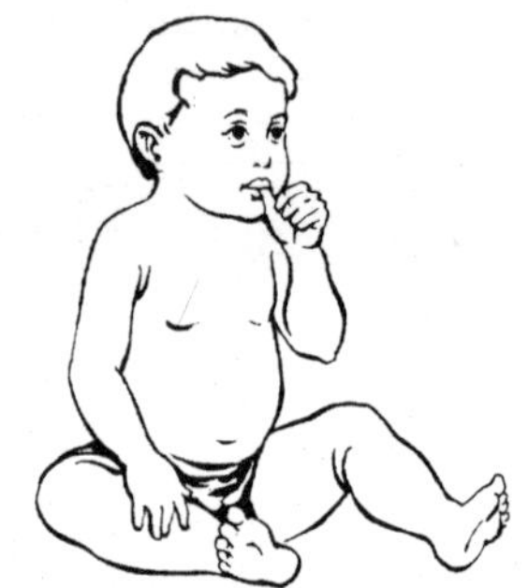

Self-nurturing: A child sucking his thumb

Nice ways to do away with thumb-sucking

Many children are born thumb-suckers. It has been observed in an unborn child too. Some infants have a strong sucking response while others have a less hearty urge.

The chances are fifty-fifty that a natural thumb-sucker will quit on his own before he is five years old. There are only two valid reasons to attempt to change the habit of thumb-sucking, one relates to dental concerns & the other is social.

Remember, while you attempt to change the habit, that, it will be a gradual process and never shame your child as you work on it.

Pacify the infant's sucking reflex: The pacifier could be a bottle with a slow-flowing nipple that can help satisfy her need.

"Don't do it".

"Here, you can use this".

Do not give the habit undue attention. It is more likely that the child will drop that habit before she is in her first standard. In any case it is better not to give unnecessary and repeated attention to the habit.

"No, no".

Make the child aware: Have him look at the mirror while sucking his thumb. Suck your own thumb and ask him what he thinks. Point out other children who are sucking their thumbs and ask your child how they look.

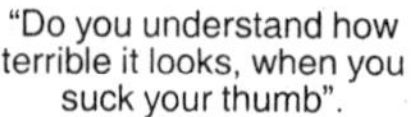

"Do you understand how terrible it looks, when you suck your thumb".

"Tell me, how do I look, when I suck my thumb".

Give the child an alternative: A less noticeable substitute may satisfy him. A

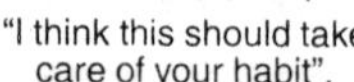

"I think this should take care of your habit".

"Take this dear, it should help you".

rabbit foot or a small furry stuffed animal (soft toy) to rub may do the trick.

Change the situation, break the association: For very young children, try to reduce the time spent sucking rather than eliminate it altogether. If your child only sucks her thumb while sitting in a particular chair and watching television, do not allow her to sit in that seat.

"Don't do it dear". "Come dear, sit down here".

Place restrictions on where she may suck her thumb: Keep a record for several days of where and when she sucks her thumb. Choose one place or time and tell her that it is no longer acceptable to suck her thumb in that place or at that time. Be sure to choose a place and time when you will be there for several consecutive days.

"I don't want you, sucking your thumb anywhere". "I don't want you, sucking your thumb while you are in the dining room".

Eliminate the habit in one place at a time: Begin with a time frame, you are fairly certain that the child can manage easily. The first day the child may earn a thumb print for not sucking his thumb for just a few minutes, while watching television. Gradually increase the length of time required to earn a thumb print.

"Good, you haven't sucked your thumb for quite some time now". "Good, you shall earn a thumb print for not sucking your thumb in the past half an hour".

Apply a natural consequence: Choose a natural consequence to follow it your child does suck her thumb in the unacceptable place. If watching television is chosen, turn off the set for five minutes when she sucks her thumb. After five minutes with no television or thumb sucking she may resume watching.

Right

"Since, you are sucking your thumb, you will not get a candy today". "Since, you are sucking your thumb, you will not get to watch television for five minutes".

When your child stops sucking his thumb, touch, hug and give him a lot of love. Positive reinforcement at this time may be helpful.

Right

"Nice to see you without your thumb in your mouth." "You look like a big boy, now".

Thumb-sucking usually starts appearing at the age of 3-4 months and may become established by the age of 7-8 months. It is a self-nurturing phenomenon used by the child to seek solace. If you remove the thumb from the child's mouth it comes out, but pronto it goes back again in his mouth as soon as your attention is diverted. It appears just like the proverbial dog's tail that cannot be straightened. Fortunately, this behaviour, though appearing "childish" and "immature" in say a 4-year-old child, tends to decrease by time and "burns out" by 5-6 years, even without any active measures. Reminding him constantly or punishing him doesn't help much, because it is a means of seeking solace and how can anyone give up something which is soothing and in which he finds mental peace and calm? Measures like putting chilli on the thumb etc. are of dubious benefit, because the child will wash it off or rub it off somehow. Thumb sucking often appears in solitude and is reduced greatly when the child is actively playing or socially interacting, because then he "forgets" about it. This is because he is now getting solace in the interesting and enjoyable company of others. The only problem is that prolonged thumb-sucking can mal-align the teeth. But since the habit usually dies out by 5-6 years, i.e. when the permanent teeth are appearing, it does not affect their development. Parents should be reassured that it is a normal part of early childhood behaviour and will resolve spontaneously by the age of 5 years. Parents' attempt to dissuade the child from this habit only reinforces it. Parents need not be much concerned about it as most of the children are happy going and cheerful, sucks mainly during bedtime and only occasionally during the day. Attention should be focussed on the child and not on the thumb-sucking. Parents should try to divert the attention of the child towards more interesting activities that he enjoys. And also they should make the child feel wanted and loved by them. Parents can substitute a pacifier for thumb-sucking. This should be done early (at the age of 3-4 months) before the child gets into a firm habit of thumb-sucking. A pacifier is a blind nipple without a hole, attached to a disk that rests against the baby's mouth. A baby who has mild periods of irritability can often be calmed by the use of a pacifier. There is no side effect of a pacifier, provided it is clean. The habit of pacifier sucking is not a permanent one and tends to recede by the age of 6 months when the instinct of the child to suck decreases. At this juncture, the child may start "spitting" out the pacifier from his mouth. The pacifier can be tied with a string around the neck so that it rests on the baby's chest and doesn't fall on the ground. This is to maintain cleanliness so that dirt and infection don't enter the child's stomach. Pacifier use should be discouraged after the age of 10 months.

11. Temper Tantrums

The child flings himself on the floor, starts screaming, and thrashes around with his hands, feet and head. Any attempt to hold the child or to lift him up is met with resistance as the child fights with you and wants to persist with his tantrums. Control is a central issue. Inability to control some aspect of the external world results in loss of internal control manifested as temper tantrums. Overtiredness, frustration, physical discomfort, fears can evoke temper tantrums. A temper tantrum once in a while is normal, because in children also, the frustration levels are bound to cross the limits once in a while and this is the way they may give vent to it. When the tantrums are intermittently or

Temper Tantrums: Don't succumb to them.

constantly rewarded by giving in to the child's demands as a means of stopping the tantrum at that moment, tantrums can become an entrenched strategy for exerting control. Tantrums normally peak during 2-4 years. If tantrums are persistent after the age of 5 years, usually it tends to persist in the whole childhood. Obviously the best way to control temper tantrums is to remain calm and aloof and not pay any attention to the child's ongoing behaviour, i.e. to ignore it completely. If it is irritating you a lot, you can just walk away from the child into another room. Once the child realises that throwing tantrums is getting him nowhere and no one is bothered or interested in his behaviour, he gives this up as a means of expressing himself, after a few trials. After the child has calmed down, the parents should try to find out what precipitates such tantrums in their child and if possible sympathise with the feelings of the child and tell him that you realize how he feels. You should then try to prevent future recurrences by striking at the cause that is precipitating them. During the tantrum don't argue with him, don't get angry or start beating him. Instead give the child a graceful way out, so that when the worst of the storm is over, the child can reconcile to you more easily.

12. Breath Holding

This is another not so uncommon complaint. To the onlooker it appears frightening. A minor injury, frustration or slapping may precipitate the episode. The child starts crying in a very prolonged fashion without "breaking" the cry. As a result, he expels out the air from his lungs and since he is not inhaling during the crying, he gets a lack of oxygen in the body. It is just like you holding your breath for a prolonged period. The child starts becoming blue, may lose consciousness and may even have a fit (convulsion) due to the lack of oxygen. Frightening as the description is, it is benign in that nothing happens to the child even if he becomes blue and has a transient fit. Parents get extremely frightened at the sight of their child getting blue and if he starts convulsing, it can drive them into a state of acute panic. So they start showering the child with all the attention, massaging and soothing him. Some of the more adventurous may even try to give him cardiac massage and mouth to mouth breathing. Paradoxically this attention is the last thing, which is desired, as the child is doing this to seek attention, and he is succeeding in it, thereby positively reinforcing the behaviour. So this behaviour will continue. The most effective way to extinguish such behaviour is to remain calm and walk out and away from the child completely ignoring him, even if he is limp or convulsing. Once the child realizes that such behaviour is not producing the desired effect i.e. gaining parental attention, after a few more trials, he will give it up. An interesting point is how to distinguish whether a child is having a fit primarily and not secondary to a "breath holding" episode. It is simple. In case of a fit, the child's body will twitch first and later on he will become blue, while in a "breath holding spell" the child will become blue first and later on have twitching i.e. it is vice-versa.

13. Aggressiveness

What constitutes aggressiveness and where to draw the dividing line between normal and abnormal aggressiveness? Some children are a bit hyperactive and aggressive by nature, and have a tendency to boss and dominate over others. As long as it remains within the limits of acceptable social behaviour and doesn't result in harm or injury to others, it is tolerable and normal. Another very important thing is that the child should not take a 'perverse' pleasure in attacking or bullying others. The parents have to teach the child that just being bigger or stronger doesn't mean that he can encroach upon the right of others and do whatever he likes, without caring for the feeling of others. He has to be taught that every child has an equal right as he has. Once he understands that what he is doing is not liked by his parents and is not correct, he will feel guilty about it and tend to avoid such type of behaviour.

14. Timidity

A child at the tender age of 2-3 years lets others take her toys away or to push her around. She may come to the parents crying and complaining every time. This may worry the parents that their child is not able to stand up on her own but always comes running seeking their intervention. In most cases, it is a temporary affair, and as the child grows older, and gains more experience in social interaction, she recognises her rights and is ready to resist. In the initial stages it is wise for the parents not to interfere too much, not to fight her battles for her and not to show too much concern as it may make the child dependent on them for petty matters. Rather tell her casually to go back and get the toy back on her own. If there is a particularly aggressive child in the neighbourhood, who bullies others and doesn't understand reason, it is wise not to let your child interact with him. If he comes and wants to play with your child, you can tell him that he should go and seek company of equal ones.

15. Jealousy and Sibling Rivalry

Jealousy is an inborn trait. It can't be prevented but can be moderated. Many children react to the coming of a new one in the family by yearning to be a baby again. So they may want the bottle again, may relapse into baby talk and act helpless about doing things for themselves. Parents should be wise enough to humour the baby at these moments. Supposing the child is old enough to undress himself, but now wants the parents to do so, the parents can do so. When the child realises that he is not being denied what he wants, but it is no delight also, he will gradually lose the habit. The older child should be made proud of his maturity and his being skilful, big and strong. At the same time, the parents, once in a while, should point out casually towards the helplessness of the younger child. This will make the child take pride in self as a "grown up" and also he will realize that there are many disadvantages in being a small baby.

One of the best ways in which to help the older child get over the pain of having a younger rival is not to make him feel a rival at all. The child should be made to feel that he is not competing in the same league with the baby; he is infact bigger than him. The child should be made to act as if he is no longer a child, but a "third" parent to the younger one. If the older child feels secure and not threatened by the baby, he will shower him with love, teach him new things, give him toys, assist in feeding, bathing and other routine chores of the smaller one, try to protect him from dangers, comfort him etc. The parents should show genuine appreciation of the efforts of the child in caring for the young one. A child always wants to hold the younger baby and kiss and cuddle him. The parents are afraid that the young one may get injured as the older child may drop him. Making them sit on the floor on a rug can eliminate this risk. In these ways the parents can help transform resentful feelings of jealousy into one of co-operation and genuine altruism.

Helping with the new baby: Let her outgrow sibling rivalry.

Parents should make the child mentally prepared for the arrival of a new baby in advance so that he gets used to the idea gradually. The arrival of the baby should change his life as little as possible. It is tactful to play down the new baby during the first few weeks. Don't get too excited over it. Don't talk a lot about it, particularly in front of the older child.

Jealousy may take on many different forms and all of them may not be manifest. Most of the parents say that the older one loves the younger one very much. If that were the case, then there wouldn't be a word like "sibling rivalry and jealousy." So it is always wise to assume that though there is a lot of love, there is a bit of jealousy, too. The child may be fond of the baby otherwise, but may sulk and feel hurt if others admire the baby and shower it with love and attention, thus not paying any attention to him. Similarly when the parents come home from their work and the first thing they want to see and love is the small baby, the older one is bound to feel resentment and hurt. Rather the parents should first enquire about and love the older one (the younger one anyhow is too small at this stage to understand all this) and only after that turn their attention towards the smaller baby.

A child may not show any overt signs of jealousy, but may suddenly, one fine day, not let the younger one touch his toys or things. Sometimes the older one in a fit of rage or jealousy may beat up the younger one or harass him. In these circumstances the parents should be very firm and let the older one know that his browbeating is something they don't appreciate, just as they won't appreciate if someone bigger than him browbeats him. At the same time they should reassure the older one that they love him a lot. In fact the older child requires this type of reassurance a lot off and on, again and again. Parents should see to it that they reassure and show their love towards him not once in a while, but as often as possible. Generally speaking,

Family ties: Interaction within the family fosters sociability.

jealousy is stronger before 5 years when the child doesn't have much of a social circle himself and is dependent on and wants the love of his parents. After the age of 6 years, the child starts having peer interaction and his attention is thus diverted.

The parents have different feelings for each of their child. Should parents love children equally? This question worries a lot of conscientious parents simply because they don't love the children equally and therefore feel guilty about it. But this is expecting the impossible. Every child is different and therefore the parent's feelings for it will also be different. It is the feeling of particular irritation towards one child that makes the parents most guilty, especially if there is no clear reason for it. The parents may try to be constantly considerate to him and to overlook his bad behaviour, yet he may rub them the wrong way often. Good parents care for their children equally and want the best out of life for each of their children and will make necessary sacrifices to do so. Never compare the children amongst themselves. For e.g. saying something like "why can't you be polite and well mannered like your sister?" is not advisable.

The children in the family often fight. Parents should keep out of it until it is harmful to one or the other child. Siding with one child or the other or trying to be judges as to what is fair and what is not, which child is to blame and which is innocent, is counter productive as the child don't care for these things. They only want to come out victorious and the parents to side them. The children may also quarrel in the hope that the parents will vindicate them and scold the other. It is better to demand an end to the hostility, to refuse to listen to any arguments and explanations, to act uninterested and neutral.

Very often parents have to buy identical things for the children, identical in all aspects including colour. This is because the children suspiciously view the other's toy, and if they find any difference, they clamour for it, thinking that it is a better one. No efforts on the part of the parents will convince them that such is not the case. They simply want the other toy. In these situations, it is not wise to force the older one to partake his toy by the oft-heard reasoning "you are older and hence should be understanding." True the older one may give it on insistence by the parents, but inside he feels resentment. He thinks that favouritism is going on. One of the ways out is to take them out to the market and let them choose for themselves what they want, so that they can't very well complain about their own choice!

Sometimes children will fight over one toy with both of them wanting it at the same time. They will pull and tug at the toy and may even break it in the process! Or one of them may get slightly injured in the process. For the parents it is a testing time and usually they will take the side of the younger one and urge the older one to give it up, of course with the promise that after some time they will restore it back to him. The older one, believe me, is not satisfied with this. To part the toy to the younger one is a "defeat" for him plus he feels resentment that the parents are always siding with the younger one, which is really the case in 99% instances. Remember that you can "fool" the younger one more easily. You can take him apart and in a conspiratorial tone tell him that you will give him something better. At the same time you can tell the older one that he will give up the toy after some time to the younger one of his own accord. Generosity of such kind i.e. giving up one's possessions to the younger one should come from within and for this the older child must be made to feel secure and loving first. Forcing a child to share or give up his possessions is not advisable, as the child will chafe at it and resent you and the younger one.

16. Bad Words, Biting and Stealing

Children at the age of 4-5 years, commonly boys, may mouth abuses and bad words. It comes as a shock to the conscentitious parents to hear such words from the mouth of their child. Do not beat the child. Rather firmly let him know that you and other people don't want to hear such words as they are bad and that he should not use them again as you don't want him to use them.

Some children have the tendency to bite others (parents or children) particularly when they are frustrated and irritable. Perhaps such children are being disciplined too much, resulting in a highly-strung child. The parents should pay attention to the environment of the child and try to make it soothing so that the child is in a more relaxed and calm state and not easily provoked. Plus they should make it clear in no uncertain terms that that they don't like and condone such "animal" behaviour and don't want him to repeat it in future.

Some children steal deliberately knowing that it is wrong, but somehow just cannot resist the impulse. It appears as if they derive satisfaction out of it. This type of stealing usually comes at the age of 6 years + when the child understands that stealing is something that is forbidden. Before that, children may sometimes take some things from others' home or from the shop just because they liked it, without being aware that it is tantamount to stealing and hence something bad. In such cases, the parents simply need to remind their child that it is not their good or toy, and that he should go and give it to the proper owner. A child who deliberately steals should be made to confess that he has done it, made to realize that it is something wrong which they don't want him to repeat in future, plus the parents should insist on restitution of the thing to its rightful owner by the child himself. Don't humiliate or beat the child, rather make it clear to him that it can't be permitted.

17. Right and Left-handedness

Many children are ambidextrous till the age of 1-2 years. Only after that they show preference towards one hand. Handedness is usually established by the age of 3 years. There is no evidence to show that a left-handed person is more or less gifted than a right-handed person. So don't make an issue and force the child to use the right hand (which parents believe is better). If you put things like toys etc. towards the right side of the child, there is a likelihood that he will use the right hand preferentially and hence will be right handed. But this should be started early before handedness is established.

18. Teeth Grinding

Teeth grinding ("bruxism") usually occurs during the night. It is because a child, who is normally submissive in the day, acts out his aggression during the night-time by grinding his teeth. The usual history is that of a docile child who is bullied and ridiculed by his peers. Thus he develops a suppressed anger, which is "vented" out in the night by teeth grinding. Helping the child in becoming more aware of his rights and telling the child to fight for his rights plus helping him to find other, alternate ways of expressing resentment may relieve this problem. Organic causes for bruxism includes worm infestations, chronic abdominal disorders, middle ear effusions, allergic rhinitis, and anal pruritus. These should be sought for and treated.

COMFORTING A HURT CHILD

When a child is hurt, physically or emotionally, the child seeks solace from the parents and they also comfort him. Since this is a normal phenomenon and comes to both the child and the parents naturally, it is correct. However, there are some parents who want their child to grow up being brave and so may resist their natural impulse to comfort the child. A child below the age of 4 months cannot be spoiled and so the parents should comfort him at the first instance. However, as the child grows older it is better not to make a fuss about small injuries, but rather just console the child and send him back to play. Parents should not desist from comforting a hurt child, thinking that this way; he will learn to be tough and brave. A secure child (secure emotionally in the family atmosphere) isn't made "timid" by comforting.

Some children start crying on the slightest pretext. They are very sensitive. Small hurts and aches mean a lot to them. This is because parents were overprotecting the child and used to fuss over him for petty things. It can happen to a child who is born after many years of marriage or to a second sibling if the parents feel guilty that there has been some lapse on their part in bringing up the first child. So they shower all their attention on the second one, don't scold or set firm limits on him, and are always taking his side. Even small complaints of the child are met with excessive attention and fuss. Such babies usually are "soft" and may be ill equipped to face the life later on, because they are so much dependent on their parents.

❖❖❖

CHAPTER 14

BABY MYTHS

Most mothers, particularly if it is their first baby are given varying advice, opinions and suggestions. Even the housemaid contributes her share of advice in baby care. These advices are often conflicting and may not be scientifically correct. There are many "well wishers" who cannot digest their meals unless they have passed some "invaluable guidance" to the mother, particularly regarding rearing of the baby.

If the baby is crying there will be different viewpoints. It is ear ache, put oil in the ear; it is a tummy ache, press the stomach, give gripe water; it is constipation, give a laxative, the baby has fever, cover him with blankets etc. Parents should be able to separate the reality from the well meant but sometimes unscientific suggestions of the "well wishers."

The scientific facts are given below and also myths exposed, so that the parents can really know what is good for their baby:

1. **Mothers cannot breast-feed immediately**: The baby should be put to the breast as soon as he and the mother are comfortable. Baby's born by operation i.e. caesarean section can be put to the breast as soon as the mother comes out of the anaesthesia and is comfortable, approximately 4 hours, even if the mother is on I.V. drip.
2. **Initial milk (colostrum) is not good for the baby:** The milk produced within 1-2 hours after parturition is less and called "colostrum". Some mothers think it as "witch milk" and discard it thinking it to be harmful. Nothing is farther from the truth. Colostrum though looks thin, sticky and yellowish is very rich in nutritional factors (richer than even milk) and should in all cases be given to the baby.
3. **A breast-fed baby needs water:** The breast milk is 99% water. So no supplementation with water is advocated during the first 4 months when the child is exclusively on a milk diet. After that as weaning starts and the baby eats semi-solid food, he requires water in order for the body and the kidneys to handle the solute load. However in very hot conditions, the baby may lose a lot of water through the skin and water supplementation becomes necessary. There is no point in adding glucose to water.
4. **A newborn requires multivitamins, gripe water, Bonnisan etc:** A baby requires only mother's milk and nothing else. The only supplementation, which is really required, is iron starting at the age of 4 months. Gripe water contains alcohol, which may be sedating.

5. **A mother ruins her figure due to breast-feeding**: Breast-feeding helps the mother to reduce weight as some of her energy and calories is "going out" in the form of breast milk.

6. **Exposure to cold, breeze, cold drinks, ice cream causes cough/cold in the child**: Coughs and colds are usually caused by viruses present in the atmosphere and not by breeze, cold drinks etc. The viruses are present ubiquitously, more so in the cold months. So parents make all types of erroneous conclusions and blame the above-mentioned things for the coughs and colds, which are anyhow more common during the winters due to the increased prevalence of the viruses. Almost every parent believes that the child gets a cold when he eats cold things like ice creams, cold drinks, curd or fruits like oranges. In fact no dietary restrictions are prescribed in respiratory infections. Children should be encouraged to take a lot of fluids, as this is the best way of liquefying and bringing out the mucus from the lungs.

7. **Swathing the baby in woollens from head to toe will prevent colds:** It can make the child comfortable. But, it cannot kill the viruses present in the air nor can it prevent the baby from contracting those viruses simply because the baby has to breathe the air. Therefore, coughs and colds cannot be prevented and all children have many episodes during their childhood.

8. **Teething causes diarrhoea and fever:** Teething causes mild irritability in the child because of the irritation of gums by the erupting teeth. It directly doesn't cause any illness.

9. **A fat baby is a healthy baby**: In fact a fat baby is more likely to be an obese adult, because there are more fat cells in the fat baby. A baby whose weight stays within the range of normalcy is absolutely healthy, even if he appears lean.

10. **Starvation is good during diarrhoea:** This is a very erroneous concept, originating because feeding during diarrhoea does increase the volume and frequency of diarrhoea. Plus the child usually passes stools every time the baby eats something and hence the parents consider that whatever he has eaten is "lost" in the stools. This is incorrect. Even during profuse diarrhoea, at least 60% of what is given to the child is absorbed in the blood and thus provides essential nutrition that is very necessary for the baby.

11. **Diarrhoea and constipation**: A common misconception is that if the baby passes 8-10 stools per day it is diarrhoea and if passes once in 2-3 days, it is constipation. More important is the consistency of the stool. It should not be liquid (semi-soft is O.K.), nor too hard, so as to cause pain to the child during evacuation.

12. **Vitamins and tonics increase the appetite and the weight of the child:** The weight of the child increases by what food he consumes and not by tonics and vitamins. These also do not increase the appetite. What increases the appetite is the quality of food, the parents removing all types of pressures on the child to "force" eat and the

child's mood and temperament. Vitamins are sought after by the parents as a must for the baby and a panacea for being fit and fine. In fact they do little but burn a hole in the parent's pockets.

13. **Only baby products should be used for the baby care:** Any ordinary soap, shampoo, oil or lotion is good enough for the baby. There is no need to go for expensive products, commercially touted as exclusive for the baby and ideal for them.

14. **Talcum powder should be applied:** It is not necessary. It only makes the baby smell good and thus there is no harm in applying it.

15. **A newborn must be massaged to strengthen his bones and muscles:** Massaging in no way strengthens the bones of the baby. It only increases the skin circulation and may make the baby look temporarily "ruddy."

16. **Circumcision is necessary if there is tight fore skin:** The foreskin over the penis in a newborn is tight and may not be retracted backwards over the glans up to the age of 5-6 years. This is normal and called "physiologic phimosis." No attempts should be made by the parents to forcibly retract it, neither is circumcision required for it. Usually it doesn't cause any problems in urination. However if there is a swelling at the tip of the penis during urination or the urinary stream is weak (i.e. urine comes in dribble) consult your doctor, as it may be a true phimosis, which requires surgical correction.

17. **Kajal is necessary for the eyes:** Kajal is powdered carbon. It also contains lead. Both of these are harmful to the eyes. Kajal can be applied anywhere on the face like the forehead, cheeks etc. but not inside the eyes.

18. **If the baby has cough, cold, diarrhoea or fever, vaccines should be postponed:** Vaccines can be given in minor illnesses without any side effects.

19. **A coin should be tied to an umbilical hernia to push it in and "cure" it:** An umbilical hernia disappears by its own by the age of 3-4 years in the vast majority of cases. Application of a coin can lead to unnecessary complications for a benign problem.

20. **Eating sweets give rise to boils and worm infestation in the child**: Boils are an external skin infection caused by bacteria and has nothing to do with eating sweets. Similarly worms don't thrive on sweets.

21. **Measles rash portends God's blessings**: Measles is caused by a viral infection and is no blessing of the god towards the child, nor it purges the body of bad omens.

22. **If the baby sleeps on one side, its head gets deformed**: It does temporarily, but not permanently. When the baby starts sitting, the head is moulded back to its natural shape.

23. **In case of earache pour oil in the ear:** It is not advisable. Advice of a doctor should be sought to diagnose the cause of earache and treat it accordingly.

24. **Antibiotics are a must for treating coughs, fevers, diarrhoeas etc.:** Antibiotics are no panacea for illnesses. Most of the infections are viral and antibiotics are of no use in them. In fact they can cause resistant strains of the bacteria to emerge. So antibiotics should be used judiciously and only when clearly indicated.

25. **Rickets:** Parents suppose that any bone problem is due to "rickets" (a disease caused by deficiency of Vitamin-D). Thus it is blamed for knock-knees, bow legs, big head, delayed eruption of teeth, short stature, slender arms and legs etc. While rickets can cause them, to attribute all bone problems to it is not correct. For e.g. delayed eruption of teeth may be normal. Symmetrical defects at and below the knee joint like knock-knee, bowing of the legs, out-toeing or in toeing in children is normal and tend to correct itself by the age of 6 years. Prescription of calcium and vitamin-D for reasons mentioned above are not justifiable.

26. **Chapping of lips:** The corners of the mouth of a child are chapped or cracked. Similarly the tongue may have some soreness or ulcers over it. It is attributed to Vitamin-B deficiency, while actually it is seldom the cause. Chapping of the lips and the corners of the mouth are frequently due to dryness and hence application of an emollient will cure it. Another common cause is drooling of the saliva or constant licking by the tongue whence it manifests as an irritant dermatitis and requires application of steroid based ointments to cure it. Tongue ulcers are called "aphthous ulcers" and are usually due to obscure reasons. It can cause a lot of pain and the treatment lies in taking soft, bland diet and analgesics. There is no cure for this and it becomes alright on its own. However chances are there that it may recur.

27. **Pitryseas Alba:** These are whitish spots encountered on the face of a lot of children and are chronic, though with time they subside of their own. Parents wrongly attribute them to calcium or vitamin deficiency or worm infestations, while actually it is a chronic allergic disorder of the skin. Moisturising lotions over it may be useful to reduce the scaling. They disappear permanently at the time of puberty.

28. **Whitish lines on the nails:** Parents attribute it to deficiency of calcium or some vitamin deficiency, while actually they are normal and seldom reflect a deficiency in the diet. Similarly, the skin at the corners of the nail beds is frequently peeled a bit, which again is attributed to a dietary deficiency. Actually it is due to a recurrent, unrecognised trauma in the day to day work and is not a sign of a nutritional deficiency.

29. **Honey:** It is a popular food item for the babies and used frequently by the parents both for its nutritional value and also in cases of constipation. Honey should not be given to a child below 1 year of age, firstly because it is not essential and secondly because rarely it can cause a serious and life threatening disease called "botulism."

30. **Treatment of constipation is a must for cure:** Many parents believe that unless the child passes normal stools, his illness will not be cured, as if the illness is "excreted" out in stools. During many illnesses, particularly associated with fever, normally there is a transient constipation that is self-limiting and doesn't require treatment. All that should be done is to increase the fluid intake of the baby, particularly in the form of soups and fruit juices.

31. **Straining and crying before urination/ passing stools is abnormal:** Both are often observed in normal infants and usually requires no remedial measures.

32. **Liver is the centre of control for many diseases**: Parents and some doctors, too, have the erroneous notion that a liver problem is responsible for all sorts of indigestion, failure to gain weight, poor appetite, thinness, chronic and recurrent pain abdomen etc. A liver problem (hepatitis) will usually manifest as jaundice, deep yellow urine and nausea/vomiting with a marked decrease in appetite. Thus to blame the liver for each and every problem is injustice being meted out to a versatile and "innocent" organ of the body.

33. **Treatment of Jaundice and Hepatitis**: It is believed that some sort of liver tonic is a must for treating jaundice e.g. Liv-52, Stimuliv etc. These liver tonics are of questionable benefit. The fact is that the liver is a very versatile organ capable of regeneration of the dead liver cells by its own and doesn't require liver tonics to keep itself fit and fine. Similarly, there is a misconception that fried and fatty food is contraindicated in liver disorder and should not be given to the child. So often parents just feed the child high carbohydrate diet (most popular being Glucon-D) and even if the child asks for it, avoid oily and fried food. It is true that in some cases fatty food can cause more nausea, but in that case the child will not ask for it. Even the sight of fatty food will repulse him. So if he asks for it, it means that he will be able to tolerate it. So it can be given. Finally many parents, even educated ones, go to "jaundice specialists" (quacks), who dip the hands of the child in water. The water as if by magic takes on a yellow colour and the "specialist" smugly tells the parent that the jaundice of the body is "removed" into the water. In fact it is nothing else but a hoax and a trick of the hand and parents should be aware of such magic.

34. **Intolerance to food & milk is responsible for diarrhoeas and allergies**: Whenever there is a change in the diet of a child, e.g. introduction of a new food substance or cow's milk, the stooling pattern of the child changes from what parents have been normally used to. Thus there may be an increased frequency, change in odour, flatulence etc. Parents blame the new food as the culprit for G.I. upsets and avoid it or change the milk. In fact change of food is seldom responsible for diarrhoeas and allergies and to curtail a food without any definite proof of its "harm" is unjustifiable.

35. **Child requires more nutrition during illness**: It is true, but the fact is that a

child's appetite (or for that matter adults also) is suppressed during an acute illness. Since there is no appetite, there is less intake of food, generating considerable anxiety in the parents who believe that good and wholesome nutrition during illness is a must for the child to fight the disease and get well sooner. The fact is that the immunity and defence mechanisms of the child do not become weak if he doesn't eat properly for 3-4 days. No attempt should be made to force feed him. As the illness subsides, the appetite of the child comes back and he starts eating ravenously and makes up for any caloric deficiency that he underwent during the acute episode of illness.

36. **For diarrhoeas, half diluted milk should be given**: In diarrhoea, there is no rational in diluting the milk. *Anyhow, how will you give breast milk half-diluted?* Another common misconception or advice is to stop milk diet during diarrhoea, as if milk is the culprit responsible for causing diarrhoea. I once again reiterate that no dietary restrictions are required during diarrhoea.

37. **For anaemia, iron is a must:** It is a common notion even amongst doctors, that iron should be prescribed as a cure for all anaemias without trying to find out the cause of anaemia. So I have seen iron being prescribed for anaemia even in an 8-year-old child. The fact is that iron deficiency is most common till 2-3 years of age. The correct approach is to search for the cause of anaemia and treat accordingly. Finally iron therapy is harmful and in fact contraindicated in a type of anaemias called "Haemolytic anaemias", the classical example of which is Thalessemia.

38. **Illness in a breast-fed baby**: If diarrhoea or other illness occurs in a breast-fed baby, the mother may believe that there is something "going out" in her milk to the baby, which he is not able to tolerate or that there is something wrong with her breast milk. Hence she goes for all sorts of self-imposed dietary restrictions. In fact, maternal food intake or breast milk has little to do with diarrhoea/illness in a breast-fed baby.

39. **Intravenous drip**: Parents believe that intravenous drip is the life-line of the child and that if it doesn't run properly, it will cause grave harm to the child. Actually a meticulous i.v. drip is required only in cases of dehydration or shock. Otherwise most of the i.v. lines are for securing a vein for the purpose of giving injections periodically. In these cases it doesn't matter if it is not running steadily. Parents also have the erroneous belief that in a child who is not eating well (as is common in illness), it is a means of nutrition for the child as it contains glucose and therefore if it is not run properly, the child will become weak. On an average, a 5% glucose drip provides 20 calories/kg/day of calories, which is very less if you compare it with the normal caloric requirement of a child and that is 100 calories/kg/day.

40. **Deviation of nasal septum, enlarged tonsils and adenoids**: These are held culprits for all types of respiratory

majority of cases, these are not responsible for the respiratory problems. The parents are often advised operations i.e. removal of the tonsils or correction of the "deviation" of the nasal septum surgically. One should desist from such operations for a child unless there is an absolute indication. The post-operative results as regards the disappearance of the chronic respiratory symptoms are frequently disappointing and parents feel duped as well as frustrated.

CHAPTER 15

MEDICINES, HOSPITALS AND CHILDREN

***"A young doctor was just setting up his clinic when his secretary told him that there was a man to see. The doctor wanted to make a good impression by having the man think that he was a very busy man. He told his secretary to show the man in.*

Just as he entered, the doctor picked up the phone and pretended to have conversation with a patient. The man waited until the "conversation" was over. Then the doctor asked "Can I help you?"

*"No, I am here just to connect your telephone", replied the man coolly. ***

Syrups: Children are fussy about taking medicines. It is a common problem and causes problems to the parents and to the treating doctor. In a not so uncommon scenario, the parents have to catch hold of the child forcefully, the child thrashing, resisting to his fullest extent. Parents have to catch hold of his arms, then his legs; one of them have to hold his face so that there is no movement of the neck and open the mouth of the child somehow. Then the spoon of the medicine is forcibly put in the child's mouth. It is amazing that even with 2 adults holding the child, many times the child somehow jerks the spoon by a sudden, unexpected motion and the medicine is spilled on the bed or the floor. Since it is syrupy, it creates quite a lot of mess and has to be cleaned up. Almost always, some medicine lands itself on the child's as well as the parent's clothes also, which also has to be cleaned. So much struggle for a spoonful of medicine does not appear justified, but mostly there is no other solution. The only advice I can give is to give it to the child quickly before the child is fully aware of it, because once he is aware of it, he will throw up a struggle. Give it in a casual, nonchalant way while engaging the child in an interesting game or conversation. Giving it quickly without much ado makes the child realize too late that he has been "cheated." Otherwise you have to convince the child that he has to take the medicine. Usually he will listen to either threat of a greater pain (i.e. injection as a substitute) or will reluctantly agree if told that after having the medicine, his symptoms will abate (he will agree only if the symptoms are causing a great anguish to him, like severe pain). Alternatively you can postpone the enjoyable activity that the child is engaged in till the less pleasurable task i.e. swallowing of the medicine is completed. The child with his mind on the enjoyable activity being denied to him temporarily may gulp down the "bitter" medicine. You can tell him that after the medicine, he can engage in the pleasurable task like playing etc (i.e. a thing which he loves very much). Finally his taking the medicines should be praised so as to act as a positive reinforcement.

It happens many times that the child, as the spoon with the medicine is forcibly put into his mouth, gags and vomits out all the medicine along with some of the stomach contents. This is due to struggle; with the child not at all wanting to swallow the medicine.

Some people recommend that you should block the nose of the child completely by pinching his nose tightly shut. The child having no alternative has to open his mouth to breathe and when he does so, the medicine can be rapidly given to the child. I don't have much experience in trying out this method. But I am wary that while the child breathes through the mouth, some of the medicine may enter the windpipe, causing a bout of extreme coughing and vomiting. Anyhow this can also happen with an extremely struggling child without pinching the nose. So parents can give it a try and see whether it works for them or not.

Parents before giving any medicine to the child should make it a point to taste it itself, because in the majority of cases what turns the child off is the taste of the medicine. If the medicine is bitter and not palatable, it is wise to ask your doctor whether a suitable alternative exists. If it doesn't, you should take steps to mask the bitterness of the medicine syrup by putting sugar, honey etc. in it. Parents also are in the habit of mixing the medicine (syrup or crushed tablet) with the milk bottle or the food of the child. I have nothing against it and do consider it as a suitable alternative with the caveat that the child should finish the whole milk; otherwise the required dose of medicine will not go!

***A patient was seen jumping up and down. On being asked the reason, he replied that the doctor had advised him to shake the bottle before taking the medicines, but he forgot it. That's why he is mixing it now in the stomach by jumping. ***

Whenever you give syrups to your child, always shake it thoroughly. Otherwise the top part of the syrup remains diluted while the bottom part of the syrup is concentrated thus giving wrong dosing to your child. Syrups are available in 2 forms, ready made and those, which has to be constituted by adding water to them. Once the ready made syrup bottle is opened, it is better to use it within 1 month. For reconstitution, you have to take clean, boiled and cooled water and add it to the powder in the bottle up to the mark specified on the bottle. After that you should close the cap and shake it thoroughly. Some mixtures take some time to dissolve and become homogenous. So be patient and go on shaking. After the powder is totally dissolved you will find that the level of the syrup has shrunken below the specified mark. This is because as the powder dissolves into water, it occupies less space. In all cases, "top up" water should be added so that the "shrunken level" is again brought up to the mark. These types of reconstituted syrups should be used quickly, preferably within 1 week.

Children are usually given syrups with a spoon. Parents use different types of spoons according to the availability in their house. So some spoons are small and some are big, i.e. there is no uniformity regarding a spoonful measure. So when the doctor writes to give your child 1 spoon three times a day, different parents depending on the size of the spoon will give different doses. This is incorrect and imprecise. Many syrups don't provide a measuring cap with the bottle and even if they do provide, it is calibrated only as 2.5 ml (=1/2 tsf), 5 ml and 10 ml. Doctors calculate the dose of a drug according to the body weight of the child and may write a prescription say, 2ml tds or 3.5 ml tds. Of course the doctor is theoretically correct and written the prescription precisely. But how will parents give 2 ml, 3.5 ml, 6ml etc.? As I have mentioned earlier giving by spoon is quite imprecise. Ideally, therefore, drug companies should come out with caps that are marked up to 10 ml and graded in ml; i.e. they should have marks at 1ml, 2 ml, 3ml...

The dose schedule is important. To give a drug 4 times a day means that it should be given 6,12, 18, 24 hours or 5, 11, 17, 23 hours etc. How can parents give a child medicine at 12 o'clock in the night or 5 o'clock in the morning without undergoing considerable trouble both for themselves and the child? Practically it is not feasible and as a result the child does not receive the required doses and thus the desired treatment. I tried myself to take drugs on a 6-hour basis and failed miserably in doing so. Even taking medicines 8 hourly i.e. three times / day was a big task for me with only 70% compliance. So it is impractical for the doctors to believe that a 6 hourly drug regime for 7-10 days will be complied with. Drug companies have to come out and promote drugs that have a longer duration of action and can be given 12 hourly or even as a single dose/day. Fortunately these types of medicines are nowadays freely available in the Indian market for practically all the common diseases and the onus now lies on the doctors to prescribe such medicines so that there is at least 80-90% compliance. Parents can also contend that since they cannot give drugs every 6 hours, the doctor choose an alternate but equally efficient drug (which is freely available) so that dosing can be 12 hourly or once a day. Even for the child it means less torture in taking medicines.

Companies are at fault in writing the doses on the bottle, for example ½ tsp till 1 year of age, 1 tsp for 2-6 years etc. This is a gross approximation and does not often tally with the dose that the doctors calculate and recommend. This is because the doctors calculate the dose according to the weight and obviously you don't expect a 2-year and a 6-year-old child to weigh the same. So how can the dose for 2-6 years be the same e.g.1 tsp? Why it is done? I think primarily to promote over the counter (called OTC) sale. Many parents directly go to a drug store and ask for fever or cough syrup for the child without having a doctor's prescription because they never visited the doctor. Drug stores are more than willing to give **a brand** in which they earn the maximum profit which usually is always 30% plus. I can only comment that parents are doing so at their own responsibility and with a risk to the child. Remember all medicines are chemicals and overdosing is potentially dangerous, while under-dosing will lead to sub-optimal cure, plus the drug brand being given to them may be of some sub-standard company.

Drops: Another form in which medicines are available is drops. I prefer them over syrups because the dose is less say 10-20 drops (0.5-1 ml), which is easy to administer (as compared to 5 ml of the syrup) and since the bulk is less; chances of the child vomiting it out are less. Plus the dose is accurate and precise. The only disadvantage is that they are a bit bitter because they are not syrupy and secondly few drugs are available in the market in form of drops that can be given on a 12 hourly basis.

Tablets: There are 2 types of tablets. One is known as the dispersible kid tablet, in which the tablet dissolves in a spoon of water, which can then be administered to the child. The dosing is precise irrespective of the size of the spoon as the tablet strength (say 125-mg) is being given to the child in the dissolved form irrespective of the spoon size. The most important advantage is uniformity of dosage i.e. it is not diluted at the top and concentrated at the bottom as happens in a bottle plus the shelf life is not limited as in the case of bottle. One tablet when opened is used immediately. Many drugs are nowadays coming in kid tablet forms and I prefer them to syrups for the reasons mentioned above.

The other form of tablet is the one that has to be swallowed. A child less than 7-8 years usually cannot swallow a tablet. So to give it to a younger child, one has to crush the tablet and make it powdered before administering. The powder doesn't dissolve in water and so the child will not like the taste plus he will feel a gritty sensation in his mouth and so may reject the medicine. The best way to administer such powders is not to use water as a medium but instead a viscous gel like thing (e.g. honey, tomato ketch-up or jam). The powder can be put at the centre i.e. it should be surrounded on all sides by the viscous liquid, which can then be administered to the child. Some children are fussy and once they know that a medicine is going to be administered, they reject it even though the viscous liquid "encapsulates" it and the child won't feel the taste of the medicine. In such cases it is best to prepare the concoction of the powder and viscous liquid away from the sight of the child and then make the child take it.

Capsules: While primarily meant for adults, there are a few situations where they have to be given to a child for want of a better or a suitable alternative. The same method as above should be followed. The capsule should be opened, the powder taken out on a piece of paper and then put in the viscous gel before giving it to the child.

Injections: It is a painful alternative for the child. As soon as the child sees a doctor or a sister, his anxiety level peaks and he starts crying, particularly if he has been sensitized to it earlier by prior injections. The injection has to be forcefully given to the child in most cases with someone holding him. As in certain cases injections cannot be avoided and are a must, parents should make the child realize that it is for his own good and will make him get well faster. Some parents want some sort of anaesthesia (i.e. pain killer) to "deaden" the pain of injection. It is practically not possible to implement. Nowadays there are some creams which when applied locally and left for half an hour, create a local anaesthesia and reduce the pain of pricking. It is suitable for intravenous injections and for starting intravenous drips. In intramuscular injections, it only anaesthetizes the skin and hence the muscular pain is still felt. Different children have different temperaments and tolerance to pain. Some may face it stoically while others may refuse to be injected and thrash around to avoid the injection. If the child is very sensitive, he may be given some sedation 1 hour before the injection so that his anxiety level is reduced.

Multiple medicines: If many medicines are to be given to a child, parents often forget which medicine is to be given when and in what dose. So they may end up giving erroneous drug therapy to their child. However much you remember and jot down, when a child is prescribed 5-6 medicines, there is always a chance of an error. The best way is to tell the doctor that he writes less medicines and gives medicines (say 2 or at the most 3 drugs) for the immediate illness and other drugs like tonics, B-complex syrups etc. can be given later on when the child is a bit better.

Caution: Do not self-drug your children. Some parents think that they are competent and give medicines to their child by their own self. I have only to state that this is hazardous and may lead to unnecessary and sometimes dangerous complications. Always ask a doctor before giving any medicines.

There are some misconceptions as to whether the medicine should be given before or after food. For most of the medicines it is better not to be empty stomach. However some medicines require an empty stomach for better absorption.

The parents should complete the whole course of the treatment and should not stop it in between, particularly when they find that the child has improved. This is because residual infection may still linger on, plus haphazard medications lead to the emergence of resistant strains of bacteria. Some of the medicines have to be given for a long duration like T.B. medicines for 6-9 months, anti-convulsants for 3 years etc. The parents should strictly comply with the whole course.

Hospital admission: If your child is advised admission to a hospital, parents are full of anxiety. There is a lot of bother in hospital admissions for a family. The normal family life is disrupted with the mother having to stay in the hospital with the child and the father having to be constantly on the run going here and there to fetch medicines, food, clothes etc. Uppermost anxiety in the parents' mind is about the child's condition. Sometimes the child is put on an intravenous line and the child may take time to become accustomed to it. During this time he may yell and want the i.v. line to be pulled out or will try to pull it out himself. The parents have to catch hold of the child and soothe him. The first day in the hospital is often the hardest and after that you also start becoming accustomed to it. The above are all part and parcel of hospitalization, which cannot be avoided or can be avoided only to some extent, but cannot be completely eliminated.

During the hospital stay, try to be relaxed and let the doctors and the nurses do their job. They are professionals trained in this field and are accustomed to dealing with such cases many times. So when an intravenous line is being put for the child, doesn't stand near the medical personnel, craning your neck to see how everything is going. It is better to let the medical personnel be alone with your child and complete whatever procedure is deemed necessary in the interests of the child. Of course there is no harm in your standing nearby (primarily to comfort and soothe the baby by the presence of a familiar face). Remember some children may start behaving just the opposite i.e. when the mother is present, they will kick up a row, while if the mother is not there, they are afraid enough to keep quiet and tolerate the procedure without much fuss. But mothers who cannot stand the sight of even a single prick and whose anxiety level increases in direct proportion to the child's crying should stay away.

Running minute to minute to the nurse with some or the other complaint not only makes the nurse harried but you also start getting paranoid and thinking how long you will be able to bear it. So try to be relaxed and listen to the reassurances from the medical personnel like the nurses and the doctors without doubting them much.

When the doctor comes for a visit, it is better to jot down whatever you want to ask on a paper so that you don't miss out on anything. It many times happens that after the doctor's visit is over, you realize that you have forgotten to ask him something that was bothering you throughout the day. The same applies when you take your child for a visit to the doctor in his clinic. Get reassurances from the doctor about the condition of your child. This will make you relaxed that there is nothing serious with the child. You can also ask the doctor whether the disease can take a serious course or become worse.

Keeping patience is very important. You cannot and should not expect that as soon as you admit the child in the hospital, he will have a magic cure in a matter of few hours. If the child is having diarrhoea along with dehydration, necessitating i.v. fluids, it is very stressful for the parents. The child will evacuate frequently and may soil your clothes, bed sheets etc. which may be quite a nuisance. But remember that though it is a nuisance, it is nothing more than that in the sense that by and large, diarrhoea is a benign disease from which the vast majority of children recover very well. It is only a matter of time. Some children may become better in 2 days; others may even take 5-7 days for the diarrhoea to stop. Once the child is off the i.v. drip and not vomiting, you can ask the doctor whether you can take the child home. Some parents prefer to take the child home and even get periodic injections from their home setting. Same thing holds true for other diseases also. By and large diseases have got an excellent prognosis in children, particularly the common ones like respiratory infections, diarrhoeas, vomiting, fever etc. which are the diseases that your child is most likely to suffer from. They have got more of a nuisance value (e.g. the child is having a troublesome cough, gets fever every 4 hours etc.) without causing any serious harm or ill effects to the child. Of course it is a testing time for parents. As mentioned above all these are trifling matters and more of a nuisance rather than a reason for serious concern.

If your child is **unfortunately serious**, then your doctor will explain to you the condition of the child. At that moment you have to decide **where** you should get your child treated. Is there a better hospital nearby with good facilities to handle such type of serious condition? You can consult your doctor who will surely guide in your decision making. It is better to get treatment for serious diseases like coma, head injury etc. at a centre with facilities to deal competently with them.

DOCUMENTED FACTS

Why observing the dog for 10 days without initiating treatment could be risky!

"Animals in canine rabies endemic areas are subjected to frequent rabies challenges."

"The result of inadequate or not frequent enough vaccination, at least in Thailand, is that up to 6% of dogs found rabid at autopsy have a reliable rabies vaccine history. 40% of dogs vaccinated only one time have lost most of their humoral immunity 4 to 6 months later."

"Furthermore, 62% of dogs found rabid at our laboratory are less than 1 year old and many are puppies between 1 and 3 months of age."

Management of rabies exposure in rabies endemic countries

TREATMENT REGIMEN For unknown, sick, proven rabid or wild mammal	WHO Category	Nature of Contact	TREATMENT REGIMEN For Healthy Animal
None	I	Petting, feeding, licking on healthy skin, no mucous membrane exposure	None+
RABIPUR Complete post exposure treatment (5 doses)	II	Superficial scratch, lick on broken skin	Modern Tissue culture rabies vaccine **RABIPUR**++
RABIPUR Complete post exposure treatment (5 doses) **& RIG**	III	Single or multiple transdermal bites or scratches at any location, or lick over mucous membrane	Modern Tissue culture rabies vaccine **RABIPUR**++ **& RIG**

+This is a good time to start pre-exposure vaccination, particularly in children and others likely to have repeated animal contacts, such as postmen, vets and others that are at a risk of dog bites.

Only for healthy animal bite (not for stray animal bite)

++Start full treatment on first day and discontinue vaccine if animal is alive and well on day 10, or if it has been found rabies negative on reliable laboratory examination. Encourage patient to return for another dose of Vaccine on day 21 so that a full pre-exposure series has been completed.

Contd...

RIG (Rabies Immune globulin) For Passive Immunization

"Human rabies immune globulin (HRIG) is given as 20 IU/kg. Equine rabies immune globulin (ERIG) is given as 40 IU/kg. Both are injected into and around all wounds with any surplus given by deep intramuscular injection. If the calculated volume is inadequate for the injection of all wounds, dilute it in normal saline to make up a sufficient volume."

Special clinical situations

"It may be appropriate to double the first dose of vaccine (whatever schedule is used) if there is significant delay in presentation or if the patient is immunosuppressed. Administration of two ampules of vaccine, one in each arm, on day 0 with the Essen schedule."

Recommendation for use of rabies vaccine in special circumstances.

DOUBLE THE FIRST DOSE

(i) in patients who attend for treatment after a delay of 48 hours or more

(ii) in the severely malnourished

(iii) in patients taking immunosuppressive drugs (including corticosteroid and anti-malarials)

(iv) in patients who are congenitally immunodefficient or suffering from Acquired Immuno-Deficiency Syndrome

(v) in patients with underlying chronic disease (e.g. liver cirrhosis)

(vi) in patients where RIG is indicated but unavailable

Important considerations while administering a rabies vaccine.

1. Prompt and thorough wound care and administration of purified Equine or Human Rabies immunoglobulin (ERIg or HRIg) and Cell Culture Rabies Vaccine, immediately after exposure, virtually guarantee complete protection.

- Wash the wound with plenty of water and soap.
- Apply an antiseptic or even alcohol.
- Do not cover the wound.

2. All intramuscular injections must be given in the deltoid region or, in small children, into the anteriolateral area of the thigh muscle.

3. The vaccine should never be administered in the gluteal region. The gluteal region is not recommended on account of high fat content in this region which retards the absorption of the vaccine.

4. Neonates can be given the anti-rabies vaccine without any additional side effects vis-a-vis older children or adults. Modern tissue culture rabies vaccine should not be given in reduced dosage, irrespective of the age and/or weight of the vaccinee. **The dosage schedule for the modern tissue culture vaccine remains same for all age groups.**

5. **Dosage:** Day 0 is the day of the first injection, preferably the day of the bite. Days 3,7, etc. are to be counted from Day 0.

For post-exposure prophylaxis one injection each on day : **0** **3** **7** **14** **30**

Day 90 (optional)

CHART-1

Coughing in Children

Coughing is a normal reaction to irritation in the throat or lungs. Coughing is unusual in babies under 6 months old and may indicate a serious lung infection. Most coughs are caused by minor infections of the nose and/or throat, but the sudden onset of coughing may be caused by choking.

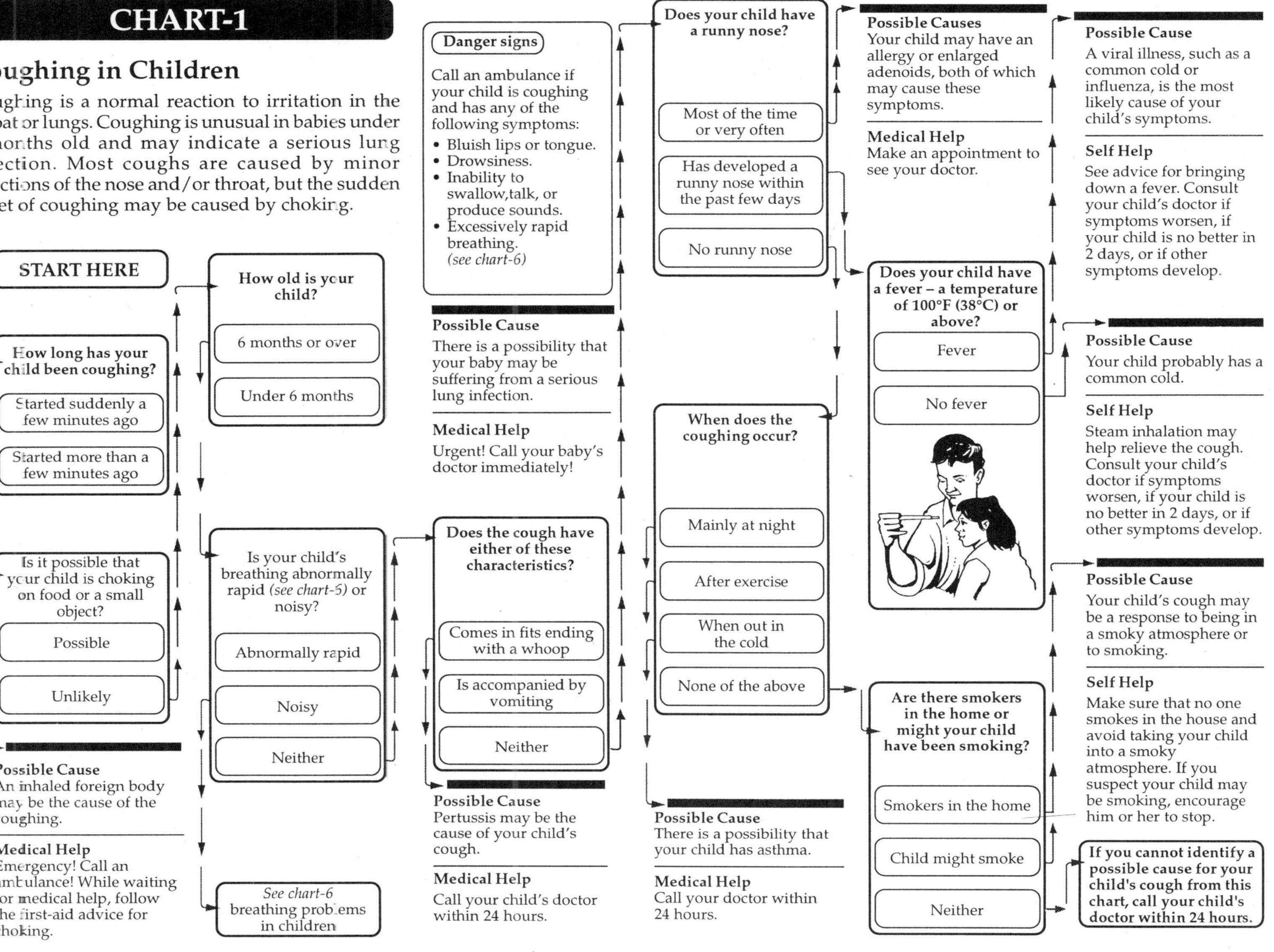

CHART-2

Abdominal Pain in Children

Every child suffers from abdominal pain at some time, and some children have recurrent episodes. Usually the cause is minor, and the pain subsides in a few hours without treatment. In rare cases, abdominal pain is a symptom of a serious disorder that requires prompt medical attention.

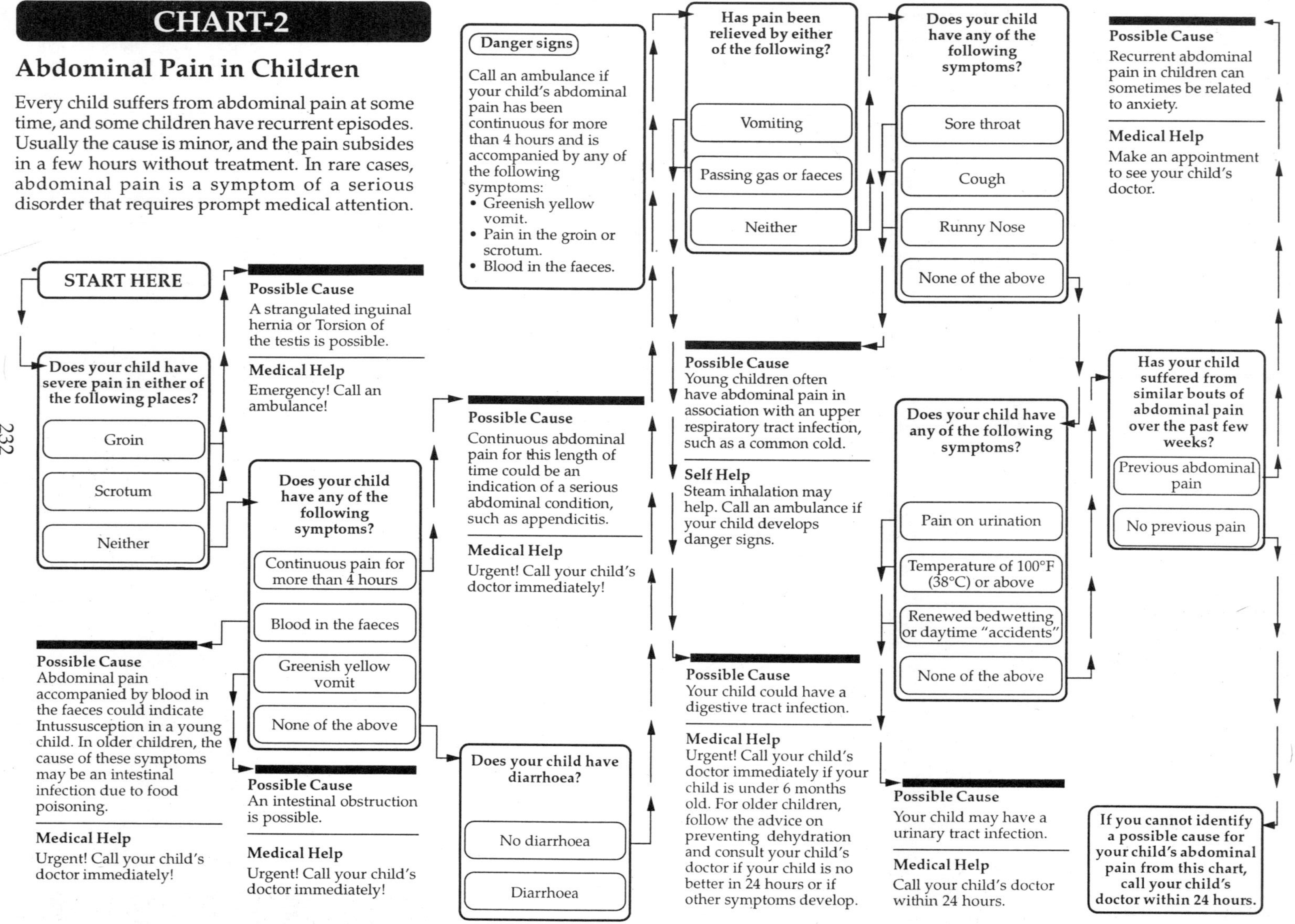

CHART-3

Weight Problems in Children

Check your child is within healthy limits by regularly measuring his or her weight and height. An abnormality in a child's weight may be due to disease. A long-term weight problem may increase your child's risk of future health problems.

Warning

Special Diets: the dietary needs of children differ from those of adults. An unbalanced diet can adversely affect growth and development. You should not put your child on a reducing diet or restrict specific food groups except on the advice of your child's doctor.

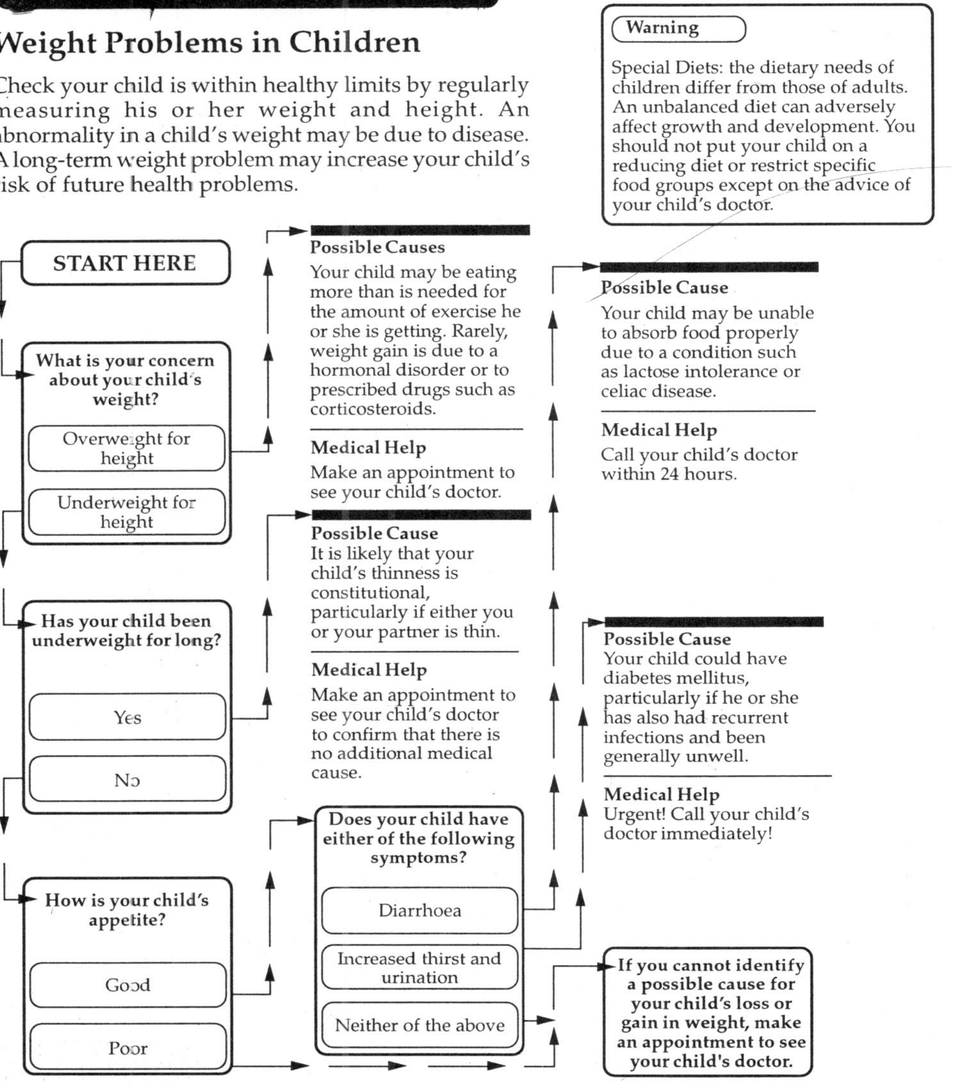

CHART-4

Diarrhoea in Children

Diarrhoea is the passage of loose or watery faeces more often than normal. Breast-fed babies may pass loose faeces several times a day, and this is normal. To avoid dehydration your child should drink plenty of fluids that do not contain milk. If symptoms do not improve, consult your child's doctor.

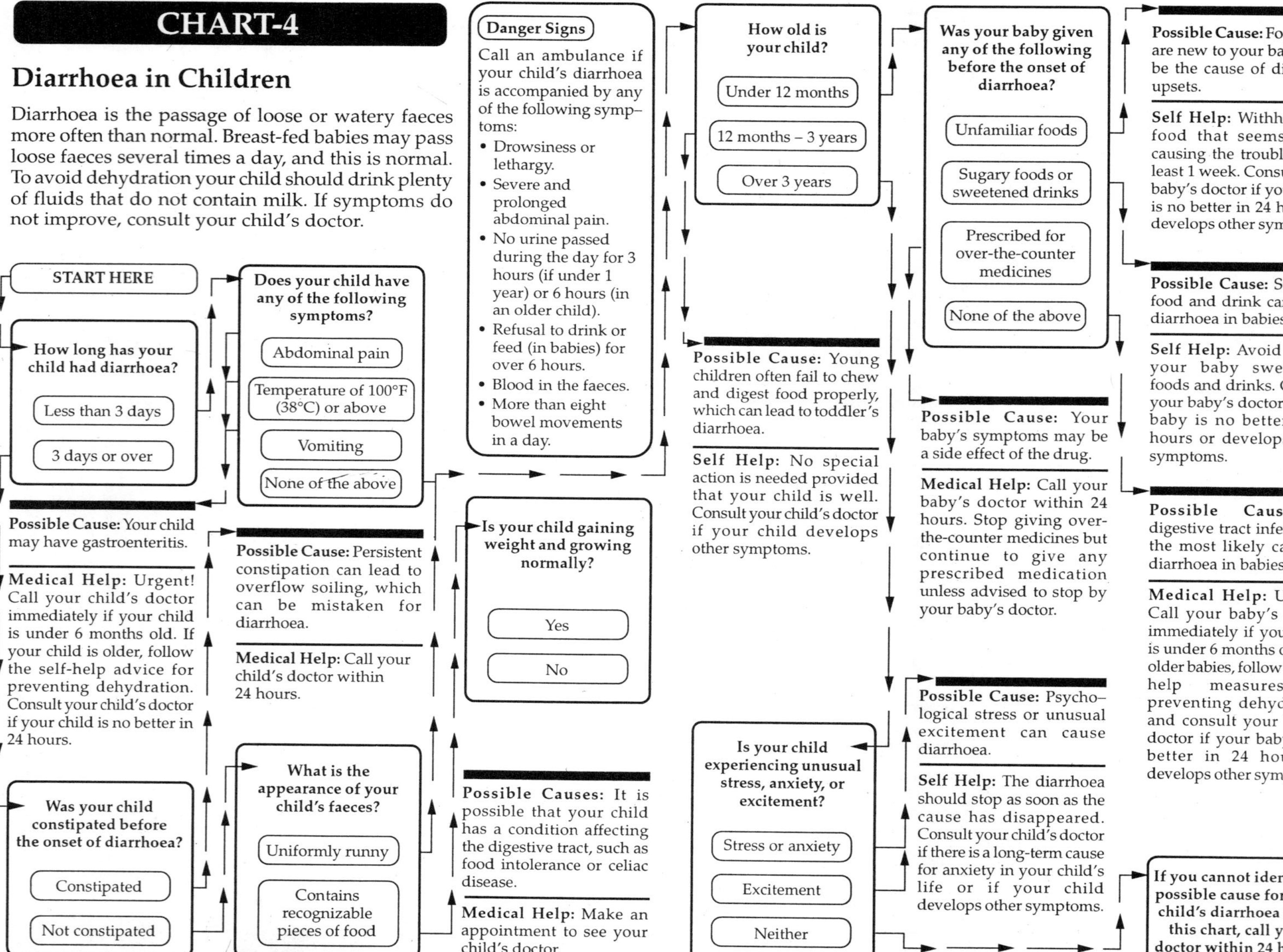

CHART-5

Fever in Children

A fever is a temperature of 100°F (38°C) or above. If your child is not well you should take his or her temperature because a high fever may need urgent treatment. If a feverish child becomes unresponsive, call an ambulance.

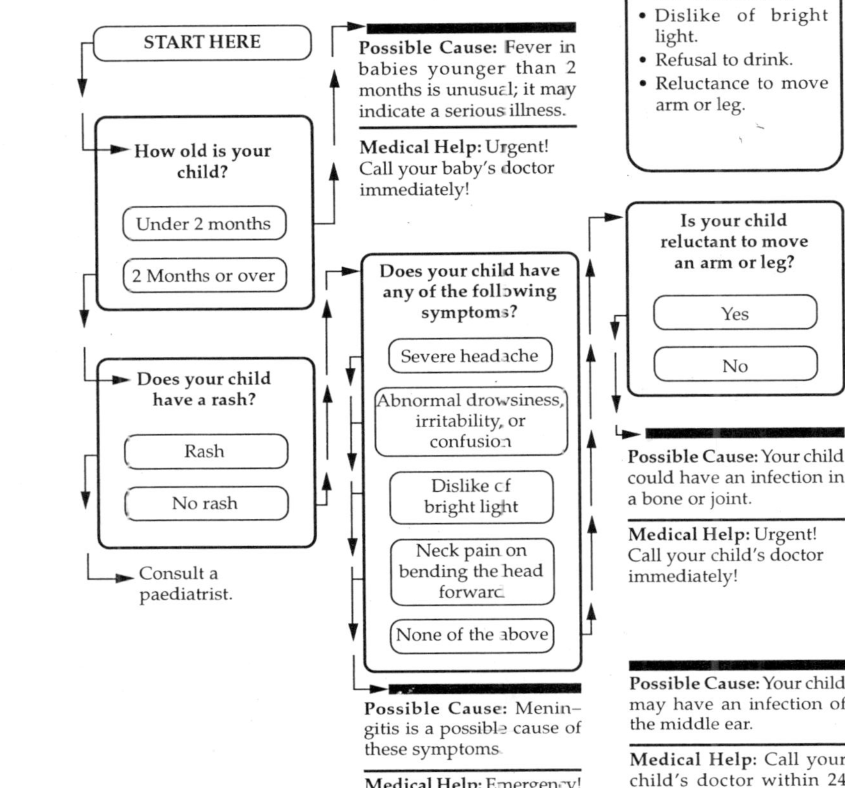

CHART-6

Breathing Problems in Children

Breathing problems include noisy or rapid breathing and shortness of breath. Shortness of breath may not be obvious because a child may simply avoid exertion. A child with severe difficulty in breathing needs urgent hospital treatment. Sudden breathing problems also need immediate attention.

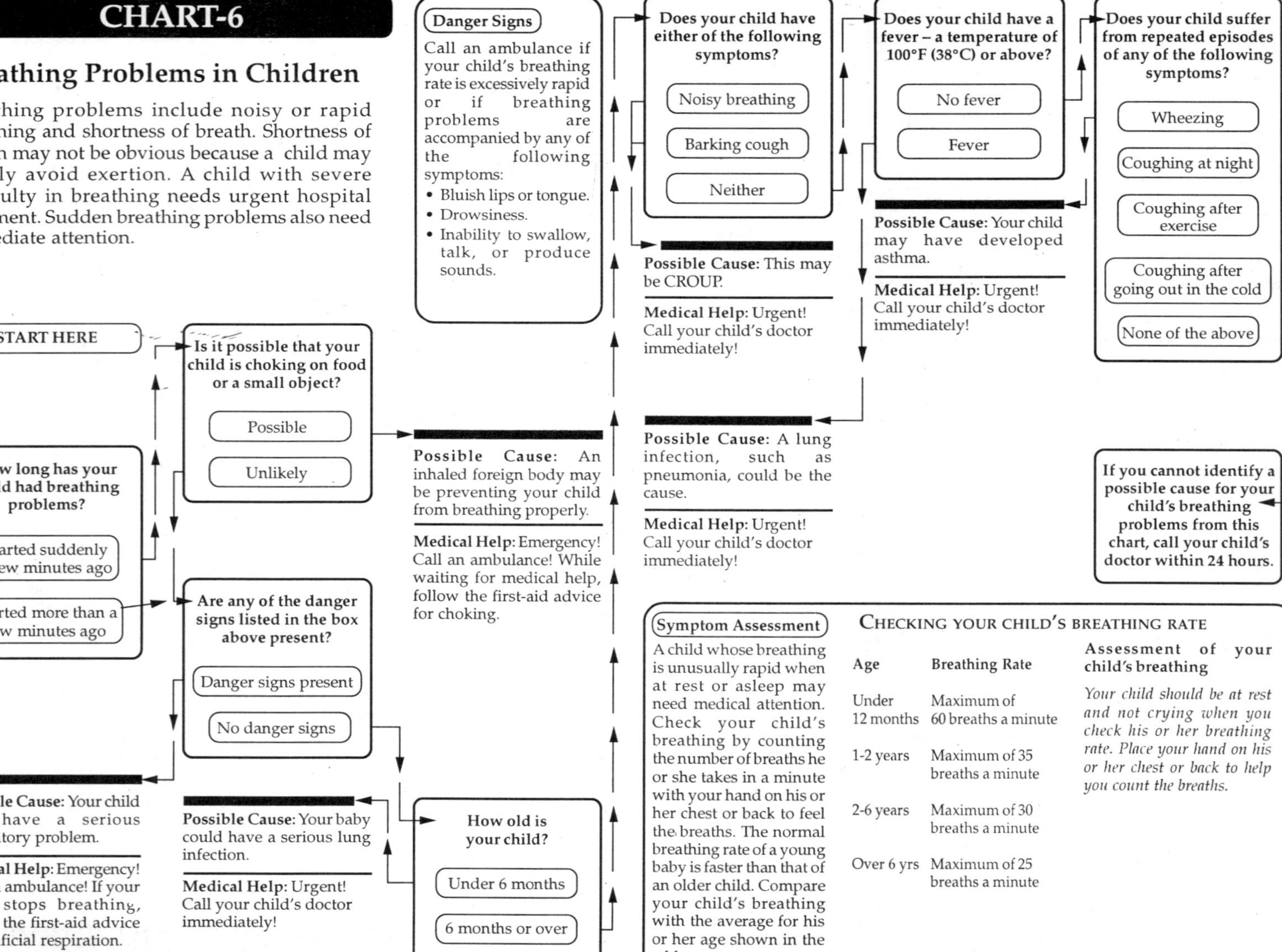

Checking Your Child's Breathing Rate

Age	Breathing Rate
Under 12 months	Maximum of 60 breaths a minute
1-2 years	Maximum of 35 breaths a minute
2-6 years	Maximum of 30 breaths a minute
Over 6 yrs	Maximum of 25 breaths a minute

Assessment of your child's breathing

Your child should be at rest and not crying when you check his or her breathing rate. Place your hand on his or her chest or back to help you count the breaths.

CHART-7

Vomiting in Children

Children vomit as a result of many illnesses, including ear infections and urinary and digestive tract disorders. Anxiety or excitement may also cause vomiting. Rarely, vomiting may be due to an infection or injury to the brain. If vomiting is persistent, you should consult your child's doctor urgently.

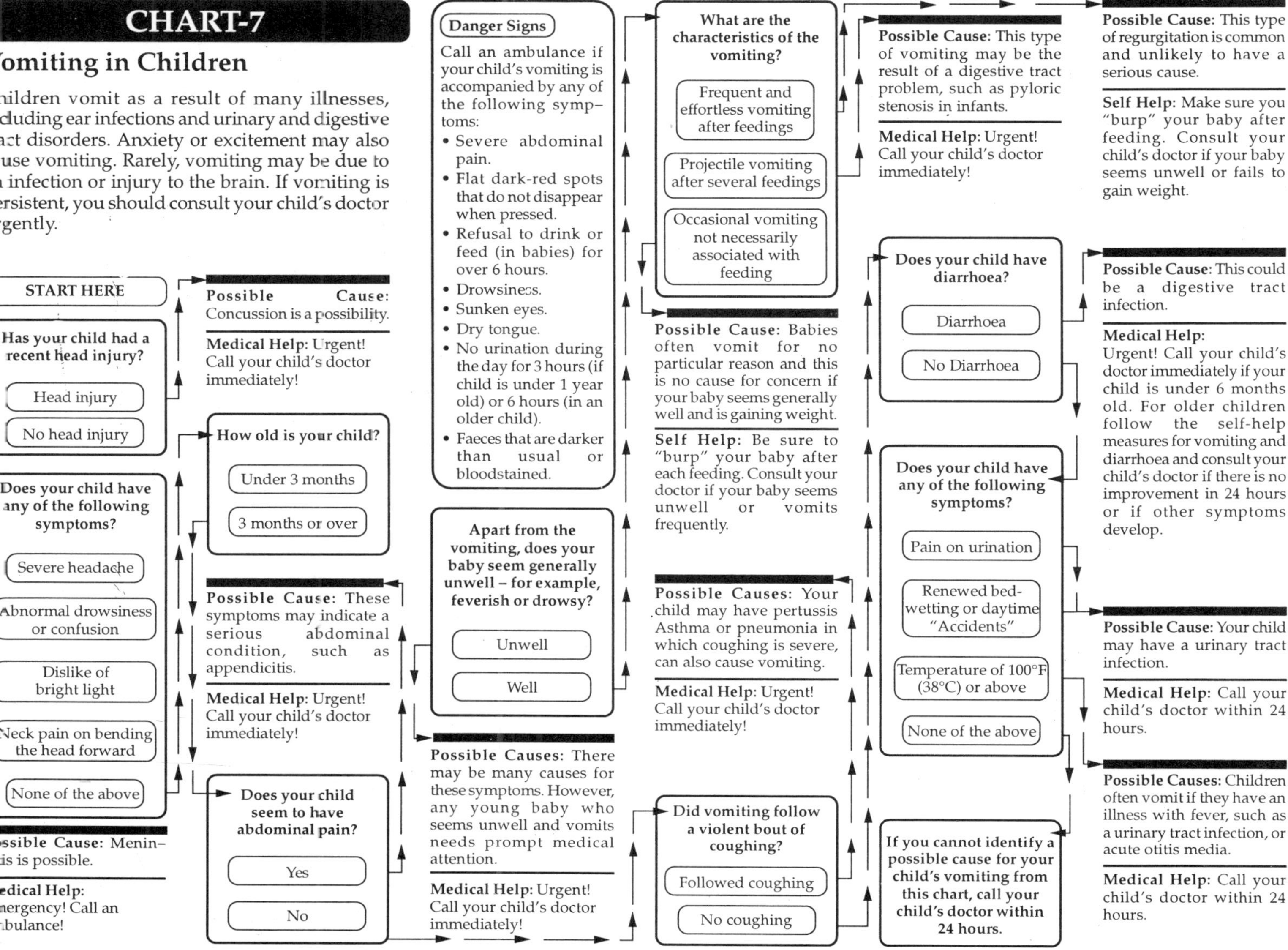

APPENDICES

Appendix 1

GROWTH CHART : WEIGHT

X-axis = age Y-axis = weight

- Weights lying in zones-B and C are normal. If it lies in zone-A, the child is obese. Weight lying in zone-D and below is abnormal and indicates that the child is undernourished. If it lies in zone-D, the child is mildly malnourished. If it lies in zone-E, the child is moderately malnourished. If it lies in zone-F, the child is severely malnourished. For example, in the graph depicted below, observe the weight of a 1-year old child. If it lies between 8-12 kilos, i.e. in zones B and C, it is normal. If the weight is more than 12 kilos, it falls in zone-A (child is obese). If it is between 7-8 kilos, it lies in zone-D (child is mildly malnourished). If it is between 6-7 kilos, it lies in zone-E (child is moderately malnourished). If the weight is less than 6 kilos, it falls in zone-F (child is severely malnourished).
- Plot the weight of your child on the above graph monthly/yearly and join the dots to form a growth curve. If it lies within the zones B & C and is growing parallel to the lines drawn in the graph, it is normal. However if the curve shows a dip, it is abnormal, even though it may lie within the specified range (Appendix 4).

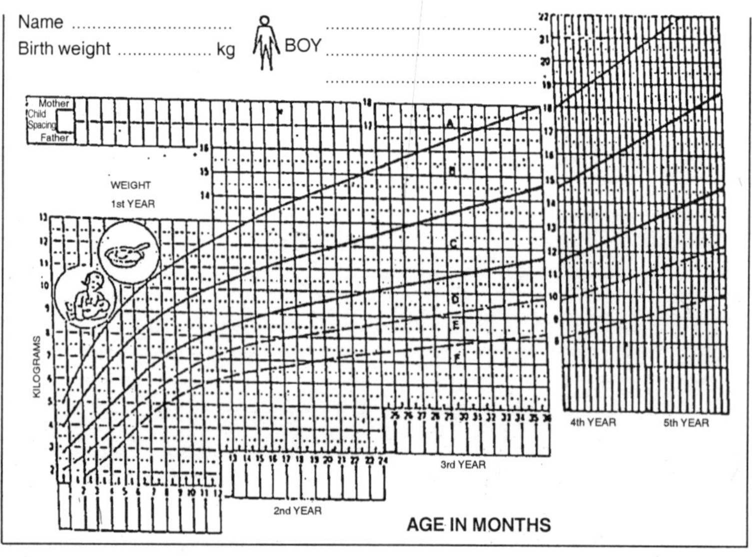

Appendix 2

GROWTH CHART : HEIGHT

X-axis = age

Y-axis = Height

- 2 graphs are shown. The graph on the left is for age 0-36 months. The graph to the right is for age groups 2-18 years.
- Height, lying between 10-99 centile is normal. For example, in the graph above, see the length of a 1-year-old child. If the length lies between 70-80 cm (i.e. 10-90 centile), it is normal. Any height above or below the 10-90 centile is a reason for medical opinion.
- As in the case of the weight graph (in the previous page), plot the height of your child periodically on the above graphs and join the dots to form a height curve of your child. If it is between 10-90 centile and growing parallel to the existing curves, it is normal. However if the curve shows a dip, it is abnormal, even though it may still be lying between the 10-90 centile.

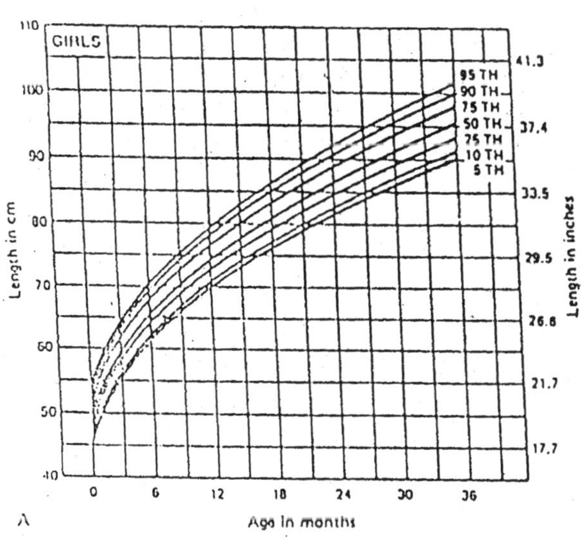

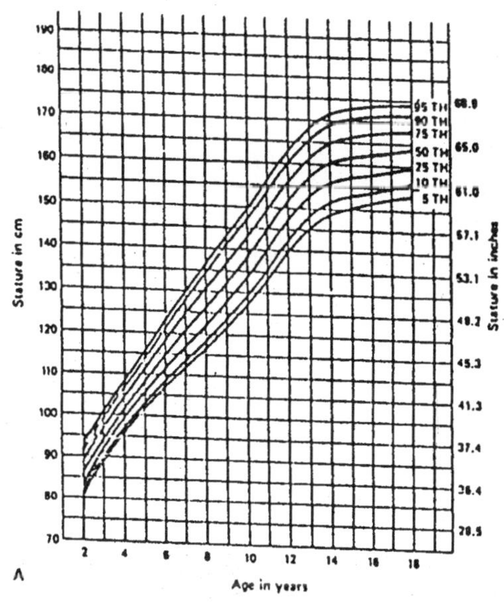

Appendix 3

GROWTH CHART : HEAD CIRCUMFERENCE

X-axis = age

❖ Head circumference lying between + 2 S.D. and - 2 S.D. is normal. For example, in the graph above, see the head circumference of a 1-year-old child. If it lies between 42.5 - 48 cm (i.e. between the S.D. curves), it is normal. Any head circumference above or below this range is an indication for medical opinion. The middle line on the graph i.e. the 50% curve shows the average head circumference of children for a particular age.

Y-axis = Head Circumference

❖ As in the case of the weight graph (Appendix-1), plot the head circumference of your child periodically on the above graph and join the dots to form a head circumference curve of your child. If it is between + 2 S.D. and - 2 S.D. and growing parallel to the existing curves, it is normal. However if the curve shows a dip, it is abnormal, even though it may still be lying between the normal range.

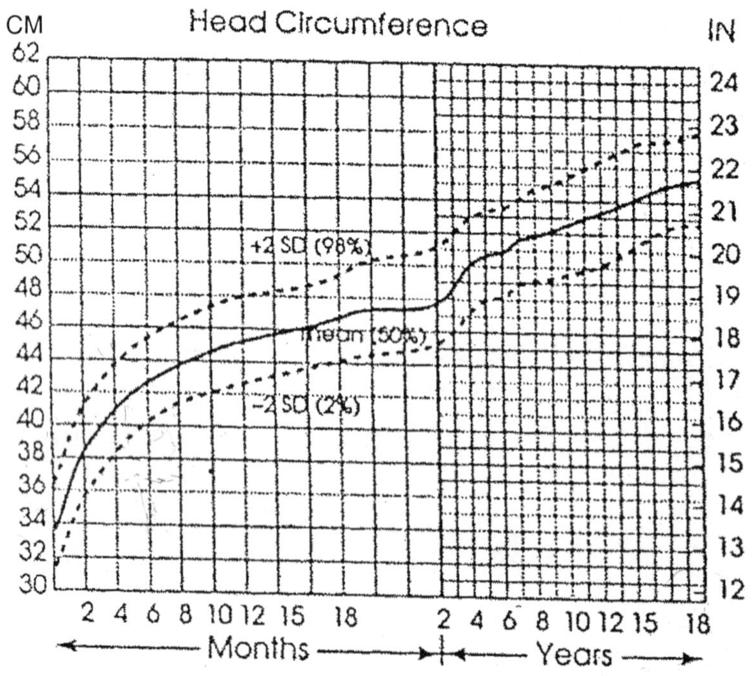

Appendix 4

DESTINED PATH OF GROWTH OF TWO CHILDREN "A" & "B"

X-axis = age

Y-axis = weight

- The graph above shows the growth curves of children "A" and "B". Weight below the 60% line is abnormal. The destined path of "A" is above the 80% line, while the destined path of "B" lies below the 80% line. For example, at the end of July i.e. when the children are 6 months old, the weight of "A" will be 7.2 kilos, while that of "B" will be 5.8 kilos. At 1 year, they will be 9.5 and 7.5 kilos respectively. NOTE : Though there is a projected weight difference of 2 kilos between the two children at the age of 1 year, yet both are normal (i.e. not growth retarded) as long as they follow a parallel curve and show no dip.
- The curve of "B" dips downwards in June (though it is still above the 60% line i.e. within the normal range). Only in July does it go below the 60% curve i.e. the child is absolutely malnourished. However a dip in the curve in June is not normal and efforts should be made to redeem it in June rather than letting it dip further in July.
- **Conclusion :** Intervention should come when the curve starts dipping. It holds true not only for weight but also for other growth parameters (i.e. height and head circumference).

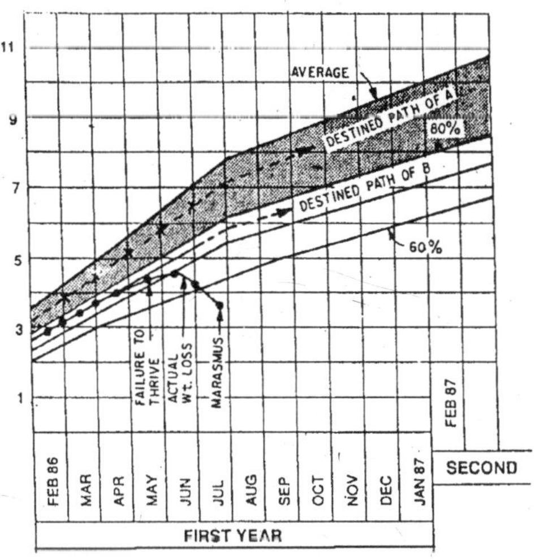

Appendix 5

HIGHLIGHTS OF CHILD DEVELOPMENT AND PARENTAL FEELINGS

Stage (Age)	Developmental Tasks	Developmental Landmarks	Developmental Concerns	Pitfall for Caregivers
Infancy (birth to 1 year)	Emotional attachment	2-3 months : responsive social smile. 7-9 months : distress in the presence of ``strangers".	Temperamental variations (including colic)	Exhaustion. Lack of emotional support. Unexpected temperament. Unfulfilled expectation and fantasies.
Toddler (1-3 years)	Beginning of the separation-individuation process	8-24 months : separation anxiety. 12 months : locomotion. 15 months : "no". 24-36 months : bowel training.	Sleep disturbances (separation or overstimulation). Breath holding and temper tantrums 'Terrible twos,' i.e. oppositional behaviour, accident proneness.	Exhaustion. Autonomous strivings of child seen as rejection or adversarial relationship. Need for parents to set limits seen as parental failure. "Permissiveness" seen as good parent-child interaction.
Preschooler (3-6 years)	Taming of the internal world of fantasy	Symbolic play	Childhood fears : bedtime, darkness, ghosts, and monsters.	Competitive strivings of child seen as personal challenge. Egocentricity of child seen as selfishness.
School age (6-11 years)	Skills development	7 years : logical thought processes (cause-and-effect thinking) ; games and organizations with rules.	Continued childhood fears. School avoidance. Learning disabilities, Primary nocturnal enuresis.	Parental discomfort with separation from child. High expectations for child's performance, which is perceived as necessary for parent's own self-esteem.

Contd...

Stage (Age)	Developmental Tasks	Developmental Landmarks	Developmental Concerns	Pitfall for Caregivers
Adolescence (11-20 years)	Continuation of the separation-individuation process. Identity formation ("Who am I ?"). Gaining independence.			
Early (11-15 years)		Puberty : "best friends" of same sex. Self-absorption. Painful concerns about appearance.	Adolescent "turmoil"	Child's attachment to peer group seen as rejection. Self-absorption seen as irresponsible disregard for others. Exasperation with the child's changing moods.
Middle (15-17 years)		Heterosexual interests. Beginning of a truce with parents.	Adolescent sexuality	Prudish indignation. Sexual stimulation of the opposite-sex parent. Envy and anger at child's youthful energy and appearance. Rivalry and competition with suitors.
Late (17-20 years)		Orientation towards future. Pursuit of an adult work-role identity.	Will the young adult "make it"?	"Empty nest syndrome". Sense of loss and grief.

- *This table shows the main categories of development that a child undergoes at different age groups (from birth to late adolescence i.e. till the age of 20 years). It also shows the developmental concerns (column 4) affecting the child e.g. childhood fears, bed wetting, sleep problems, school avoidance, turmoil etc.*

- *Column 5 shows the parental feelings, concerns and pitfalls e.g. parental exhaustion, unfulfilled expectations from their child, high expectations from their child, personal challenge perceived by the parents from their child etc.*

Appendix 6

COMMON FOODSTUFFS WITH PROTEIN AND ENERGY CONTENT

Food	*Quantity (household measure)*	*Ingredients*	*Weight (gm)*	*Protein (gm)*	*Energy (KCal)*
Boiled rice	1 plate	Rice	60	4.1	207
Chapati	1 med-size	Wheat flour	25	3.0	85
Parantha	-do-	Wheat flour Fat	30 5	3.6	150
Poori	-do-	Wheat flour Fat	15 3 to 4	1.8	65-70
Idli	2 or 3 pcs	Rice Black gram	40-45 15-20	7.8	190-230
Dosa	2 dosas	Rice Black gram Fat	40-45 15-20 5	6.8	240-270
Apple	1 med-size	Apple	100	0.2	60
Guava	1 med-size	Guava	150	1.4	75
Bread	1 big slice 1 small slice	Flour Flour	30 20	2.3 1.5	75 50
Sweet biscuit Salted biscuit	2-3 3-4	Flour, Sugar Flour, Salt	20 20	1.3 1.3	107 90
Bengal gram dal (cooked)	1 bowl	Bengal gram	20	6.2	100
Black gram dal (cooked)	1 bowl	Black gram	30	7.2	103

Contd...

Food	*Quantity (household measure)*	*Ingredients*	*Weight (gm)*	*Protein (gm)*	*Energy (KCal)*
Moong dal (cooked)	1 bowl	Moong dal	30	7.2	103
Milk (cow)	1 small glass	Milk Sugar	200 5	6.4	150
Milk (buffalo)	1 small glass	Milk Sugar	200 5	8.6	250
Curd (cow's milk)	1 bowl	Milk	150	4.2	90
Egg (hen)	1	Egg	50	6.6	85
Mutton	1 piece	Mutton	20	2.7	40
Fish	1 piece	Fish	20	3.0	16
Potato	1 med-size	Potato	75	1.2	75
Banana	1 med-size	Banana	70	0.8	80
Almonds (shelled)	7-8 large	Almonds	10	2.1	66
Cashew nuts	6 large	Cashew nuts	10	2.1	69
Walnuts (shelled)	4 halves	Walnuts	10	1.6	69
Peanuts (shelled)	25-30	Peanuts	10	2.5	67

Appendix 7

AVERAGE MILK FEEDS/DAY (UPTO 1 YEAR OF AGE)

AGE OF BABY	NO. OF FEEDS/DAY	AMOUNT TAKEN/FEED (Oz)**
0-2 weeks	6-10	2-3 oz
2 weeks-2 months	6-8	4-5 oz
2-3 months	5-6	5-6 oz
3-6 months	4-5	6-7 oz
6-9 months	3-4	7-8 oz
9-12 months	3	7-8 oz

1 Oz (ounce) = 30 ml.

Note : The amount and number of feeds may vary from child to child. In case of doubts regarding your baby's intake of milk, kindly contact your paediatrician.

NORMAL CALORIC AND PROTEIN REQUIREMENT OF CHILDREN

Age	Calories	Proteins (g/kg/day)
0-3 months	120 cal/kg	2.2
3-6 months	115 cal/kg	1.8
6-9 months	110 cal/kg	1.5
9-12 months	105 cal/kg	1.5
1-3 years	1300-1400 Kcal	1.2
4-6 years	1700-1800 Kcal	1.1
6-9 years	2100-2200 Kcal	1.0
9-12 years	2500-2600 Kcal	1.0

Appendix 8

NEONATAL DISCHARGE CARD (A SPECIMEN)

Name : .... Sex : .... Reg. No. ....

Address : ....

Name of mother : .... Name of father : ....

Any significant maternal history : ....

Date of Birth : .... Time : ....

Type of Delivery : Normal / Breech / Vacuum / Forceps / Caesarean

Apgar at 1 minute : ....at 5 minutes : ....

Birth Weight : .... kg Weight at discharge : .... kg

Length : .... cms Head Circumference : .... cms.

Blood Group of baby : .... Mother : ....Father : ....

Date of Discharge : .... Follow-up on : ....

Diagnosis at Discharge : ....

Rx (treatment) on discharge :

1) ....

2) ....

Details of siblings and abortions :

1) ....

2) ....

Date : .... Medical Officer : ....

Advice on Discharge :

- ***Umbilical Cord :*** *Apply spirit over it and leave it open to air and dry till the stump falls off.*
- ***Immunisation :*** *Immunisation is prevention, better than cure. Get your child immunised.*
- ***Breast feeds :*** *Ideal for your baby. Never start milk tins without your doctor's consultation and advice. Breast milk is nature's gift for the baby; don't deny him this gift.*
- ***Weaning :*** *Exculsively breast-feed your baby upto 3-4 months (even water is not necessary). Only after that, give other foodstuffs, a process called weaning.*
- ***Regurgitation :*** *Babies usually bring out some white curdled milk after feeds, a process called regurgitation. It is not vomiting and is normal.*
- ***Stools and urine :*** *Babies usually pass stools by 24 hours of birth and urine by 48 hours of birth. Babies may cry and strain a bit on passing urine or stool. Frequency of stooling may range from once every alternate day to 10-12 times per day.*
- ***Jaundice :*** *Mild yellowness of the skin of babies is normal and called physiologic jaundice.*
- ***Nasal problems :*** *Sneezing/stuffiness of the nose during the initial few days are normal.*

Appendix 9

IMMUNISATION SCHEDULE

AGE	VACCINE	DUE DATE	DATE GIVEN
Birth	*Polio*		
	BCG		
1 ½ months	*Polio*		
	DPT		
	Hepatitis – B		
	HIB		
2 ½ months	*Polio*		
	DPT		
	Hepatitis – B		
	HIB		
3 ½ months	*Polio*		
	DPT		
	Hepatitis – B		
	HIB		
9 months	*Measles*		
1 year	*Chickenpox*		
	Hepatitis-A		
18 months	*Polio*		
	DPT		
	MMR		
	HIB		
	Hepatitis-A		
2 years	*Typhoid*		
5 years	*Polio*		
	DPT		
	Typhoid		

- DT (and not DPT) is given at the age of 10 years, 16 years and thereafter after every 10 years.
- Typhoid vaccine (injectable) has to be given every 3 years. Oral typhoid vaccine (in the form of 3 capsules to be taken on alternate days) can be given only after the age of 6 years. Its protection lasts for 5 years.
- Hepatitis-A is given as a 2 dose schedule 6 months apart.

IMMUNISATION GUIDELINES

- *Immunisation can be safely given in the presence of minor illnesses like cough, cold, diarrhoea & low- grade fever.*
- *Anyone at any age can be immunised, if not immunised before. The same schedule is followed.*
- *It is not necessary to restart an interrupted schedule from the beginning. Continue as if no interruption has occurred.*
- *Multiple vaccines can be given together on the same visit without any problem.*
- *For preterm babies, the same schedule as for term babies is followed. No adjustments for prematurity are made.*
- *Vaccines, particularly DPT, can cause local pain, fever and irritability in the child. Sometimes a few days after DTP injection, parents may feel a small, firm nodule at the site of injection. It doesn't require any treatment.*

Appendix 10

NORMAL PARAMETERS OF A NEWBORN

Four parameters (gestational age, birth weight, length and head circumference) are important at the time of birth. Three parameters (weight, height and head circumference) should be monitored regularly (once every 1-2 months till the baby is 1-year old and twice a year thereafter) and plotted on a "growth card". These parameters are the most accurate indicators of the normal progression of the physical growth of a child. Hence all parents must keep a serial and accurate record of their child's weight, height and head circumference.

1. GESTATIONAL AGE OF A BABY

A term pregnancy is typically of 40 weeks.

1. *If the baby is 37 - 42 weeks' gestation, it is a* ***full term baby.***
2. *If the baby is born before 37 weeks, it is a* ***preterm baby.***
3. *If the gestation period is more than 42 weeks, it is a* ***post-term baby.***

- **EDD** *(expected date of delivery) = {LMP (last menstrual period) + 9 months and 7 days}.*
- *Supposing a pregnant woman had her LMP on 11.1.96. Her EDD will be 1.1.96 + 9 months and 7 days = 8.10.96, which is equal to 40 weeks of pregnancy.*
- *If the baby is born between 17.9.96 (i.e. 3 weeks prior to 8.10.96 = 37 weeks) and 22.10.96 (i.e. 2 weeks after 8.10.96 = 42 weeks), it is term baby. Else it is preterm/ post-term.*

2. WEIGHT OF A BABY AND ITS PROGRESSION

1. *A baby between 2.5 kilos to 3.8 kilos is* ***"appropriae for date (AFD / AGA)."***
2. *A baby weighing less than 2.5 kilos is* ***"small for date (SFD / SGA)."***
3. *A baby weighing more than 3.8 kilos is* ***"large for date (LFD / LGA)."***

- *A term baby loses 7-10% of its birth weight during the initial 3-4 days and regains it by 7-10 days. So a baby may weigh the same as at birth even at 10 days.*
- *After this, the baby gains approximately 20 grams/day till the child becomes 5 months of age (initially it may even gain 30 grams/ day for the first 1-2 months). It translates to a weight gain of 20 × 140 days = 2.8 kilos. Thus the baby's birth weight doubles at 5 months.*
- *After this, the child gains approximately 15 grams/day till the age of 1 year. It means a gain of 15 × 210 days = 3 kilos approximately. That's why the birth weight triples at 1 year.*

- *It quadruples at the age of 2 years. After that it grows approximately 2 kilos/year till the age of 6 years and then 3-3.5 kilos/year till adolescence.*

TABLE FOR CALCULATING WEIGHT INCREMENT

WEIGHT	KILOGRAMS
At birth	2.6 - 3.8 kilos
3-12 months	age (months) + 9 / 2
1-6 years	age (years) x 2 + 8
7-12 years	age (years) x 7 - 5 / 2

3. LENGTH OF A BABY AND ITS NORMAL PROGRESSION

- *A newborn (full term) has a length of 48-52 cm. It becomes 1.5 times (i.e. 75 cm) at the age of 1 year, doubles (i.e. 100 cm) at the age of 4 years and triples (i.e. 150 cm) by 13 years.*
- *A child gains approximately 4-5 inches (10-12 cm) during the second year and thereafter grows approximately 2 inches (5-6 cm) / year till adolescence. Gain in height can be expected upto the age of 16 years in females and 18 years in males.*
- *An absolute less height is less indicative of a problem than the annual increment in height. If the child is gaining 5-6 cm / year, it usually indicates no problems (even if the child is short as he may be a "late bloomer" i.e. may have a spurt at puberty).*

Formula for calculating the predicted adult height :

Girls : (father's height – 13 cm) + (mother's height) / 2

Boys : (mother's height + 13 cm) + (father's height) / 2

N.B. : A child's predicted adult height generally falls within 5 cm above or below the height calculated by the above formula.

TABLE FOR CALCULATING HEIGHT INCREMENT

HEIGHT	CENTIMETRES
At birth	50 cms
At 1 year	75 cms
2-12 years	age (years) x 6 + 77

4. HEAD CIRCUMFERENCE (HC) OF A BABY AND ITS PROGRESSION

The normal HC at birth is 33-35 cm in a full term healthy baby.

During first 3 months, it increases 2 cm/month, so that at 3 months, it should be 39-41 cm.

During next 3 months, it increases 1 cm/month, so that at 6 months, it should be 42-44 cm.

During next 6 months, it increases 0.5 cm/month, so that at 1 year, it should be 45-47 cm.

It becomes 47-49 cm at the end of the 2nd year and after that it gradually increases to the adult HC of 51-53 cm.

Appendix 11

RESUSTICATION OF A CHILD

(STEP 1 - OPENING THE AIRWAY)

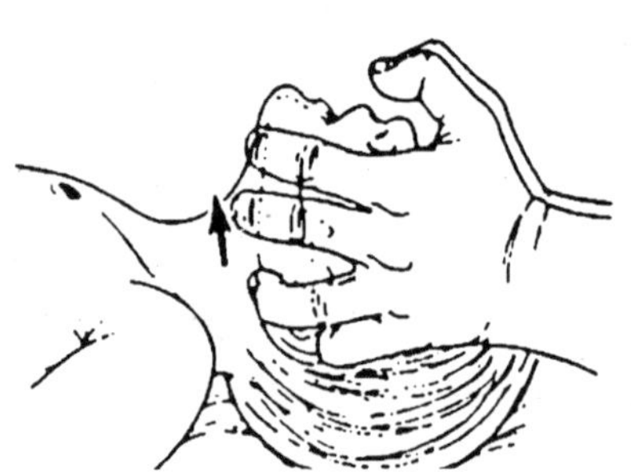

Combined jaw thrust-spine stabilization manoeuvre for the paediatric trauma victim.

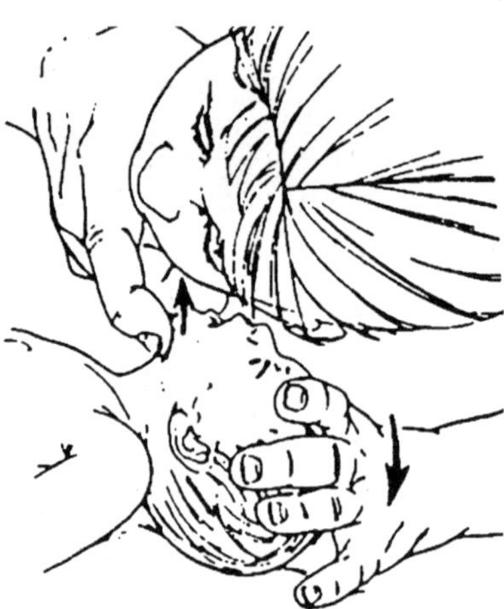

Opening the airway with the head tilt-chin lift manoeuvre: One hand is used to tilt the head, extending the neck. The index finger of the rescuer's other hand lifts the mandible outward by lifting on the chin. Head tilt should not be performed if cervical spine injury is suspected.

- *Cardio-pulmonary resustication involves basically 3 steps : (i) Securing an open airway (ii) Artificial respiration, most commonly mouth to mouth (iii) Cardiac massage.*
- *The above two diagrams show the first step, i.e. securing an open airway.*
- *Fig. 1 (left side) : It depicts "jaw thrust" manoeuvre for opening the airway. Both the hands are used with placement as shown (note that the little and the ring fingers are below the angle of the jaw). Both hands (see direction of arrow) make an upward movement (thrust). This extends the neck and opens up the airway.*
- *Fig. 2 (right side) : It depicts the head tilt - chin lift manoeuvre. The left hand is put on the forehead and the head tilted downwards and backwards (in the direction of the arrow). The index finger of the right hand is put below the chin and it is lifted upwards. These 2 movements act like a couple and extend the neck, so opening the airway.* ***Avoid head-tilt if a person has suffered head or neck trauma.***
- *Once airway is open, one proceeds with the step-2 i.e. artificial respiration (see next page).*

Appendix 12

RESUSTICATION OF A CHILD

(STEP 2 - ARTIFICIAL RESPIRATION)

- *The below diagrams show step no. 2 of resustication i.e. artificial respiration.*
- *Mouth to mouth respiration is ideal for first aid. One hand pinches the nose of the patient shut. The other hand opens the mouth of the patient slightly. The rescuer's mouth covers the patient's mouth so as to make an airtight seal. Then he blows air into the patient's mouth. His eyes should be looking at the patient's chest and as he blows in air, the patient's chest should rise (as it does in normal breathing). If it doesn't rise, either the pressure that the rescuer is using in blowing the air is less or the seal between the lips is not airtight. Once the chest rises, the rescuer should terminate his blowing in of the air and open the nose of the patient. The patient will exhale passively as can be judged by the downward movement of the risen chest wall. The process is repeated at the rate of 30 breaths / minute. There is no need to take the mouth off the patient's mouth, because then the rescuer will have to make an airtight seal between the lips again.*

Rescue breathing in an infant: The rescuer's mouth covers the infant's nose and mouth, creating a seal. One hand performs head tilt while the other hand lifts the infant's jaw. Avoid head tilt if the infant has sustained head or neck trauma.

Rescue breathing in a child: The rescuer's mouth covers the mouth of the child, creating a mouth-to-mouth seal. One hand maintains the head tilt; the thumb and forefinger of the same hand are used to pinch the child's nose.

Appendix 13

RESUSTICATION OF A CHILD

(CARDIAC MASSAGE = STEP 3 OF CPR)

- This should be done after step 1 (i.e. clearing of the airway) and step 2 (i.e. giving artificial respiration). This is because the function of the heart is to distribute Oxygen to the body and hence first artificial respiration has to be given first so that the lungs have oxygen to be distributed.
- The technique of cardiac massage differs in newborns/ infants, and that applied to older patients.
- **Newborn/infant:** The heart is compressed by 2 fingers (see illustration). The 2 fingers are put on the breast bone and then rhythmic compression is given at the rate of 120/minute. Respiration is given at the rate of 30/mt. So the ratio is 4:1.

Older children: The heel of the hand is placed 2 fingers above the lower end of the breast bone (called sternum) and then the heel of the other hand is placed on top of it (see illustration). Compressions are applied without bending the elbows (i.e. with the shoulders and the body weight). 80 rhythmic compressions are applied/minute. Artificial respiration is given at a rate of 16/minute. So the ratio translates to 5:1.

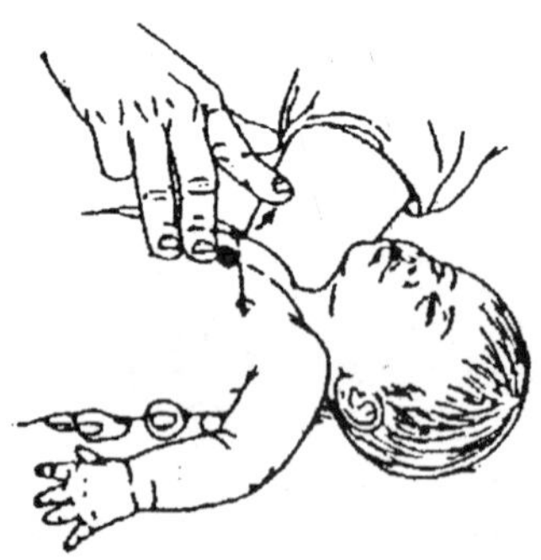

Cardiac compressions, infant supine on palm of rescuer's hand.

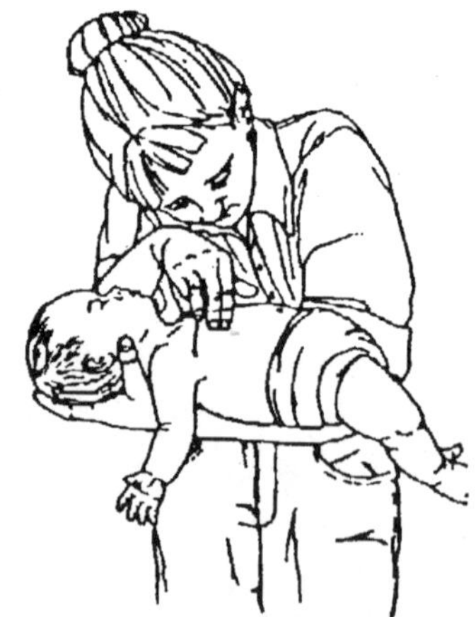

Performing CPR while carrying the infant or small child. Note that the head is kept level with the torso.

Appendix 14

(FIRST AID DURING CHOKING)

- *The two figures below show the manoeuvres during choking by a foreign body. They are meant to expel the foreign body and clear the airway so that the child can breathe. It is different in children under 1 year and those above 1 year. The figure on the left shows the manoeuvre for a child less than 1 year while the figure on the right shows it for a child more than 1 year.*
- *Child is less than one year : Give 4 blows on the back of the child followed by 4 blows to the front of the child's chest. The blows are given with the heel of the hand. The child is positioned face downwards on the rescuer's arm, so that the face is lower than the rest of the body. After giving these blows, the child's mouth should be opened and the back of the throat examined for any foreign body. If seen it can be removed by forceps or even by a "scoop" of the finger (here you are able to see the object and therefore it is not blind finger sweeping, which is contraindicated). In case the object is not expelled, the rescuer should give artificial respiration (described earlier) and repeat the blows.*
- *Child is older than one year : In this case, instead of chest thrusts, abdominal thrusts are used. The heel of one hand is kept on the abdomen between the navel and the end of the breastbone. The heel of the other hand is placed on top of the first hand and a thrust is given in an upward and inward direction. Six rapid thrusts are recommended after which the mouth is examined as stated above. If the object is not seen, artificial respiration is given and the sequence is repeated. Abdominal thrusts can be given in a standing position with the rescuer standing behind the victim (as in the diagram) or if the child is unconscious by making him lie down on the ground.*

Back blows (top) and chest thrusts (bottom) to relieve foreign-body airway obstruction in the infant.

Abdominal thrusts with victim standing or sitting (conscious).

Appendix 15

DEVELOPMENT RECORD

(MAKE SURE YOUR CHILD SEES, HEARS AND LISTENS)

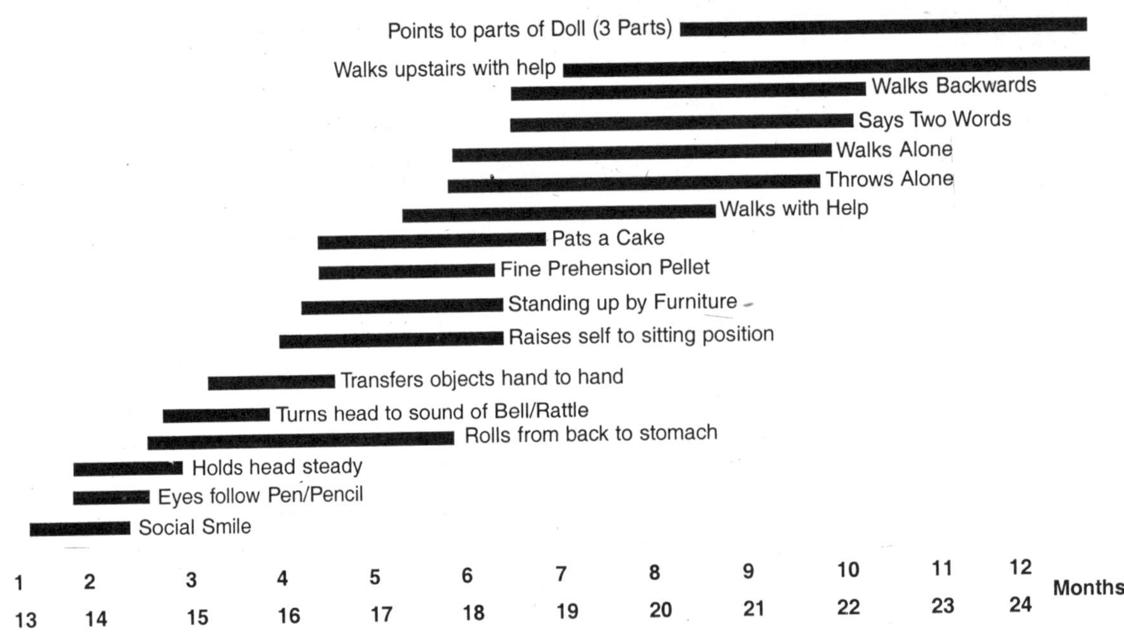

Note: To use this chart, keep a pencil vertically on the age of the child. All milestones falling to the left of the pencil should have been achieved by the child.

Based on BSID Baroda norms & Trivandrum Development Screening Chart (TDSC)

More Books on Beauty Care/Parenting

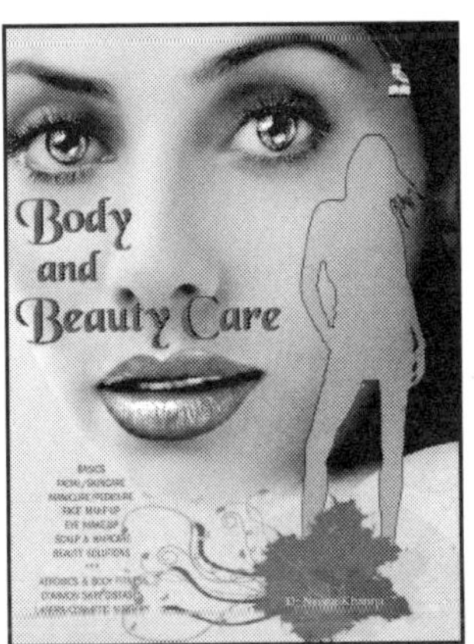